The Fast Track to New Skills

The Fast Track to New Skills

Short-Cycle Higher Education Programs in Latin America and the Caribbean

María Marta Ferreyra, Lelys Dinarte Díaz, Sergio Urzúa, and Marina Bassi

 **WORLD BANK GROUP**

Contents

Boxes

Figures

Map

Tables

Foreword

The COVID-19 pandemic has unleashed an unprecedented crisis in Latin America and the Caribbean (LAC)—a severe shock to a region that was already struggling to regain its footing after the collapse of commodity prices in 2013. The crisis has severely affected aggregate employment and production and has thrown millions of people into poverty. Yet, while the crisis has destroyed many jobs and businesses, it has also created others. Over the past year, machines and electronic platforms have replaced workers in some sectors, and we have also seen people with analytical skills fare well during the pandemic. Although these trends were already evident before the pandemic, they have become even stronger over the past year.

In this context, investing in the skills for the jobs of the future has become both critical and urgent. It is already clear that labor markets will emerge from the pandemic irreversibly changed. Many of the jobs that have disappeared may not come back. As firms begin to hire, many will seek new skills. Upskilling and reskilling the population will be critical—not just for economic recovery and transformation but also for equity and inclusion.

Developing skilled human capital is a fundamental role of higher education systems. Are LAC systems up to the current challenge? Can they accompany the ongoing structural transformation and provide for the needs of the new labor market, or will they remain focused on the labor market of the past? Can they respond flexibly and fast, or will they take many years to adapt?

This book argues that short-cycle programs (SCPs), a type of higher education program, are particularly well suited to address these challenges. These programs, which have been relatively overlooked by researchers and policy makers, have a clear focus on labor markets and helping students get jobs. And a major advantage is that they develop skilled human capital in only two or three years.

The evidence presented in this book shows that, on average, these programs deliver good academic and labor market outcomes. Moreover, their providers respond nimbly to the needs of local labor markets, and many SCPs implement specific practices that contribute to good student outcomes. Although not all SCPs are equally good, clear and vigorous policy can mitigate SCP shortcomings and help them fulfill their promise.

A 2017 World Bank study on higher education in the region, *At a Crossroads: Higher Education in Latin America and the Caribbean*, noted that higher education faced a defining moment, because the prevailing model was not delivering what the region wanted and needed—an education capable of promoting growth, innovation, and inclusion.

As the region seeks to build better and more adequate higher education systems, this report advocates for new actions and ideas supported by evidence, not simply to overcome the current crisis but also to set the foundations for a more productive economy and a more equitable society.

The findings of this report can help create an environment where good programs that students can attend are offered across the region—which is critical, given LAC's urgency to skill, upskill, and reskill its population. SCPs can be extremely valuable: they are oriented to the labor market and specific skills or occupations, and their providers are flexible and adapt easily to new realities. In addition, the total cost and time commitment per student are lower than those of bachelors' programs.

As LAC emerges from the COVID-19 pandemic, the region has the opportunity to chart a new future with more equitable and sustained economic growth. Building human capital with the skills demanded for the jobs of the future will be key. This report offers new evidence and ideas on how SCPs can help achieve this goal.

Carlos Felipe Jaramillo
Vice President
Latin America and the Caribbean Region
The World Bank Group

Acknowledgments

This report was prepared by a team led by María Marta Ferreyra. The core team also consisted of Lelys Dinarte Díaz, Sergio Urzúa, and Marina Bassi, and received excellent research assistance from Andrea Franco, Manuela Granda, Angelica Sánchez, and Gabriel Suárez. The work was conducted under the general guidance of Martín Rama, current Chief Economist for the Latin America and the Caribbean (LAC) Region of the World Bank, and Carlos Végh, former LAC Chief Economist of the World Bank, with substantial inputs from Rita Almeida, former LAC acting practice manager for the Education Global Practice of the World Bank, and Emanuela Di Gropello, current LAC practice manager for the Education Global Practice of the World Bank.

Preparation of the book was informed by a series of background papers. Authors of these background papers who have not been already named include Juan Esteban Carranza, Stephanie Cellini, Camila Galindo, Ana Gazmuri, Hernando Grueso, Macarena Kutscher, and Tatiana Melguizo. Empirical work for the book was underpinned by an extensive survey to directors of short-cycle programs in LAC, the World Bank Short-Cycle Program Survey (WBSCPS), developed by the team and conducted by SIMO Consulting under the leadership of Mayra Benítez and Azucena Cháidez. The team is grateful to Diego Angel-Urdinola, Ciro Avitabile, Marcelo Becerra, Sebastián Burgos, Pedro Cerdán, Veronica Díaz, Eric Jardim, Ildo Lautharte, Andre Loureiro, Carlos Medina, Rafael Santos, and Alexandria Valerio, who facilitated contacts with government agencies and provided institutional information. For providing access to administrative information and supporting the WBSCPS, the team is grateful to the Ministries of Education of Brazil, Colombia, and Peru; the Ministry of Finance, Planning and Development, Dominican Republic; and the Secretariat of Higher Education, Science, Technology and Innovation (SENESCYT) in Ecuador. *Servicio Nacional de Aprendizaje* (SENA) in Colombia provided administrative data. *Instituto Nacional de Estudos e Pesquisas Educacionais Anisio Teixeira* (INEP) in Brazil provided access to restricted data, which were used to conduct on-site estimation by Renato Vieira.

The team was fortunate to receive excellent advice and guidance from three distinguished peer reviewers: Omar Arias, Nina Arnhold, and Kevin Stange. While the core team is very grateful for the guidance received, these reviewers are not responsible for any remaining errors, omissions, or interpretations.

Additional insights from Matías Busso, Jean-Francois Houde, Renata Lemos, Hugo Ñopo, Juan Esteban Saavedra, Di Xu, and other participants of an online workshop on October 27, 29, and 30, 2020, are gratefully acknowledged.

In preparing this book, the team benefited from conversations with Susan Ambrose, Martin Borchardt, Anthony Carnevale, Ruth Graham, Karen Kelly, C. J. Libassi, Armando Mendoza, Angélica Natera, Juan Carlos Navarro, Christopher Neilson, Ricardo Paredes, Lino Pujol, Grant Taylor, Jorge Téllez, Daniel Toro, and Jaime Torrado. Comments from Andrés Bernasconi and Pablo Landoni, participants at the CACES conference in Guayaquil (November 2019), and participants at the APICE and Laspau-World Bank online events (November and December 2020, respectively) are also gratefully acknowledged. The team is grateful for the support and insights provided by senior management of the World Bank's Education Global Practice, including not only Reema Nayar but also Global Director Jaime Saavedra and Regional Director Luis Benveniste.

Sandra Gain edited the manuscript. Patricia Katayama (acquisitions editor), Mary Fisk (production editor), and Deborah Appel-Barker (print coordinator) of the World Bank's Formal Publishing Program were responsible for managing the design, typesetting, and printing of the book. Sergio Andres Moreno Tellez provided the cover design. Carlos Molina, Shane Kimo Romig, and Gonzalo Villamizar contributed to design and communication. Sara Horcas-Rufián translated the volume into Spanish, and Leonardo Padovani translated it into Portuguese. Last, but not least, the team thanks Jacqueline Larrabure for unfailing administrative support.

About the Authors

Marina Bassi is a senior economist in the Education Global Practice of the World Bank for East and Southern Africa. Before joining the World Bank in 2017, she worked at the Inter-American Development Bank, focusing on operational and analytical work on education in LAC. Her work has been published in journals and books on such areas as teaching practices, gender gaps in education, skills, and impact evaluation of education programs. She is a coauthor of *Disconnected: Education, Skills and Employment in Latin America* (Inter-American Development Bank 2012). She holds a PhD in economics from the University of California at Los Angeles.

Lelys Dinarte Díaz is a research economist in the Human Development Team of the World Bank's Development Research Group. Her primary research fields are development economics and economics of education and crime. Combining experimental and nonexperimental approaches, one strand of her research agenda studies how educational interventions implemented in developing countries can modify at-risk youth performance, including academic performance, socioemotional skills, and violent behaviors. She also conducts research on quality determinants for higher education in LAC. Her current research involves projects in multiple Latin American countries, including El Salvador, Guatemala, Honduras, Jamaica, Mexico, and Peru. She holds a PhD and an MSc in economics from the Pontifical Catholic University of Chile.

María Marta Ferreyra is a senior economist in the Office of the Chief Economist for Latin America and the Caribbean (LAC) of the World Bank. Her research specializes in the economics of education. She has conducted research on school choice, accountability, and finance in primary and secondary education in the United States (US); child care markets in the US; higher education in LAC; and cities in LAC. Her research has been published in journals such as the *American Economic Review*, the *Journal of Public Economics*, and the *American Economic Journal: Economic Policy*. She is the lead author of *At a Crossroads: Higher Education in Latin America and the Caribbean* (World Bank 2017), and the co-lead author of *Raising the Bar for Productive Cities in Latin America and the Caribbean* (World Bank 2018). Before joining the World Bank, she served as a faculty member at the Tepper School of Business at Carnegie Mellon University. She holds a PhD in economics from the University of Wisconsin–Madison.

Sergio Urzúa is an associate professor in the department of economics at the University of Maryland, where he teaches labor economics and applied econometrics. He is also an international research fellow at Clapes UC, research associate at the National Bureau of Economic Research (NBER), Research Fellow at the Institute of Labor Economics (IZA), and research director of RIDGE. His research focuses on labor economics, development, and applied econometrics. He has published widely in leading peer-reviewed journals (more than 40 publications) and is a former editor-in-chief of *EconomiA*. He has published three books, including *At a Crossroads: Higher Education in Latin America and the Caribbean* (World Bank 2017). He currently coordinates the Latin America and the Caribbean Economic Association's (LACEA) Labor Network. He has served as a member of the steering committee of the NBER Program for Children and as a member of LACEA's executive committee. He earned a PhD from the University of Chicago in 2007.

Abbreviations

APICE	Pan-American Association of Educational Credit Institutions (*Asociación Panamericana de Instituciones de Crédito Educativo*)
CACES	Council for Higher Education Quality Assurance (*Consejo de Aseguramiento de la Calidad de la Educación Superior*) (Ecuador)
Cedefop	European Centre for the Development of Vocational Training
CEDLAS	Center for Distributive, Labor and Social Studies
CEFET	Federal Centers for Technological Education (*Centros Federais de Educação Tecnológica*) (Brazil)
CFT	technical training center (*centros de formación técnica*) (Chile)
CINDA	Inter-University Center of Development (*Centro Interuniversitario de Desarrollo*)
CPC	Preliminary Course Score (*Conceito Preliminar de Curso*) (Brazil)
ENADE	National Exam of Student Achievement (*Exame Nacional de Desempenho dos Estudantes*) (Brazil)
ENEM	National Assessment of Secondary Education (*Exame Nacional de Ensino Médio*) (Brazil)
ETG	extra time to graduate
FIES	Student Financing Fund (*Fundo de Finaciamiento Estudantil*) (Brazil)
FUNDAPEC	Pro-Education and Culture Action Educational Credit Foundation (*Fundación Acción Pro Educación y Cultura [APEC] de Crédito Educativo*) (Dominican Republic)
GDP	gross domestic product
HEI	higher education institution
HQA	high-quality accreditation

ICETEX	Colombian Institute of Educational Credit and Technical Training Abroad (*Instituto Colombiano de Crédito Educativo y Estudios Técnicos en el Exterior*) (Colombia)
IDB	Inter-American Development Bank
IF	Federal Institute (*Instituto Federal*) (Brazil)
IGC	General Course Index (*Índice Geral de Cursos*) (Brazil)
INEP	National Institute of Educational Research and Studies (*Instituto Nacional de Estudos e Pesquisas Educacionais Anísio Teixeira*) (Brazil)
IP	professional institute (*institutos profesionales*) (Chile)
ISCED	International Standard Classification of Education
LAC	Latin America and the Caribbean
LASSO	Least Absolute Shrinkage and Selection Operator
MESCyT	Ministry of Higher Education, Science and Technology (Dominican Republic)
MRI	magnetic resonance imaging
nini	neither working nor studying (*no estudia, ni trabaja*)
OLE	Labor Observatory for Education (*Obsevatorio Laboral para la Educación*) (Colombia)
PAA	Academic Aptitude Test (*Prueba de Aptitud Académica*) (Dominican Republic)
POMA	Orientation and Academic Measurement Test (*Prueba de Orientación y Medición Académica*) (Dominican Republic)
PPP	purchasing power parity
PRONABEC	National Program of Scholarships and Educational Credit (*Programa Nacional de Becas y Crédito Educativo*) (Peru)
SABER	Systems Approach for Better Education Results
SCP	short-cycle program
SEDLAC	Socio-Economic Database for Latin America and the Caribbean
SENA	National Learning Service (*Servicio Nacional de Aprendizaje*) (Colombia)
SENATI	National Industrial Work Training Service (*Servicio Nacional de Adiestramiento en Trabajo Industrial*) (Peru)
SENESCYT	Secretariat of Higher Education, Science, Technology and Innovation (Ecuador)
SIES	Higher Education Information Service (Chile)
SIGETI	Database of Registered Degrees (*Sistema de Gestión de Títulos*) (Peru)

SNIES	National Higher Education Information System (*Sistema Nacional de Información de la Educación Superior*) (Colombia)
SP	São Paulo (Brazil)
STEM	science, technology, engineering, and mathematics
UNESCO	United Nations Educational, Scientific and Cultural Organization
WAP	working-age population
WBSCPS	World Bank Short-Cycle Program Survey

Overview

Following the collapse of commodity prices in the early 2010s, Latin America and the Caribbean (LAC) countries have been seeking new engines of growth, which, in addition to raising productivity, would preserve and enhance the equity gains attained in the previous decade. By developing skilled human capital, higher education could be a formidable engine of economic and social progress.

A specific type of higher education program forms skilled human capital relatively fast—the so-called short-cycle programs (SCPs). Unlike bachelor's programs (which usually last five or six years in LAC), SCPs are short (two or three years long), eminently practical, and have a clear goal of training students for work in a relatively short time. SCPs are similar to short technical and vocational postsecondary courses in their practical focus, yet are different in that, by being a form of higher education, they are longer (at least two years long) and provide broader training.[1] SCPs are known by different names throughout the region, such as *programas técnicos y tecnológicos, carreras técnicas, tecnicaturas, carreras terciarias, carreras de nivel técnico superior, cursos tecnológicos, cursos técnico-profesionales, carreras profesionales*, and *cursos superiores de tecnología*. Some SCPs focus on traditional fields such as advertising, hospitality, physical therapy, logistics, graphic design, and electronics. Others focus on more recent, innovative fields such as app design, digital animation, big data, web design, cybersecurity, and social networks.

SCPs are attractive to a wide variety of individuals. These include those who are not able to pursue a bachelor's program due to other responsibilities or poor academic preparation; those who might succeed in a bachelor's program but are not willing to invest time and resources in it; and those who already have a bachelor's degree but are seeking short, specific training in their broad area of knowledge (for example, a computer scientist interested in learning computer animation) or a different one (for example, a historian interested in marketing). More generally, SCPs can help individuals enhance their skills for a similar occupation ("upskilling") or acquire new skills for a different one ("reskilling").

Because firms and the economy need a variety of skills—those of engineers as well as technicians and economists as well as marketing specialists—through SCPs the higher education system can provide a greater variety of options than those limited to bachelor's programs.

The wide attractiveness of SCPs contrasts with the prevailing view in the region, where SCPs bear the stigma of being the lesser higher education choice. If they are well-designed, SCPs have the potential to become a crucial tool for workforce development in the new world of work—where individuals can be expected to switch occupations, and perhaps careers, multiple times over their lifetime, and where training must be fast, efficient, and closely connected to the labor market.

Although LAC has been in need of skilled human capital for the past few years—particularly since the end of its "Golden Decade"—the need has become decidedly urgent following the COVID-19 pandemic.[2] Even before the pandemic, machines had been replacing humans in routine tasks through automation; the internet had been replacing personal interaction through electronic platforms; and the productivity and market value of workers who produce intangible value added, such as researchers, programmers, and designers, was already on the rise. Rather than creating new trends, the pandemic has merely accelerated the preexisting ones.[3]

Although the pandemic has damaged aggregate employment and output, not all firms and workers have fared equally. Many jobs and firms have been destroyed, yet many others have appeared. At the same time, the jobs that have disappeared are not likely to come back. To return to employment, those individuals will need to acquire the skills relevant to the new world of work in order to perform nonroutine, complex tasks that cannot be automated or executed by electronic platforms. Recovery from the COVID-19 crisis will depend crucially on upskilling and reskilling the workforce in order to support economic transformation.

Since governments are facing extremely severe fiscal constraints, workforce development can hardly count on additional resources. By definition, SCPs should be able to satisfy the skill needs fast and efficiently, but only to the extent that they can supply high quality and respond flexibly to the needs of the market. That is why this study investigates SCP outcomes, quality, and supply in LAC. The focus on SCPs is novel, as neither policy makers nor researchers have previously devoted much attention to them.

The study shows that SCPs have several strengths but also shortcomings. On average, SCPs have good academic and labor market outcomes, and many implement practices or have inputs associated with good outcomes. Further, the SCP market is dynamic and providers respond nimbly to labor market needs. However, SCP outcomes and practices vary greatly among programs, and providers often open low-cost, low-value programs.

To some extent, these shortcomings might be due to poor policy. Thoughtful policy design and diligent implementation might mitigate them, thereby realizing the SCP potential at this time of great need. As a recent study on higher education in LAC shows,[4] higher education is at a crossroads, with policy makers, institutions, firms, and students seeking a new, more effective type of higher education—one that fits the current realities and promotes growth, innovation, and inclusion. To attain this new type of higher education, new actions are needed. The evidence presented in this study can inform the new, bold actions required at this critical juncture.

The remainder of this overview begins by describing the novel data collected in order to answer the study's novel questions, and describes the general landscape of SCPs in LAC—both from an institutional and economic perspective. It summarizes various measures of SCP outcomes and quality and describes aspects of SCP supply such as new program entry, competition, and program design. It presents the main findings from the analytical work seeking to identify the program characteristics, inputs, and practices that contribute to good student outcomes. It concludes by offering some policy considerations.

New Data to Answer New Questions

Consider a program that is "good," in the sense that it provides good outcomes, after accounting for student characteristics. What makes it good? What specific practices does it use? For example, does it communicate frequently with local companies to assess their skill needs, update the curriculum in response to industry feedback, or hire faculty with industry experience?

Entering the "black box" of program quality is fundamental for the design and replication of high-quality programs. However, the ability to do so is severely limited by standard data sets, which do not report program practices. To overcome this limitation, the study designed and implemented the World Bank Short-Cycle Program Survey (WBSCPS) in Brazil (in the states of São Paulo and Ceará), Colombia, the Dominican Republic, Ecuador, and Peru (for licensed programs). These five countries account for 54 percent of all SCP students in LAC. The survey took place by phone, online, and in person and obtained an unusually high response rate (70 percent on average), for a total of approximately 2,100 effective interviews.

The survey covers a broad range of topics, including student demographics and readiness for the program; admission and graduation requirements; faculty characteristics, hiring, and evaluation; curriculum and practical training; infrastructure; online teaching; costs and financing; oversight and regulation; institutional governance; interaction with industry; job search assistance; competition; and academic and labor market outcomes.

To our knowledge, this is the first attempt to learn about SCP practices and characteristics systematically, in LAC or elsewhere. This wealth of information allowed for characterizing the SCP sector well beyond what had been possible previously and to delve into the question of what makes a program good.

General Landscape of SCPs in LAC

In the new millennium, higher education in LAC has experienced a large, rapid expansion, with gross enrollment rates rising from 23 to 52 percent in less than 20 years (figure O.1, panel a). Nonetheless, throughout this expansion, enrollment has grown faster at bachelor's programs than at SCPs. As a result, today's share of SCP students in higher education enrollment is lower in LAC, at 9 percent, than in most other regions (figure O.1, panel b).

SCPs are a relatively late addition to LAC's higher education landscape, and their enrollment share varies widely across countries (figure O.2, panel a). Countries also vary in the types of institutions they authorize to provide SCPs (universities, non-universities, or both). On average, about half (48 percent) of SCP students are enrolled in private higher education institutions (HEIs) in LAC, yet the enrollment share in private institutions varies widely throughout the region (figure O.2, panel b).

SCPs usually fall under the purview of the Ministry of Education, which authorizes openings and conducts quality assurance (accreditation). Although many SCPs nominally provide pathways (or credits) toward more advanced degrees, in reality, these are not effective and only few SCP students pursue longer degrees. This "dead end" quality of SCPs might have contributed to their stigma.

Figure O.1 In LAC, Higher Education Enrollment Has Grown Rapidly, but There Are Relatively Few Students in SCPs

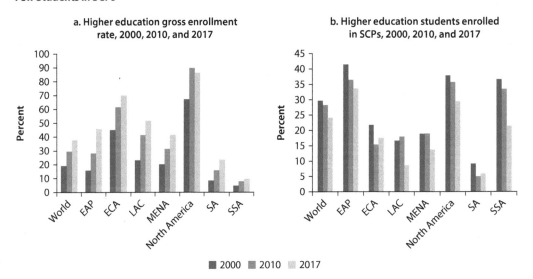

a. Higher education gross enrollment rate, 2000, 2010, and 2017

b. Higher education students enrolled in SCPs, 2000, 2010, and 2017

■ 2000 ■ 2010 ▨ 2017

Source: World Development Indicators, based on data from the United Nations Educational, Scientific and Cultural Organization, and National Center for Education Statistics for the United States (2000 and 2010).
Note: In panel a, gross enrollment rate is the number of students enrolled in higher education relative to the total population in the relevant age range (usually 18–23 years old). Panel b shows the share of SCP students relative to all higher education students. In each panel, the region-level indicator is a weighted average across the region's countries. EAP = East Asia and the Pacific; ECA = Europe and Central Asia; LAC = Latin America and the Caribbean; MENA = Middle East and North Africa; SA = South Asia; SCP = short-cycle program; SSA = Sub-Saharan Africa.

Figure O.2 SCP Enrollment Share and Private Sector Participation Vary Widely among LAC Countries

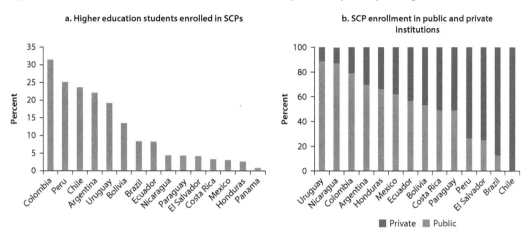

a. Higher education students enrolled in SCPs

b. SCP enrollment in public and private institutions

■ Private ■ Public

Source: World Bank calculations based on Socio-Economic Database for Latin America and the Caribbean (SEDLAC) and administrative data for Brazil and Colombia (see annex 1A of the book).
Note: Panel a shows the percentage of individuals ages 18–24 years who are enrolled in an SCP relative to all individuals ages 18–24 years enrolled in higher education, circa 2018. Panel b shows the percentage of all SCP students, regardless of age, enrolled in public or private HEIs, circa 2018. For Colombia, "public" includes *Servicio Nacional de Aprendizaje* (SENA). HEI = higher education institution; LAC = Latin America and the Caribbean; SCP = short-cycle program.

On average, students in SCPs are more disadvantaged and less traditional than those in bachelor's programs (table O.1). Students in SCPs are slightly older, come from lower income households, and are more likely to be married and work while studying. Students enter most SCPs with serious deficits in math, reading, and writing. As a result, the vast majority of SCPs conduct remedial activities.

Despite their disadvantage, SCP students obtain, on average, favorable academic and labor market outcomes. On the academic side, they graduate at higher rates than bachelor's students (57 versus 46 percent; see figure O.3). On the labor market side, although they earn lower wages than graduates from bachelor's programs—as expected—they obtain better outcomes than *dropouts* from bachelor's programs (figure O.4). Their unemployment rate is lower (3.8 versus 6.1 percent), their formal employment rate is higher (82 versus 67 percent), and their wages are higher (by 13 percent). Since dropouts from bachelor's programs account, on average, for a staggering 49 percent of all higher education students, such favorable outcomes for SCP programs are a promising starting point for the more detailed analysis presented in the next sections.

Program costs to students are an important element of the SCP landscape. Policy makers subsidize public HEIs both for SCPs and bachelor's programs, leading to an average tuition that is well below cost (figure O.5, panel a). In contrast, they rarely provide funding to private HEIs or their students. Some policy makers provide, guarantee, or subsidize student loans, yet these cover only a small fraction of students in the vast majority of countries. As a result, students pay tuition mostly out of their own pockets. Further, the policy maker's subsidy for an SCP student is lower than for a student at a bachelor's program (figure O.5,

Table O.1 In LAC, Students in SCPs Are More Disadvantaged and Less Traditional Than Those in Bachelor's Programs

	Bachelor's students	Short-cycle students
Female (%)	54.4	63.1
Age (years)	24.0	24.9
Urban (%)	90.3	80.8
Married (%)	14.5	22.6
Employed (%)	41.8	43.6
Income Q1 (%)	8.9	14.4
Income Q2 (%)	13.1	17.0
Income Q3 (%)	19.0	23.5
Income Q4 (%)	23.9	25.9
Income Q5 (%)	35.0	19.3

Source: World Bank calculations based on Socio-Economic Database for Latin America and the Caribbean (SEDLAC).
Note: The table shows averages of characteristics of students enrolled in bachelor's and short-cycle programs (SCPs), regardless of age, circa 2018. Simple averages over LAC countries are shown. "Urban" denotes the percentage of students residing in urban areas. "Employed" denotes whether the student works, full or part time. A part-time (full-time) worker works less than (at least) 40 hours a week. "Income Q1" denotes the percentage of students in quintile 1 of the income distribution (bottom 20 percent), and similarly for the remaining quintiles. The quintiles of the income distribution correspond to total household income *(ingreso total familiar)*. Differences in average characteristics between SCP and bachelor's students are significantly different from zero. LAC = Latin America and the Caribbean. Countries included are Argentina, Bolivia, Chile, Costa Rica, Ecuador, El Salvador, Honduras, Mexico, Nicaragua, Panama, Peru, and Uruguay.

Figure O.3 In LAC, SCPs Have Higher Completion Rates Than Bachelor's Programs

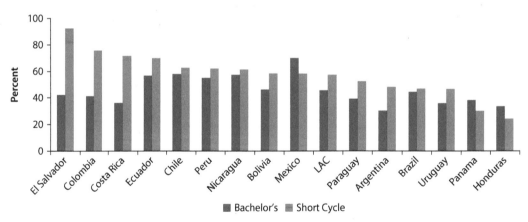

Source: World Bank calculations based on the Socio-Economic Database for Latin America and the Caribbean (SEDLAC). and administrative data for Brazil and Colombia.
Note: For each country, the figure shows completion rates for students enrolled in bachelor's and short-cycle programs (SCPs), circa 2018. Completion rates are estimated as the ratio of the number of individuals ages 25–29 years who have completed a higher education program to the number of individuals ages 25–29 years who have ever started a higher education program. For each country, the difference between the two graduation rates is significantly different from zero. For Colombia and Brazil, completion rates for bachelor's programs are the ratio of the average number of graduates in 2014, 2015, and 2016 to the number of incoming students in 2010; the completion rates for SCPs are the ratio of the average number of graduates in 2012, 2013, and 2014 to the number of incoming students in 2010. "LAC" indicates the simple average over all countries depicted in the figure.

Figure O.4 In LAC, SCP Graduates Attain Better Labor Market Outcomes Than Dropouts from Bachelor's Programs

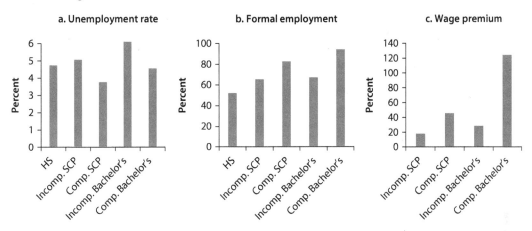

Source: World Bank calculations based on the Socio-Economic Database for Latin America and the Caribbean (SEDLAC).
Note: The figures depict average labor market outcomes, circa 2018, for the working-age population, defined as individuals between ages 25 and 65, given educational attainment. Complete bachelor's includes individuals with graduate degrees. For each educational attainment, the corresponding bar shows the simple average outcome over countries. Panel a shows the unemployment rate (percentage of unemployed individuals relative to the labor force). Panel b shows the percentage of individuals who have formal employment. Informal workers include salaried workers in firms with up to five employees, self-employed workers with at most a high school diploma, and workers with no reported income. In panel c, the premium in each category reflects the percent by which the average (hourly) wage in the category exceeds the average (hourly) wage for high school graduates. The difference between outcomes for complete SCP and incomplete bachelor's is significantly different from zero in panels a, b, and c. The difference between outcomes for complete SCP and complete bachelor's is significantly different from zero in panel c, but not in panels a or b. Comp. = complete; Incomp. = incomplete; LAC = Latin America and the Caribbean; SCP = short-cycle programs.

panel b), even though the former is more disadvantaged. The gap is only larger when considering total per-student subsidy, since bachelor's programs last longer than SCPs.

SCPs are relatively affordable in some countries but less so in others (figure O.6 panels a, b). For an individual who earns the monthly minimum wage, the average tuition is below 15 percent of annual wages in the Dominican Republic and Ecuador, but is above 50 percent in Peru and Brazil, where public provision is relatively small. Not surprisingly, 75 percent of the program directors that responded to the WBSCPS reported that the main reason for student dropout is financial hardship (figure O.6, panel c). Even when tuition is relatively affordable, the financial struggle—and overall vulnerability—of these students and their families is a major obstacle for human capital accumulation.

Labor Market Outcomes of SCP Graduates

The favorable SCP labor market outcomes described above might not be due to the programs themselves but to the characteristics and effort of their students. After accounting for observed student characteristics, the favorable labor market outcomes remain: on average, SCP graduates in LAC earn 60 percent more than

Figure O.5 Public Subsidies for SCP Students Are Lower Than for Bachelor's Students in LAC Countries

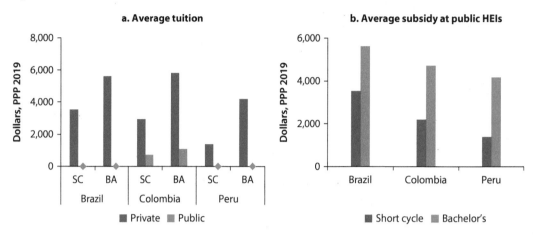

Sources: Countries' administrative information (see annex 1A of the book).
Note: All averages are simple averages over programs. In panel a, the orange diamonds indicate zero average tuition. For Colombia, average tuition at public institutions includes *Servicio Nacional de Aprendizaje* (SENA) programs, which charge zero tuition. In panel b, for a given country, the average subsidy at public HEIs for bachelor's programs equals average tuition in private HEIs – average tuition in public HEIs, and similarly for SCPs. The figure includes all states in Brazil and all programs (licensed and nonlicensed) in Peru. All monetary values are in dollars (PPP 2019). BA = bachelor's; HEI = higher education institution; LAC = Latin America and the Caribbean; PPP = purchasing power parity; SC = short cycle; SCP = short-cycle program.

Figure O.6 Average SCP Tuition Varies across LAC Countries, but Financial Hardship Is the Main Dropout Reason Everywhere

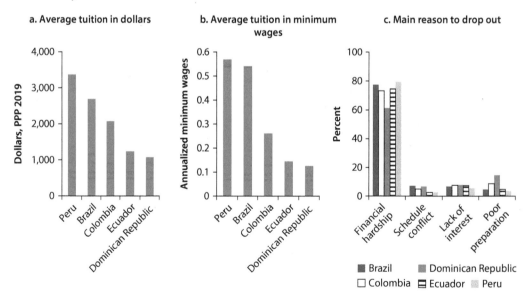

Source: Administrative data for panels a and b (see annex 1A of the book); World Bank Short-Cycle Program Survey (WBSCPS) for panel c.
Source: The figure shows the program-level (simple) average tuition, expressed in 2019 PPP dollars (panel a), or as a proportion of the country's annual minimum wage, equal to 12 times the monthly minimum wage (panel b). Panel c shows the percentage of program directors that report each reason as the main one to explain student dropout ("other reasons" are omitted from the figure). WBSCPS includes only São Paulo and Ceará for Brazil, and licensed programs for Peru. PPP = purchasing power parity.

high school graduates (figure O.7, panel a) and 25 percent more than bachelor's dropouts (figure O.7, panel b). These (Mincerian) returns have been decreasing since the early 2000s for bachelor's programs, yet they have risen for SCPs in more than half of the countries.

Beyond Mincerian returns, additional SCP quality measures tell a consistent story: on average, SCP returns are positive and relatively high, yet their variation—across fields, institutions, students, and regions—is also high. For a student with little information, this high variation poses considerable risk. Taking costs into account (direct costs such as tuition as well as the indirect costs of forgone earnings), SCPs have, on average, a positive net lifetime return relative to a high school diploma. In other words, they provide higher salaries over the life cycle than a high school degree. Net lifetime returns vary greatly among SCPs and bachelor's programs—across and within fields and HEI types—ranging from high, positive returns to negative ones (figure O.8). As a result, some SCPs provide higher returns than many bachelor's programs. Part of the SCP stigma, then, might arise from students' lack of information on returns.

Similarly, SCPs vary widely in their value added, that is, in how much they contribute to a student's labor market outcomes above and beyond the contribution made by the student or their peers (figure O.9). Program-level value-added varies across fields, but it varies much more within fields—depending, for instance, on the characteristics of the institution and the program itself.

Figure O.7 SCPs Command a Different, Generally Positive Premium across LAC Countries

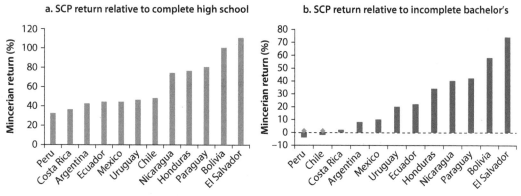

Source: Kutscher and Urzúa (2020), background paper for this book, based on the Socio-Economic Database for Latin America and the Caribbean (SEDLAC).
Note: Panel a reports the Mincerian returns to an SCP degree relative to the alternative of a high school diploma in the late 2010s. They are computed based on regression coefficients, which represent the average difference of (ln) monthly earnings between workers with an SCP degree and workers with a high school diploma, controlling for gender, age and its square, urban area indicators, and regional indicators by country. The returns are then computed as the exponential function of the coefficient minus 1. The estimation considers the potential impact of self-selection into employment. Panel b reports the Mincerian returns to an SCP degree relative to an incomplete bachelor's program; estimation is similar to the one for panel a. The diamonds above the estimates for Peru and Chile in panel b indicate that the estimates are not significantly different from zero. LAC = Latin America and the Caribbean; SCP = short-cycle program.

Figure O.8 Despite Good Averages, SCP Net Returns in LAC Vary Greatly among Programs—as Do Returns to Bachelor's Programs

Program net returns in Chile, by field

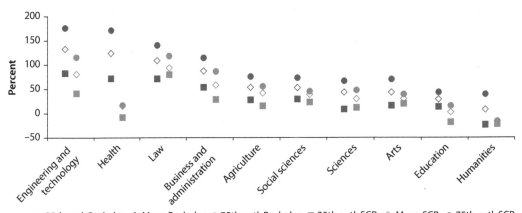

■ 25th pctl. Bachelor ◇ Mean Bachelor ● 75th pctl. Bachelor ■ 25th pctl. SCP ◇ Mean SCP ● 75th pctl. SCP

Sources: World Bank calculations based on individual-level data from the Ministry of Education of Chile, Higher Education Information Service (SIES), and *Mi Futuro*.

Note: The figure shows the average, 25th percentile, and 75th percentile of the distribution of (average) program lifetime net returns by field. "Pctl.": percentile. Program lifetime net return = [(present discounted value of lifetime earnings as a program graduate net of tuition / present discounted value of lifetime earnings as a high school graduate) − 1] * 100. LAC = Latin America and the Caribbean; SCP = short-cycle program.

Figure O.9 SCPs Vary Widely in Their Contribution to Student Outcomes in LAC—Especially within Fields

Program value-added contribution to wages in Colombia, by field

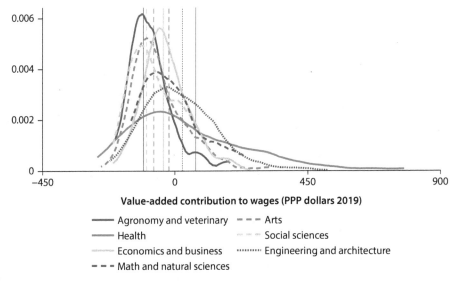

Value-added contribution to wages (PPP dollars 2019)

———— Agronomy and veterinary   – – – Arts
———— Health   ‒ ‒ ‒ Social sciences
———— Economics and business   ·········· Engineering and architecture
– – – Math and natural sciences

Source: Ferreyra et al. 2020, background paper for this book.

Note: The figure shows the distribution of program-level value-added to wages, by field of study. Wages are expressed in dollars (PPP 2019). Program-level contributions are the program value-added fixed effects, adjusting for student and peer characteristics, estimated in the regression reported in box 2.4 of the book. Their overall average is zero. SCPs taught by *Servicio Nacional de Aprendizaje* (SENA) are included. LAC = Latin America and the Caribbean; PPP = purchasing power parity; SCP = short-cycle program.

Further, SCP returns vary among students, depending on what they would choose if they did not enroll in an SCP (namely, their fallback or second-best option) and on their background characteristics. For male students with poor academic preparation, who come from disadvantaged families in small or medium-size municipalities, SCPs provide better employment and salary outcomes than the fallback option of a bachelor's program. For female students from disadvantaged, large families, SCPs provide better labor market outcomes than the fallback option of not enrolling in higher education at all. In other words, by providing a variety of quality offerings, including SCPs as well as bachelor's programs, a higher education system allows individuals to find their best, most productive match while also fulfilling employers' needs.

SCP graduates are in high demand relative to graduates from bachelor's programs, as illustrated by vacancies posted on online portals (table O.2). Nevertheless, demand for SCP graduates varies across economic sectors and geographic locations. The same two sectors of the economy concentrate most of the vacancies for SCP and bachelor's graduates—management, business and finance, and computer, engineering, and science. This might indicate segmented labor markets, where, for instance, a computer scientist and a network maintenance specialist perform different tasks based on their distinct skills. However, it might also indicate that at a time of high unemployment, the job ladder could unravel—with a computer scientist, for instance, being assigned to network maintenance. Further, the largest (most populated) area of each country concentrates the highest shares of vacancies and recent SCP graduates (the demand and supply for SCP graduates, respectively; see figure O.10). Nevertheless, demand is more concentrated than supply. In other words, there might not be enough SCP graduates relative to jobs in the largest areas, whereas there might be too many in the smaller ones. As a result, many SCP graduates in less populated areas might not find a job suited to their skills, whereas firms searching for SCP graduates in more populated areas might not find suitable candidates.

Table O.2 In LAC, SCP Graduates Are Employable and in High Demand
Minimum Educational Level Required as Posted on Online Vacancies, by Country

Minimum level of education required	Argentina	Chile	Colombia	Mexico	Peru
Primary	0.03	0.02	0.03	0.04	0.01
High school degree	0.40	0.60	0.56	0.58	0.53
SC degree	0.20	0.14	0.26	0.08	0.25
Bachelor's degree	0.12	0.07	0.04	0.09	0.04
Graduate degree	0	0	0.01	0.01	0.01
No information	0.25	0.15	0.11	0.20	0.16
Number of vacancies	580,820	1,148,359	1,896,277	2,032,132	1,290,437

Source: Galindo, Kutscher, and Urzúa (2021), background paper for this book, based on the Latin American and Caribbean Economic Association–Inter-American Development Bank Job Vacancy Project data set.
Note: For each country, the table shows the proportion of total vacancies posted online by minimum level of education required. The proportions sum to 1 (100 percent) by country. LAC = Latin America and the Caribbean; SC = short-cycle; SCP = short-cycle program.

Figure O.10 Within LAC Countries, Demand and Supply of SCP Countries Vary—and May Not Match Each Other—by Location

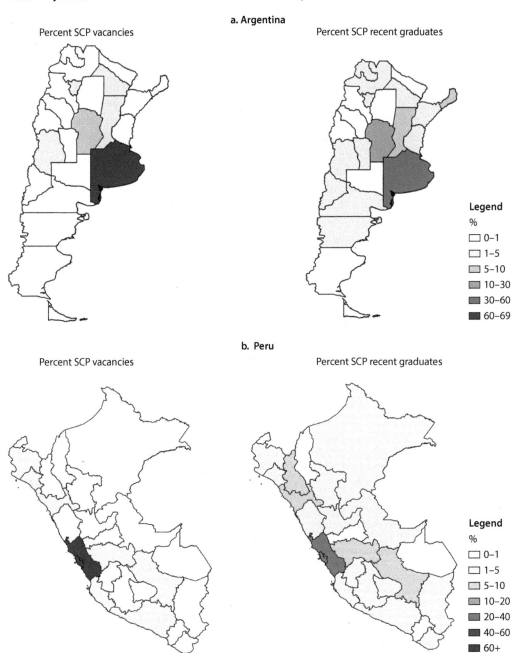

a. Argentina

Percent SCP vacancies   Percent SCP recent graduates

Legend
%
- 0–1
- 1–5
- 5–10
- 10–30
- 30–60
- 60–69

b. Peru

Percent SCP vacancies   Percent SCP recent graduates

Legend
%
- 0–1
- 1–5
- 5–10
- 10–20
- 20–40
- 40–60
- 60+

Sources: Galindo, Kutscher, and Urzúa (2021), background paper for this book, based on the Latin American and Caribbean Economic Association–Inter-American Development Bank Job Vacancy Project data set, Argentina's Statistical Annals of Higher Education (2018) and Peru's Database of Registered Degrees (2019), SIGETI.

Note: In panel a, the figure shows, for Argentina, the percentage of vacancies requesting SCP degrees posted by firms from each location (left map) and the percentage of individuals from each location who graduated from an SCP in 2017–18 (right map). Both percentages are relative to the whole country. The location is the level-1 administrative division. Panel b displays similar information for Peru. LAC = Latin America and the Caribbean; SCP = short-cycle program.

Overall, the evidence on SCP outcomes indicates that, on average, SCPs are capable of enhancing individuals' human capital and meeting employers' needs—but not all to the same extent. In the current context, then, only some SCPs are worth supporting, expanding, or emulating.

Supply of SCPs

If SCPs are to form skills for the current context and beyond, it is critical that they respond nimbly and rapidly to labor market needs. In LAC, the SCP supply is indeed dynamic—more so than that of bachelor's programs—as SCPs enter and exit the market ("churn") more frequently than bachelor's programs (table O.3). When deciding whether to open a new program in a particular location and field, HEIs respond to local economic conditions, such as the activity level in various sectors of the economy and the demand for the field's graduates —and, importantly, SCPs are more responsive than bachelor's programs (figure O.11, panel a). However, not all HEIs offering SCPs are equally responsive. Private HEIs and non-university HEIs are the most responsive (figure O.11, panels b and c). In general, SCPs' ability to respond to local labor markets suggests that they might adapt nimbly to the current needs.

Institutions also factor in their costs when they decide whether to open new programs, adding programs in fields where they already have a presence, or offering low-cost programs. Costs are particularly relevant for private HEIs, which rely almost entirely on tuition revenue. In contrast, government transfers allow public HEIs to offer relatively costly programs, such as those in computing or technology. Institutions are more likely to open new programs if they enjoy greater market power due to fewer competing programs or a higher enrollment share in the field's local market. From the point of view of public policy, the issue is that some HEIs might open low-value programs just because they are profitable.

SCPs are not equally distributed across space, as the supply of higher education programs is much greater in large cities than smaller ones. Distance and online programs have recently mitigated this inequality by expanding the options in small cities beyond face-to-face programs. The concern remains, however, that SCP markets in small cities are less competitive than those in larger ones because

Table O.3 SCPs Have a Dynamic Supply in LAC, with Lots of "Churn" among Programs

	Colombia		Chile	
	SCPs	Bachelor's programs	SCPs	Bachelor's programs
Average program life (years)	7.5	13.7	11.3	19.6
New programs per year (%)	20.8	7.2	12.0	5.9
Programs exiting per year (%)	18.0	5.5	10.3	4.7

Sources: Carranza et al. (2021), background paper for this book, based on Higher Education Information Service (SIES), from 2005 to 2018 for Chile, and National Higher Education Information System (SNIES), from 2003 to 2017 for Colombia.
Note: The table shows country-level averages for the variables listed in the rows; averages are taken over programs and years. LAC = Latin America and the Caribbean; SCP = short-cycle program.

Figure O. 11 SCP Openings Respond to the Local Economy in LAC Countries

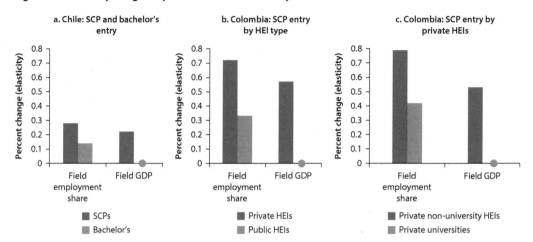

Source: World Bank calculations based on Carranza et al. (2021), background paper for this book.
Note: The figure shows the average percentage change in the probability that an HEI opens at least one new program in its geographic location (department for Colombia, region for Chile) in a given field. Probability is associated with a 1 percent increase in the (lagged) field GDP or field employment share for that location and field. A dot on the horizontal axis indicates that the corresponding estimate is not significantly different from zero. Panel a compares entry on the part of SCPs and bachelor's programs in Chile. Panel b compares SCP entry on the part of public and private HEIs in Colombia (public HEIs do not include *Servicio Nacional de Aprendizaje* (SENA)). Panel c compares SCP entry among private HEIs (universities and non-university HEIs). Field GDP is the portion of the location's GDP that can be associated to the field; association is proportional to the field's employment share by economic sector. Field employment share is the share of employed SCP graduates who completed a program in the field, relative to all employed SCP graduates. GDP = gross domestic product; HEI = higher education institution; LAC = Latin America and the Caribbean; SCP = short-cycle program.

small cities have fewer providers and, perhaps, their students are less familiar with higher education.

The presence of public, subsidized institutions in some countries decisively shapes market structure, especially with institutions that are large and have national coverage (for example, Colombia's National Learning Service, SENA). Although private HEIs can hardly compete with public HEIs in terms of tuition, they can differentiate their product in other ways, such as program content, geographic coverage, competencies taught, student services, and, in general, "product design."

The WBSCPS offers a wealth of data to investigate product design. The average program in the WBSCPS has 222 students. Consistent with their dynamism, SCP providers are young institutions, most having been established in the past 30 or 40 years. The programs are young and frequently updated. On average, the programs have desirable traits—but also substantial variation (table O.4). They mostly teach a fixed curriculum with little room for electives, which is preferable to a more flexible one, as has been shown by the US experience with community colleges.[5] They teach both cognitive and socioemotional competencies and provide remedial education, before and/or during the program. On average, they place strong emphasis on practical training. They usually require mandatory internships and have good infrastructure in workshops and labs. Nonetheless, a full 66 percent of the programs taught no classes online before the

Table O. 4 On Average, SCPs in LAC Have Good Curriculum, Infrastructure, and Faculty—but with Much Variation

Program characteristic	Mean	S.D.
Curriculum is fixed (%)	70.19	45.75
Teaches cognitive competencies (%)	79.34	40.49
Teaches socioemotional competencies (%)	94.69	22.42
Offers remediation during the program (%)	57.55	49.44
Percent of time assigned to practical training	46.70	16.86
Internships outside institution are mandatory (%)	57.75	49.41
Number of students per lab or workshop	59.43	133.25
Did not teach online classes before pandemic (%)	65.64	47.50
Student-faculty ratio	13.30	23.28
Percent of part-time faculty	61.54	30.28
Percent of faculty with more than 5 years of experience	55.74	33.12
Percent of faculty working in the industry	42.13	30.92
Percent of faculty with a bachelor's degree	82.11	29.50
Evaluate faculty at least once a year (%)	86.32	34.37
Almost all/all faculty had professional training in the previous year (%)	54.83	49.78
HEI has a governing body beyond rector/provost (%)	89.13	31.13

Source: World Bank Short-Cycle Program Survey (WBSCPS).
Note: The table shows the mean and standard deviation of some program characteristics related to curriculum and training, infrastructure, faculty, and governance, as reported by program directors. WBSCPS includes only São Paulo and Ceará for Brazil, and licensed programs for Peru. HEI = higher education institution; LAC = Latin America and the Caribbean; SCP = short-cycle program; S.D. = standard deviation.

COVID-19 pandemic and, among the online programs, quality is uneven—it is higher, for instance, in synchronous programs. Thus, the adjustment to online teaching may have posed a significant challenge for the programs in the region.

In general, the programs have low student-to-faculty ratios. Most instructors are part time, with substantive industry experience and good academic qualifications. Most are evaluated at least once a year based on multiple criteria, including student evaluations, faculty peer evaluations, and class planning assessment. About half of them provided professional training to all or almost all of their faculty in the previous year. Most programs are provided by HEIs that have a governing body beyond the rector/provost, thereby giving a voice to multiple stakeholders such as faculty, students, and firms.

On average, the programs engage with industry and assist students in their job search (figure O.12). They assign a specific person (board member, program director, or staff) to interact with firms. They tend to have internship agreements with private companies, which often provide equipment for practice, train faculty, collaborate in curriculum design or student evaluation, and have agreements to hire program graduates. The programs communicate with firms to find out their needs and request feedback on recent hires from the program.

Figure O.12 On Average, SCP Programs in LAC Engage with Industry and Assist Students in Their Job Search

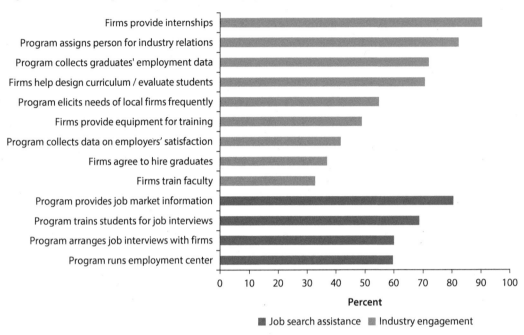

Source: World Bank Short-Cycle Program Survey (WBSCPS).
Note: The figure shows the sample mean of some program characteristics related to engagement with industry and job search assistance for students, as reported by program directors. "Frequently" means more than once per year. WBSCPS includes only São Paulo and Ceará for Brazil, and licensed programs for Peru. LAC = Latin America and the Caribbean; SCP = short-cycle program.

The programs support students' job search in multiple ways, yet the most common one is relatively passive—providing job market information. Less common are services that are more immediately useful, such as arranging job interviews, bringing recruiters to campus, or preparing students for a job search. And, although the vast majority of programs evaluate student and faculty performance more than once a year, programs engage less frequently in activities related to students' labor market outcomes, such as eliciting firms' opinions of their graduates, inquiring about firms' skill needs, or collecting data on graduates' job placement and employment.

The SCPs in the survey countries tend to believe that students care mostly about training quality (figure O.13, panel a), which might explain why the programs seem to be more attentive to curriculum, faculty, and practical training than to students' job search and labor market outcomes. Perhaps for this reason, the programs tend to view themselves as better than their competitors in training quality but not in employment outcomes (figure O.13, panel b). This suggests that although SCPs are responsive to the local economy and attempt, on average, to provide good training, they might need incentives to place greater emphasis on students' labor market outcomes.

Figure O.13 Employment May Not Be the Top Priority for SCP Students or Providers in LAC

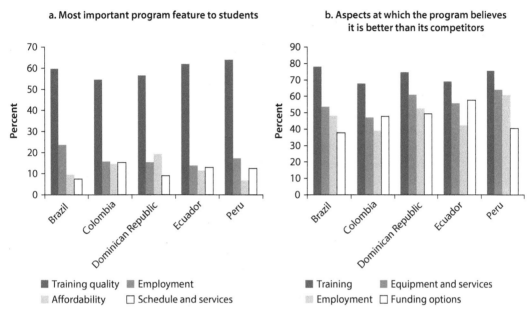

a. Most important program feature to students

b. Aspects at which the program believes it is better than its competitors

■ Training quality ■ Employment
▨ Affordability ☐ Schedule and services

■ Training ■ Equipment and services
▨ Employment ☐ Funding options

Source: World Bank Short-Cycle Program Survey (WBSCPS).
Note: Panel a shows the percentage of programs that report each feature as the most important for their students. Features are training quality, affordability, schedule and student services, and employment. Panel b shows the percentage of programs that view themselves as better than similar SCPs in each of the following categories: training, employment, equipment and services, and funding options. "Training quality" includes faculty quality, practical training, and academic quality; "Affordability" includes program cost and financial aid from the HEI; "Schedule and services" includes class schedule and quality of student services; "Employment" includes employment prospects after graduation, internship opportunities, job search assistance, and HEI connections with potential employers; "Equipment and services" includes infrastructure and student academic services. A program can view itself as better than its competitors in more than one aspect. Only São Paulo and Ceará are included for Brazil, and licensed programs for Peru. HEI = higher education institution; LAC = Latin America and the Caribbean; SCP = short-cycle program.

What Makes a Program "Good"?

The rich data collected through the WBSCPS allow for identifying the SCP practices (for example, how the program relates to industry), inputs (for example, labs for practical training), and characteristics (for example, program age) that are associated with good student outcomes, after accounting for student characteristics. The analysis focuses on four outcomes: dropout rate, time to degree, and graduates' formal employment and wages. It groups the quality determinants into six areas: infrastructure; curriculum and training; cost and financing; engagement with industry (including job search assistance); faculty; and practices related to admission, graduation, and governance. Although the data do not allow for asserting the causal impacts of the quality determinants, their associations with the outcomes are nonetheless informative.

Based on the statistical analysis, the dropout rate and time to degree are lower in programs that teach a fixed curriculum, evaluate their faculty using peer evaluation, and hire faculty with industry experience (figure O.14). Formal employment and wages are higher in programs that have sufficient

Figure O.14 SCPs with Good Outcomes Have Specific Inputs, Practices, and Characteristics

Categories	Quality determinants	Dropout rate	Time to graduate	Formal employment	Wages
Infrastructure	Internet available onsite for faculty and students			green	
	Has enough materials for practice			green	
Training and curriculum	Curriculum is fixed	green			
	Teaches numerical competencies				green
	Offers credits for longer degrees				green
	Offers remediation classes during the program				green
	Thesis or research project is a graduation requirement		red		green
Costs	Annual tuition	green			
	At least some students use HEI scholarships			green	
Link with industry	HEI has an employment center			green	
	Industry lends/provides equipment for student training			red	
	Agreements with firms to hire graduates				red
Faculty	Peer evaluation used to evaluate faculty	green			
	Class planning is very important in faculty evaluation			green	
	Percent of faculty working in industry	red			
	Percent of female faculty		green		
	Percent of faculty with 5+ years of experience		green		
	Percent of faculty < age 40 years			red	
Other practices	Admission uses a general or specific knowledge test		green		green
	Admission uses an interview			green	
	HEI has a governing board beyond rector/provost	green			

Source: World Bank calculations based on Dinarte et al. (2021), background paper for this report.
Note: The table presents a summary of the results on the correlates of the quality determinants and program academic and labor market outcomes (estimation described in chapter 4 of the book); program-level quality determinants and average labor market outcomes are reported by program directors. Green (red) indicates that the feature improves (worsens) the outcome. HEI = higher education institution; SCP = short-cycle program.

infrastructure for practical training, provide onsite internet access, teach numerical competencies, offer remediation during the program, run an employment center, have faculty with industry experience, and provide HEI scholarships to students. Giving an admission test and having a governing board beyond the provost or rector are also associated with better academic and labor market outcomes, as is having a higher tuition, which might put pressure on students to graduate or might provide better inputs. At the same time, some practices seem to hurt student outcomes. For instance, requiring a thesis for graduation delays it, and certain types of industry engagement (for instance, agreements whereby firms provide equipment or hire graduates) seem to hurt wages.

Of course, practices and inputs vary substantially across programs (table O.4, "S.D." column). These results suggest that some programs might be able to improve student outcomes by adopting practices and inputs that are associated with good outcomes. In so doing, they might help shrink the large, worrisome quality variation among programs—the gap between "good" and "bad" programs.

An important caveat is in order. To measure outcomes, the analysis relies on average program outcomes that SCP directors reported to the WBSCPS. Ideally, the analysis would rely on administrative data at the student level—background characteristics, SCP completed, and labor market outcomes. In most of LAC countries, this type of data does not exist or is not made available for research. Hence, although the WBSCPS contributed to making progress on the issue of what makes a program "good," further progress remains hampered by lack of data. Providing these data would be of help not just to researchers but to *all* stakeholders, as discussed below.[6]

Policy to Realize the Potential of SCPs

Taken together, results from this study indicate that, although SCPs appear promising, they also have shortcomings. To some extent, policy failures might be responsible for the latter. For example, regulators might believe that some programs take advantage of students, but they might lack the information necessary to identify such programs or the willingness to take action against them. Regulators might believe that students should not choose low-return programs, but they might not collect and disseminate the information that students need to make good choices. And regulators might recognize students' financial struggles, but they might not be willing to reallocate public funding toward those who need it most. They might favor the idea of SCPs providing credits for bachelor's programs but not keep track of how this works in practice. They might endorse the notion of flexible pathways among various degrees but regulate them through overly rigid norms.

Rather than dismissing or relegating SCPs—as may have been the tendency in the past—policy makers can instead address the policy failures behind the shortcomings of SCPs and provide an environment in which institutions offer good programs, students make informed choices, and the needs of individuals, firms, and the economy are met. At this critical juncture, given the region's urgent need for skills, realizing the SCP potential emerges as a key policy issue.

The study focuses on four policy categories: information, funding, oversight and regulation, and skill development pathways. The option of using a single policy instrument is not viable; multiple policy instruments are needed to face the multiple shortcomings, complement instruments' strengths, and mitigate the possible unintended effects that a particular instrument might have.

Program-level information is necessary for policy makers—who must regulate the sector and hold SCPs accountable—and for students—who need to make informed choices. This information must include average graduates' salaries and formal employment rates, as well as costs, funding options, and academic requirements. It must also be made easily available, for instance, on a website. However, existing evidence indicates that merely providing information is not sufficient to affect student choices. Instead, students must be engaged directly (for example, through counseling or interactive websites) to ensure that they receive and process relevant, timely, and useful information.

Funding inequities must be corrected, both to restore equity in access to higher education and to bring the economy closer to its optimal skill level and composition. Given the current fiscal constraints, this can be accomplished by redistributing funding across students of different incomes, program types (bachelor's and SCPs), and institution types (public and private HEIs), with the goal of providing the greatest assistance to the students who most need it. Since public funding might not be sufficient, carefully designed income-contingent loans, given by public or private institutions, might be a viable option for additional resources. Ultimately, SCP funding—and, more generally, skill development— might be viewed as a countercyclical component of the social protection system, rising during recessions to help individuals regain employment.

Oversight and regulation are fundamental in order to eliminate the lowest quality programs and promote an environment where only good programs are supplied. The regulator must establish outcome-based accountability standards—for instance, a "do no harm" rule whereby students' labor market outcomes are such that students do not, on average, lose money through the program. The regulator must also screen the entry of new programs and authorize only those with good expected outcomes. It must monitor programs periodically (for example, annually), using outcome-based accountability standards, and publish the results. Most importantly, it must close poorly performing programs. Indeed, a realistic goal for regulation—and the "first line of attack"—might simply be the elimination of the worst-performing programs.

Flexible pathways should be encouraged to facilitate skill acquisition in blocks or modules as part of lifelong learning. Completing a block would award a credential that would count toward a degree. Flexible pathways in the United States include transfers from SCPs to bachelor's programs, stackable certificates, digital badges, and the certificate-first approach.[7] While all these pathways are worth exploring, perhaps more important than adjusting SCPs to feed into bachelor's programs is adjusting bachelor's programs to absorb SCP students. The negative experience of community colleges in the United States, which give SCPs the greatest flexibility to facilitate transfers to bachelor's programs, suggests that greater SCP flexibility might not be the answer.[8] Given the good average outcomes currently accomplished by SCPs in LAC, it seems as though bachelor's programs—and not necessarily SCPs—might need greater flexibility. Streamlining programs is another way to inject greater flexibility into higher education, as many programs—particularly bachelor's—might just be too long.

Returning to the issue of the SCP stigma, is it fair and realistic in light of the evidence? Although SCPs have shortcomings that may have contributed to their stigma—including, perhaps, the poor quality of the worst-performing programs—they also have strengths that many students may currently ignore. The policies described here should help mitigate the SCP stigma. Information campaigns to promote SCPs—particularly if private firms serve as SCP "champions"—should also help.[9] But perhaps a new mindset for higher education is needed as well, one that prizes variety in offerings so that all students can find their best match.[10] The policy maker's goal should not be to maximize the number of bachelor's graduates, but to maximize individuals' potential through quality higher education programs, regardless of their type. Similarly, a student's goal should not be to obtain a bachelor's degree at any cost, but rather to graduate from the program that best matches their needs, academic preparation, and interests.

SCPs entered the LAC higher education scene relatively late. They have not had a prominent role in this region where bachelor's programs have been held as the superior—and perhaps only—key to social and economic mobility. Nonetheless, SCPs might prove to be extremely helpful in the current moment—not only to overcome the employment and production crisis generated by the COVID-19 pandemic, but also to prepare individuals for today's world of work. Succeeding at this juncture would generate a different public perception of SCPs—no longer as the lesser choice, but as the right choice for many at a time of great need. Now is the time for SCPs. If not now, when?

Notes

1. The United Nations Educational, Scientific and Cultural Organization classifies SCPs as International Standard Classification of Education (ISCED) 5, which is a type of higher education. Shorter courses and certificates are classified as ISCED 4.

2. LAC's "Golden Decade" (2003–13) was characterized by high commodity prices and growth rates. Following this period, both commodity prices and growth rates have fallen and have not returned to their previous levels.

3. Beylis et al. (2020).

4. Ferreyra et al. (2017).

5. Bailey, Jaggars, and Jenkins (2015).

6. At the time of writing this book, only Brazil had made administrative data available. Chapter 4 shows the results for Brazil using these data.

7. For further details on these pathways, see chapter 5.

8. Community colleges provide the greatest possible flexibility by letting students choose classes almost freely ("cafeteria style"), but most students who intend to transfer do not achieve this goal, and many drop out (Bailey, Jaggars, and Jenkins 2015).

9. For examples of these campaigns, see chapter 5.

10. This is in line with Ferreyra et al. (2017), who indicate three features of a good higher education system–quality, variety, and equity.

References

Bailey, T., S. Jaggars, and D. Jenkins. 2015. *Redesigning America's Community Colleges: A Clearer Path to Student Success.* Cambridge, MA: Harvard University Press.

Beylis, G., R. Fattal-Jaef, R. Sinha, M. Morris, and A. Sebastian. 2020. *Going Viral: COVID-19 and the Accelerated Transformation of Jobs in Latin America and the Caribbean.* World Bank Latin American and Caribbean Studies. Washington, DC: World Bank.

Carranza, J. E., J. M. Ferreyra, A. Gazmuri, A. Franco. 2021. "The Supply Side of Short-Cycle Higher Education Programs." Unpublished manuscript. World Bank, Washington, DC.

Dinarte, L., M. M. Ferreyra, M. Bassi, and S. Urzua. 2021. "What Makes a Program Good? Evidence from Short Cycle Higher Education Programs in Latin America and the Caribbean." World Bank, Washington, DC.

Ferreyra, M., C. Avitabile, J. Botero, F. Haimovich, and S. Urzúa. 2017. *At a Crossroads: Higher Education in Latin America and the Caribbean.* Washington, DC: World Bank Group.

Ferreyra, M., T. Melguizo, A. Franco, and A. Sanchez. 2020. "Estimating the Contribution of Short-Cycle Programs to Student Outcomes in Colombia." Policy Research Working Paper 9424, World Bank, Washington, DC.

Ferreyra, M., C. Galindo, and S. Urzúa. 2020. "Labor Market Effects of Short-Cycle Programs: Challenges and Evidence from Colombia." World Bank, Washington, DC.

Galindo, C., M. Kutscher, and S. Urzúa. 2021. "Online Job Vacancies and Short-Cycle Programs in Latin America." Background paper for this book, World Bank, Washington, DC.

Kutscher, M., and S. Urzúa. 2020. "An Economic Argument for Short-Cycle Programs in Latin America and the Caribbean." World Bank, Washington, DC.

Introduction

Following the collapse of commodity prices in the early 2010s, countries in Latin America and the Caribbean (LAC) have been seeking new engines of growth that, in addition to raising productivity, would preserve and enhance the equity gains attained in the previous decade. By developing skilled human capital, higher education can be a formidable engine of economic and social progress.

A specific type of higher education program forms skilled human capital in two or three years—so-called short-cycle programs (SCPs). Unlike bachelor's programs (which usually last five or six years in LAC), SCPs are short, are eminently practical, and have a clear goal of training students for work in a relatively short time. Their providers, who are interested in attracting students, have incentives to track new developments in the labor market and incorporate new technologies, practices, and knowledge into their curricula.

As a form of postsecondary training, SCPs are attractive to a wide variety of individuals. A first category is individuals who are not able to pursue a bachelor's program because of work or family responsibilities, or because of poor academic preparation. A second category is those who might succeed in a bachelor's program but are not willing to spend the time and resources necessary for it, opting instead for shorter, more practical, and perhaps higher paying training. A third category is those who may already have a bachelor's degree but are seeking short, specific training in their broad area of knowledge (for example, a computer scientist interested in learning computer animation) or a different one (for example, a historian interested in marketing).

More generally, individuals who wish to enhance their current skills for a similar occupation ("upskilling") or acquire new skills for a different occupation ("reskilling") might gravitate to SCPs. The wide attractiveness of SCPs contrasts with the prevailing view in the region, where SCPs bear the stigma of being the lesser choice for higher education. If they are well designed, these programs have the potential to become a crucial tool for workforce development in the new world of work—where individuals can be expected to switch occupations, and perhaps careers, multiple times over the course of a lifetime,[1] and where training must be delivered fast, efficiently, and in close connection with the labor market.

SCPs are not only attractive to individuals, they are also attractive to employers, who struggle to find skilled labor. According to the 2019 World Bank Enterprise Survey, 24 percent of firms in the world report that a workforce with inadequate education is a major constraint. In LAC, however, this rises to 32 percent—the highest of all regions. Providing the variety of skills demanded by the labor market—engineers as well as technicians and physicians as well as x-ray technologists—is a vital role of a functional, dynamic higher education system.[2]

Although LAC has needed skilled human capital for the past few years—particularly since the end of its "Golden Decade"—the need has become decidedly urgent following the COVID-19 pandemic.[3] Yet, as serious as the ensuing economic crisis has been, it has only accelerated structural labor market changes that were already underway (Beylis et al 2020). Even before the pandemic, machines had been replacing humans in routine tasks through automation, and the internet had been replacing personal interaction through the rise of electronic platforms. The productivity and market value of workers who produce intangible value added, such as researchers, analysts, programmers, and designers, was already on the rise thanks to new technologies and increased competition.

The pandemic has merely deepened these trends. Faced with quarantine and social distance requirements, some companies have replaced workers with machines for repetitive tasks, or with electronic platforms for high-contact tasks. In contrast, workers producing intangible value added have faced increasing demand and have been able to telework. Other workers who cannot be replaced by a machine or the internet, such as those in health care, have also faced increasing demand. In other words, although the pandemic has damaged aggregate employment and output, not all firms and workers have fared equally. While many jobs and firms have been destroyed, many others have appeared.

The jobs that disappeared are not likely to come back. To return to employment, those individuals need to acquire the skills relevant to the new world of work. These include cognitive skills (such as critical thinking, analytical capacities, and problem solving) as well as interpersonal skills (such as teamwork, communication, and management) that allow them to perform nonroutine, complex tasks that cannot be automated or executed by electronic platforms. In the aftermath of the COVID-19 crisis, the recovery will crucially depend on upskilling and reskilling the workforce to support economic transformation.

Recent economic crises in LAC provide an additional reason why skills must figure prominently on the path to recovery from the current one. Following such crises, some workers managed to recover employment or earnings quite well while others were permanently "scarred" or damaged, never able to recover previous employment or earnings (Silva et al. 2021). As it turns out, workers without higher education were more likely to be permanently scarred. In the current crisis, training those workers through SCPs—which are a particularly convenient form of higher education—would equip them with the skills needed to reenter the labor market soon, suffering few or no scars.

Since governments are facing extremely severe fiscal constraints, workforce development can hardly count on additional resources. Using the existing resources efficiently is of paramount importance. By being short and eminently practical, SCPs could develop skills fast and efficiently. Therefore they constitute a promise, a silver lining in the midst of an otherwise bleak landscape.

Defining SCPs

It is important to establish what SCPs are and what they are not. In defining SCPs, this book follows the United Nations Educational, Scientific and Cultural Organization's (UNESCO's) International Standard Classification of Education (ISCED). This classification describes SCPs (ISCED 5) as programs designed to provide students professional knowledge, skills, and competencies; oriented toward specific occupations; shorter, more practical, and less theoretical than bachelor's programs; and whose primary goal is student preparation for the labor market.

SCPs are higher education programs. They last at least two years and are usually two or three years long. Although shorter than bachelor's programs, they are long enough to be considered higher education programs. For this reason, they do not include short vocational or technical training courses (lasting, for instance, a few weeks or months).[4] SCPs are known by different names throughout the region, such as *programas técnicos y tecnológicos, carreras técnicas, tecnicaturas, carreras terciarias, carreras de nivel técnico superior, cursos tecnológicos, cursos técnico-profesionales, carreras profesionales*, and *cursos superiores de tecnología*.

Throughout this book, a program is defined as an institution-degree-major combination.[5] Examples of SCP degrees range from dental hygienist, physical therapist, and nurse to network technician, marketing specialist, design technician, and management specialist. In several countries, SCPs include teaching. Although some SCPs focus on rather traditional fields, such as advertising, hospitality, nursing, physical therapy, logistics, graphic design, and electronics, others have emerged in more recent, innovative fields such as app design, digital animation, big data, web design, cybersecurity, and social networks.

What Is a "Good" SCP?

To address the needs of individuals, employers, and policy makers, SCPs in LAC must be "good," that is, of high quality. The question, then, is how to tell whether a program is good.

Higher education may benefit an individual in multiple ways. It may raise her skills, improve her employment prospects, and offer a higher salary. It may also broaden her social network, expose her to alternative viewpoints, and enrich her cultural life. Not only can higher education benefit the individual, it can also benefit society as a whole. For example, a highly educated individual may be more involved with her local community and contribute to a richer exchange of ideas and information.

However, several of these personal and social benefits are extremely hard to measure. Further, in the case of SCPs, their immediate goal—as stated by UNESCO's definition—is training the individual for the labor market. Therefore this book focuses primarily on labor market outcomes such as employment and wages. It also examines mediating academic outcomes such as graduation rates and time to degree.

A program is viewed as good when it produces good outcomes, after accounting for students' backgrounds and characteristics. This qualification is important. For instance, if a recent graduate obtains a high initial wage after graduation, is it because she was already highly skilled, that is, well prepared before she started the program, or because the program substantially enhanced her skills? In this example, a good program would be one that contributed substantially to her skills and helped her reach a high wage regardless of her initial background. In other words, good (or high-quality) programs have high value added.

To measure a program's value added, the gold standard would be a large-scale experiment—randomly assigning some individuals to the program while assigning others to a control group (consisting, for instance, of not pursuing higher education at all). If individuals in the first group attained better outcomes than those in the second, it could be concluded that the program has positive value added, making a positive contribution to student outcomes.

However, randomized experiments are rare. They are also not practical, for instance, for estimating the value added of hundreds or thousands of programs in a country. Even when experimental settings might be exploited that do not require randomization, these are not always available. Given that the analysis generally must rely on nonexperimental data, measuring value added requires student-level information that is unavailable or extremely difficult to obtain, such as background characteristics, academic readiness for the program, and outcomes. Although data sets might contain information on students' socioeconomic status, they usually do not record other important aspects, such as motivation or work habits.

Depending on data availability and the specific question of interest, this study uses multiple proxies for SCP quality, including aggregate employment and wages, Mincerian returns, program net lifetime returns, job openings (vacancies), average program outcomes, program value added, and returns (treatment effects) relative to the student's second best option, which might consist of not pursuing higher education at all or pursuing a bachelor's degree.

World Bank Short-Cycle Program Survey

Consider a program that is "good." What makes it good? What specific practices does it use to yield good outcomes, after accounting for student characteristics? For example, does it communicate frequently with local companies to assess their skill needs? Does it update the curriculum in response to industry feedback? Does it hire faculty with industry experience? Does it run an employment center to assist students in their job search?

Entering the "black box" of program quality is fundamental to design and replicate high-quality programs. However, program practices are usually not reported in standard data sets, which at most contain program characteristics such as duration or number of faculty. This lack of data severely limits the ability to understand what makes a program good.

To overcome this limitation, this study designed and implemented the World Bank Short-Cycle Program Survey (WBSCPS) in Brazil, Colombia, the Dominican Republic, Ecuador, and Peru. These countries account for 54 percent of all SCP enrollment in LAC. In Brazil, the survey focused on the states of São Paulo and Ceará; in Peru, it focused on licensed programs.

The survey was administered to program directors by phone, online, and in person. It had an unusually high response rate (70 percent on average), for a total of approximately 2,100 effective interviews. About half of the interviews took place during the COVID-19 lockdown. In an effort to encourage truthful responses, program directors were informed that the survey was part of a World Bank study and not a joint effort with any government authority; that responses were confidential and would not be shared with third parties (including government); and that responses would not be individually reported in the study. Additional technical information on the WBSCPS can be found in Box I.1.

Box I.1 Some Technical Aspects of the World Bank Short-Cycle Program Survey

The World Bank Short-Cycle Program Survey (WBSCPS) was implemented in five countries in Latin America and the Caribbean: Brazil, Colombia, the Dominican Republic, Ecuador, and Peru. In Brazil, given the size of the country, the survey focused on the states of São Paulo and Ceará, which are markedly different from each other. While São Paulo captures 22 percent of Brazil's population, Ceará captures 4 percent. Relative to Brazil as a whole, the per capita gross domestic product of São Paulo is about 50 percent higher; in Ceará, it is 50 percent lower. In Peru, the survey focused on licensed short-cycle programs (SCPs) as of October 2019 (17 percent of all the SCPs in the country). Licensed programs have higher enrollment and charge higher tuition than nonlicensed programs. Throughout this book, on the WBSCPS, "Brazil" refers to São Paulo and Ceará, and "Peru" to licensed programs.

The sources and years of the SCP universe for the purpose of the WBSCPS are as follows:

• Brazil: Higher Education Census (*Censo da Educação Superior*), 2017
• Colombia: National Information System of Higher Education (*Sistema Nacional de Información de la Educación Superior*), 2017
• Dominican Republic: Ministry of Economics, Planning, and Development, 2019
• Ecuador: Secretariat of Higher Education, Science, Technology and Innovation, 2019
• Peru: Ministry of Education, 2019

---

box continues next page

Box I.1 Some Technical Aspects of the World Bank Short-Cycle Program Survey *(continued)*

As the survey was conducted, the team learned that some programs had been closed and new ones had opened, so the universe of SCPs was adjusted accordingly. Given universe sizes (see table BI.1.1), random samples were surveyed in Brazil and Colombia, whereas the universe of SCPs was surveyed for the remaining countries. The samples were stratified by location (five regions in Colombia; the two states in Brazil); institution type (three types in Colombia—*institución universitaria+escuelas* and *institutos tecnológicos, institución técnica profesional*, and *universidades*—and four types in Brazil—*universidade, centro universitário, faculdade*, and *instituto* or *centro federal*); and administration type (public or private). Because of the lack of a geographic identifier in Brazil's universe for online programs, these were not included in the survey. Table BI.1.1 shows the universe and sample sizes, as well as the response rates.

Since information on the surveys is reported by program directors, the team followed best practices to mitigate typical problems in self-reported surveys. First, respondents received a letter from the team leader indicating that their responses would be confidential, anonymous, and reported only in an aggregate fashion, thus favoring truth telling. Second, in the letter, respondents were told that the survey was being conducted by the World Bank and not a unit of their government (such as the Ministry of Education), thus eliminating possible gains from misreporting and also favoring truth telling. Third, questions were designed so as to avoid some common biases. For example, they refer to a specific period (such as the previous academic year) to address memory biases; are not open ended, and, where possible, include drop-down menus with specific options. Where possible, the team cross-checked responses with administrative data.

The team conducted tests to evaluate the representativeness of the samples given the appropriate calibration of sampling weights. In the case of Brazil and Colombia, the issue is whether effective surveys are representative of the universe. In the remaining cases, the issue is whether effective surveys are representative of their samples (which, in turn, are representative of their universes). In all cases, the team found that the effective surveys were representative of their universes (in Brazil and Colombia) or samples (in the remaining countries). In their background paper for this report, Dinarte et al. (2021) provide further information on representativeness tests.

Table BI1.1 Universes, Samples, and Response Rates, by Country

Country	Universe size	Sample size	Closed programs	Effective surveys	Response rate (%)
Brazil	2,388	1,205	266	603	64
Colombia	2,130	1,314	207	900	81
Dominican Republic	209	209	116	80	86
Ecuador	543	543	59	294	61
Peru	387	387	9	228	60
Total	**5,657**	**3,658**	**657**	**2,105**	**70**

Source: Staff calculations based on data from the World Bank Short-Cycle Program Survey.

The survey asked 65 questions covering a broad range of topics, including student demographics and readiness for the program; admission and graduation requirements; faculty characteristics, hiring, and evaluation; curriculum and practical training; infrastructure; online classes; costs and financing; oversight and regulation; institutional governance; interaction with industry; job search assistance; competition; and academic and labor market outcomes.

The WBSCPS has generated a wealth of information and allowed for characterizing the SCP sector well beyond what had been possible previously. The information is presented throughout the book.

Framework of the Book

To address the needs of individuals, employers, and policy makers, SCPs in LAC must be of high quality and respond flexibly to market needs. Hence, this study describes the SCP sector in LAC and investigates SCP outcomes, quality, and supply.

Just as SCPs have not received a great deal of policy attention in the past, neither have they received much research attention.[6] Since the bulk of higher education research investigates bachelor's programs, both in the developing and developed worlds, SCPs are an understudied segment of the higher education market. During the dissemination of previous work on higher education in LAC,[7] focused mostly on bachelor's programs, conversations with policy makers, business leaders, and higher education administrators and faculty revealed how important—and little known—the SCP segment is. This study seeks to fill that void. Further, the study makes a unique contribution to the SCP literature because of its geographic scope, data, and focus. While the best current research on SCPs for the developed world tends to focus on a single area within a country (for example, one state within the United States),[8] this study focuses on multiple LAC countries. It exploits and combines rich data from several sources, including administrative data and the novel WBSCPS. And, while previous research has placed little focus on the heterogeneity across programs—particularly in practices—this study documents and examines SCPs' variation across countries, higher education institution (HEI) types, fields, and subnational locations.

The book is organized as follows. Chapter 1 depicts the SCP landscape in LAC. It presents key stylized facts for SCPs in LAC relative to other regions and provides initial evidence of their academic and labor market promise. The chapter also describes SCP students, funding, and institutional arrangements.

Chapter 2 examines one dimension of the quality of SCPs, namely, their economic returns. The chapter examines multiple metrics: Mincerian returns, net lifetime returns, value-added contributions, and treatment effects. It also analyzes the demand for SCP graduates through the use of job vacancy data.

Chapter 3 investigates the supply side of the sector. It examines how institutions decide on the opening or closing of SCPs, how they compete with each other, and how SCP supply varies across locations of different sizes. Drawing from the WBSCPS, the chapter looks at aspects of program design—the features and practices that programs choose to have, including students, faculty, curriculum and training, infrastructure, connections with the private sector, and job search assistance for students.

Given the program features and practices documented in chapter 3 and the economic returns documented in chapter 2, chapter 4 investigates what program features and practices are associated with good outcomes. Drawing from the study's findings—which, to anticipate, show that SCPs are indeed promising yet suffer from several shortcomings—chapter 5 discusses possible policies to address the shortcomings of SCPs and realize their promise.

Notes

For their excellent research assistance, Andrea Franco, Manuela Granda, Angelica Sánchez, and Gabriel Suárez are gratefully acknowledged.

1 The World Bank's 2019 World Development Report explores these issues (World Bank 2019).

2. In a previous World Bank report on higher education in LAC, Ferreyra et al. (2017) stress the importance of variety, along with quality and equity, to a good higher education system.

3. LAC's "Golden Decade" (2003–13) was characterized by high commodity prices and growth rates. Following this period, both commodity prices and growth rates have fallen and have not returned to their previous levels.

4. UNESCO establishes that the ISCED 5 level has a minimum duration of two years and, for the case of higher education systems where credentials are based on the accumulation of credits, a comparable time period and intensity are required to complete the ISCED 5 level. See http://uis.unesco.org/sites/default/files/documents/isced-2011-sp.pdf.

5. Examples of programs are interior design technician at Autonomous University of Santo Domingo (Dominican Republic), early stimulation technologist at Riobamba Technological Institute (Ecuador), and human resources technologist at Paulista University (Brazil). In some LAC countries, programs are known as *carreras*.

6. One exception is de Moura Castro and Garcia (2003), who explore whether community colleges constitute a viable model for LAC.

7. Ferreyra et al. (2017.)

8. See, for instance, Jepsen, Troske, and Coomes (2014); Liu, Belfield, and Trimble (2015); Xu and Trimble (2016); Belfield (2015); and Dadgar and Trimble (2015).

References

Belfield, C. 2015. "Weathering the Great Recession with Human Capital? Evidence on Labor Market Returns to Education from Arkansas." A CAPSEE Working Paper. Center for Analysis of Postsecondary Education and Employment, New York, NY.

Beylis, G., R. Fattal-Jaef, R. Sinha, M. Morris, and A. Sebastian. 2020. *Going Viral: COVID-19 and the Accelerated Transformation of Jobs in Latin America and the Caribbean.* World Bank Latin American and Caribbean Studies. Washington, DC: World Bank.

Dadgar, M., and M. J. Trimble. 2015. "Labor Market Returns to Sub-Baccalaureate Credentials: How Much Does a Community College Degree or Certificate Pay?" *Educational Evaluation and Policy Analysis* 37 (4): 399–418.

de Moura Castro, C., and N. M. Garcia. 2003. *Community Colleges: A Model for Latin America.* Washington, DC: Inter-American Development Bank.

Dinarte, L., M. M. Ferreyra, M. Bassi, and S. Urzúa. 2021. "What Makes a Program Good? Evidence from Short-Cycle Higher Education Programs in Latin America and the Caribbean." World Bank, Washington, DC.

Ferreyra, M., C. Avitabile, J. Botero, F. Haimovich, and S. Urzúa. 2017. *At a Crossroads: Higher Education in Latin America and the Caribbean.* Washington, DC: World Bank.

Jepsen, C., K. Troske, and P. Coomes. 2014. "The Labor-Market Returns to Community College Degrees, Diplomas, and Certificates." *Journal of Labor Economics* 32 (1): 95–121.

Liu, V. Y., C. R. Belfield, and M. J. Trimble. 2015. "The Medium-Term Labor Market Returns to Community College Awards: Evidence from North Carolina." *Economics of Education Review* 44: 42–55.

Silva, J., L. Sousa, T. Packard, and R. Robertson. 2021. *Crises and Labor Markets in Latin America and the Caribbean: Lessons for an Inclusive Recovery from the COVID-19 Pandemic.* Washington, DC: World Bank.

World Bank. 2019. *World Development Report 2019: The Changing Nature of Work.* World Development Report. Washington, DC: World Bank. https://openknowledge.worldbank.org/handle/10986/30435 License: CC BY 3.0 IGO.

Xu, D., and M. Trimble. 2016. "What about Certificates? Evidence on the Labor Market Returns to Nondegree Community College Awards in Two States." *Educational Evaluation and Policy Analysis* 38 (2): 272–92.

CHAPTER 1

Landscape of Short-Cycle Programs in Latin America and the Caribbean

María Marta Ferreyra

Introduction

In its quest to form skilled human capital fast, Latin America and the Caribbean (LAC) looks to short-cycle programs (SCPs), which promise not only higher productivity but also greater social and economic mobility to potentially millions of individuals. SCPs' current labor market outcomes provide a first glimpse into their ability to deliver on these goals—and so does their institutional context, which can enhance or curtail that ability.

This chapter describes the landscape of SCPs in LAC. It begins by describing their institutional context. Then it presents some stylized facts. First, the chapter benchmarks the prevalence of SCPs in LAC relative to other regions in the world. Second, it compares SCP students with students in bachelor's programs and high school graduates who do not pursue higher education. Third, it compares graduation rates for SCPs and bachelor's programs. Fourth, it compares labor market outcomes for SCPs and bachelor's programs, distinguishing between bachelor's graduates and bachelor's dropouts. The chapter then examines a particularly important institutional aspect, namely per-student public funding for SCPs vis-à-vis bachelor's programs. The chapter closes with a description of the institutional framework, students, tuition, and funding in the survey countries (Brazil, Colombia, the Dominican Republic, Ecuador, and Peru.)

The main findings are as follows:

- SCPs are relatively less prevalent in LAC than in other regions of the world, as the share of SCPs in higher education enrollment is lower in LAC than in most other regions. Moreover, the large expansion of higher education that has taken place in LAC since the early 2000s has been heavily biased toward bachelor's programs.

- Students in SCPs are more disadvantaged and less traditional than those in bachelor's programs. They are slightly older, more likely to be female and married, and come from lower income households. However, they are less disadvantaged than individuals who do not pursue higher education at all.
- Despite their disadvantage, SCP students graduate at higher rates, on average, than bachelor's students. Moreover, SCP graduates attain better labor market outcomes (unemployment rate, formal employment, and wages) than bachelor's dropouts. This is a particularly important finding, as bachelor's dropouts account for about half of all the individuals that start higher education in LAC.
- Governments provide a lower per-student annual subsidy to SCPs than to bachelor's programs. Since bachelor's programs last longer than SCPs, the gap is even larger in terms of total per-student subsidy. This might have created a public perception of bachelor's programs as being more socially valuable than SCPs, perhaps contributing inadvertently to the preexisting SCP stigma.
- In the survey countries, the average SCP has a student body that consists mostly of male students and students who are younger than age 25. In Brazil and the Dominican Republic, most students are enrolled part time; in the other survey countries, they are mostly enrolled full time. Students enter most programs with deficits in math, reading, and writing. On average, the programs are relatively affordable in Colombia, the Dominican Republic, and Ecuador but less so in Peru and Brazil. Although students have access to some funding mechanisms, for the most part, they self-fund their studies in SCPs. Not surprisingly, the program directors reported that the main reason for student dropout is financial hardship. Although the programs claim to provide a pathway toward more advanced degrees, few students pursue these, suggesting that the pathways might not be smooth.

Institutional Landscape

Before starting, a clarification is in order on the definition of SCPs. This book follows the United Nations Educational, Scientific and Cultural Organization's (UNESCO) International Standard Classification of Education (ISCED), which describes SCPs (ISCED 5) as programs that are designed to provide students professional knowledge, skills, and competencies; oriented toward specific occupations; shorter, more practical, and less theoretical than bachelor's programs; and whose primary goal is student preparation for the labor market.[1] ISCED 5 programs are higher education programs; they last at least two years and do not include shorter vocational or occupational training programs.[2]

In LAC, the institutional landscape of SCPs is quite complex. Examples of SCP degrees range from dental hygienist, physical therapist, and nurse to network technician, marketing specialist, design technician, and management specialist. In several countries, they also include teaching.[3] Further, they span a range of traditional and innovative programs. Traditional programs include advertising, hospitality and tourism, nursing, auto mechanics, logistics, culinary arts, fashion design, graphic design, and electronics. Innovative programs include aeronautics, app design, digital logistics, digital animation, video game design, data science, information security, web design, cytohistology, cybersecurity, biotechnology, and social networks.

SCPs usually take two or three years, although in some countries they can take as long as four.[4] They are mostly offered by non-university higher education institutions (HEIs), such as technical institutes and professional training centers, although in some countries they are also offered by universities.[5] For instance, in Brazil, Chile, and Colombia, university and non-university HEIs can offer SCPs, yet only non-university HEIs can do so in Peru. In some countries, the non-university sector includes an institution with national coverage, which is public in Colombia (the National Learning Service [SENA, *Servicio Nacional de Aprendizaje*]) and private in Brazil (the S System) and Peru (the National Industrial Work Training Service [SENATI, *Servicio Nacional de Adiestramiento en Trabajo Industrial*]).[6]

Figure 1.1 shows the number of non-university HEIs in each country. For comparison, it also shows the number of universities regardless of whether they offer SCPs. Different HEI types prevail in different countries. Universities outnumber non-university HEIs in Mexico and Costa Rica, but the reverse happens in Argentina, Brazil, and Peru. Perhaps because of this institutional variety, in practice, there is usually no pathway from SCPs to bachelor's programs—particularly across different HEIs—and universities rarely coordinate with non-university HEIs. Students in SCPs usually follow a structured curriculum, with little margin for curriculum customization or elective classes. For

Figure 1.1 University and Non-University Higher Education Institutions, circa 2019

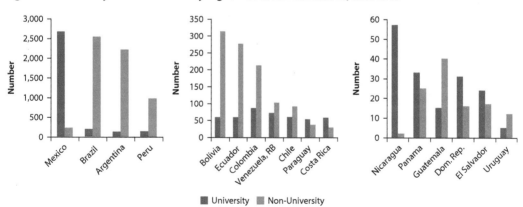

■ University ■ Non-University

Sources: Administrative information for Brazil, Chile, Colombia, and Ecuador (see annex 1A for detailed information); Brunner and Miranda 2016 for the other countries.
Note: The data are for the following years: Argentina (2014), Bolivia (2014), Brazil (2018), Chile (2019), Colombia (2019), Costa Rica (2014), Dominican Republic (2014), Ecuador (2018), El Salvador (2014), Guatemala (2014), Mexico (2014), Nicaragua (2014), Panama (2014), Paraguay (2014), Peru (2014), Uruguay (2014), and República Bolivariana de Venezuela (2014). In Chile and Colombia, institutions with multiple branches are counted as one.

comparison, box 1.1 provides a brief description of the institutional landscape in the United States and Germany.

In LAC, most students attend higher education locally (Ferreyra et al. 2017), particularly for SCPs. A variety of public and private HEIs provide SCPs. SCPs in public HEIs are free or highly subsidized. Private institutions charge tuition, although in countries such as Brazil, Chile, Colombia, Ecuador, and Peru, governments facilitate access to private SCPs by providing scholarships, tuition subsidies, or student loans (Sevilla 2017). Only Brazil, Chile, Costa Rica, Haiti, Mexico, and Peru allow for-profit HEIs. For the most part, SCPs are open enrollment, nonselective programs, although they do have some admission requirements.

SCPs usually fall under the purview of the Ministry of Education. They are subject to similar quality assurance procedures as bachelor's programs—procedures that, in general, do not consider program outcomes such as employability and initial earnings. However, in recent years, Colombia, Chile, and

---

Box 1.1 Short-Cycle Programs in the United States and Germany

United States. Short-cycle programs (SCPs) include two-year programs leading to associate degrees taught at non-university institutions such as community or junior colleges, vocational technical institutes, and career colleges.[a] Community colleges are public institutions run at the state level; other providers include for-profit and not-for-profit private institutions. Community colleges and for-profit and not-for-profit providers capture 96, 3, and 1 percent of the market share, respectively. As of 2017–18, 44 percent of US undergraduates were enrolled in community colleges.

In community colleges, associate degrees in principle offer a pathway to bachelor's programs, although the coordination necessary between community colleges and universities is not equally successful across states and institutions (Bailey, Jaggars, and Jenkins 2015). Associate degrees typically feature a highly flexible, "cafeteria-style" curriculum that allows students to choose among a wide variety of courses and fashion their own degree. Bailey, Jaggars, and Jenkins (2015) discuss the negative consequences of this model and present successful cases of structured curricula.

Germany. Vocational education and training are widely popular in Germany, as many students from lower and upper secondary school opt for the dual system, which provides on-the-job and classroom training. In addition, vocational education is also offered at the postsecondary, non-higher education level. At the higher education level, this type of training is provided in SCPs taught at two-year institutions *(fachschulen)* that specialize in one or several subjects and frequently offer dual training. Most vocational and technical education in Germany does not take place in a higher education setting, but rather in secondary or postsecondary, non-higher education training.

Sources: National Center for Education and Statistics (https://nces.ed.gov/ipeds/TrendGenerator/app/answer/2/3?f=1%3D5&rid =5&cid=16); Community College Research Center (https://ccrc.tc.columbia.edu/Community-College-FAQs.html); Country Note for Germany, Education GPS, OECD (https://gpseducation.oecd.org/Content/EAGCountryNotes/EAG2020_CN_DEU.pdf).
Note. a. In Latin America and the Caribbean, only the Caribbean countries have community colleges.

Peru have developed information systems that report outcomes on public websites, at the program or more aggregate level.

Private HEIs absorb 48 percent of SCP students in LAC (figure 1.2). Nonetheless, the enrollment share of private HEIs varies widely across countries, from more than 75 percent in Brazil, Chile, El Salvador, and Peru to less than 20 percent in Colombia, Nicaragua, and Uruguay.

Five Stylized Facts

This section describes salient stylized facts about SCPs in LAC. Some definitions are in order. For a given country, the working-age population (WAP) is defined as the set of individuals between ages 25 and 65 years. For some analyses, the focus is on individuals in the WAP with at least a high school diploma, and they are classified into five levels of educational attainment: high school, incomplete SCP ("SCP dropout"), complete SCP ("SCP graduate"), incomplete bachelor's program ("bachelor's dropout"),[7] and complete bachelor's program ("bachelor's graduate").[8] Individuals who have started higher education, whether they completed it or not, are considered to have "at least some higher education." Statistics at the country level reflect an average over individuals; statistics for the whole region reflect a simple average over countries except when indicated otherwise. Several facts reported below and in other parts of this book draw from a critical data source, SEDLAC (box 1.2).

Figure 1.2 Enrollment in Short-Cycle Programs in Public and Private Institutions, circa 2018

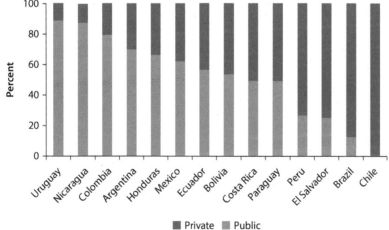

Sources: World Bank calculations based on the Socio-Economic Database for Latin America and the Caribbean and administrative data for Brazil and Colombia (see annex 1A).
Note: For each country, the figure shows the percentage of all short-cycle program (SCP) students, regardless of age, enrolled in public or private higher education institutions (HEIs). For Colombia, "public" includes *Servicio Nacional de Aprendizaje* (SENA). The data are for the following years: Argentina (2018), Bolivia (2018), Brazil (2018), Colombia (2018), Chile (2017), Costa Rica (2018), El Salvador (2018), Honduras (2016), Mexico (2018), Nicaragua (2014), Paraguay (2018), Peru (2018), and Uruguay (2018).

Box 1.2 Fundamental Data Source: SEDLAC

Much of the analysis in this book draws on household survey microdata for countries in Latin America and the Caribbean (LAC). The data come from the Socio-Economic Database for Latin America and the Caribbean (SEDLAC). This database was constructed by the Center for Distributive, Labor and Social Studies at the Universidad National de La Plata (Argentina) and the World Bank's Poverty Group for the LAC region. Since the raw microdata from household surveys are not uniform across LAC countries, SEDLAC harmonizes them to provide information that is comparable across countries and over time, "by using similar definitions of variables in each country/year, and by applying consistent methods of processing the data" (CEDLAS and World Bank 2014).

The harmonized data are extremely useful for many analyses. Indeed, Ferreyra et al. (2017) rely heavily on these data to study higher education in LAC. Nonetheless, the usefulness of these data is limited for the present book, because the harmonized data remove the distinction between bachelor's programs and short-cycle programs (SCPs), lumping them together under a single higher education category. As a result, it is not clear whether a higher education student is enrolled in an SCP or completed an SCP. To overcome this obstacle, the book uses the raw, unharmonized data and relies on the country-specific questionnaires in the household surveys to identify SCP enrollment and SCP degrees.

Still, a couple of issues remain. First, the original survey does not separately identify SCP enrollment in Brazil, Colombia, the Dominican Republic, and Guatemala, or SCP graduates in Brazil, the Dominican Republican, and Guatemala. Thus, the book uses administrative data whenever possible (see annex 1A). Second, the data do not reveal whether individuals have graduated from higher education in Bolivia, Mexico, and Nicaragua, but rather the type of program (SCP or bachelor's) in which they were enrolled and for how many years. Completion is imputed based on the number of years enrolled in higher education, with different windows for SCP and bachelor's completion.

Stylized fact 1. LAC has experienced a large, rapid expansion of higher education since the early 2000s.

In the new millennium, gross enrollment rates in higher education have grown in every region of the world (figure 1.3). Their worldwide average has doubled, going from 19 percent in 2000 to 38 percent in 2017. Growth over the same period was even greater in LAC, where the gross enrollment rate more than doubled, from 23 to 52 percent (Ferreyra et al. 2017).

Stylized fact 2. LAC has relatively few students enrolled in SCPs.

On average, 24 percent of students in higher education in the world are currently enrolled in SCPs (figure 1.4). The share of higher education students who are enrolled in SCPs (namely, the SCP enrollment share) declined in almost all regions between 2000 and 2017. In other words, in the recent worldwide expansion of higher education, enrollment in bachelor's programs has grown more than enrollment in SCPs.

Figure 1.3 Higher Education Gross Enrollment Rate, 2000, 2010, and 2017

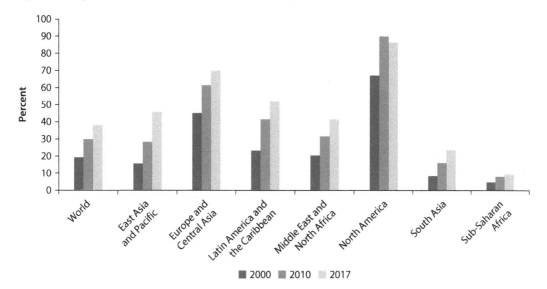

Source: World Development Indicators, based on data from the United Nations Educational, Scientific and Cultural Organization.
Note: For each region, the gross enrollment rate corresponds to the weighted average across the region's countries.

Figure 1.4 Students Enrolled in Short-Cycle Programs Relative to Total Higher Education Enrollment, 2000, 2010, and 2017

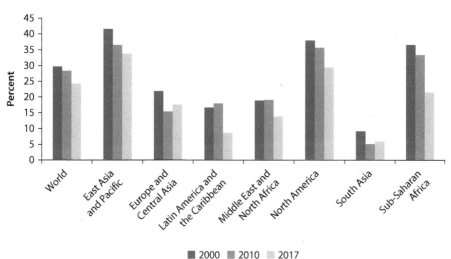

Source: World Bank calculations based on data from the United Nations Educational, Scientific and Cultural Organization and the National Center for Education Statistics for the United States (2000 and 2010).
Note: The figure shows the percentage of students enrolled in short-cycle programs (SCPs) (ISCED 5) relative to total enrollment in higher education (ISCED 5-8), regardless of age. Total enrollment includes postgraduate programs. Each region shows the weighted average of the corresponding countries.

Despite this worldwide decline, the current SCP enrollment share varies widely across regions. Among the seven regions depicted in figure 1.4, East Asia and the Pacific has the highest SCP enrollment share (34 percent), while LAC has the second lowest (9 percent). Further, LAC's SCP enrollment share has almost halved since 2000, and it has fallen in about two-thirds of LAC countries (figure 1.5).

Stylized fact 3. SCPs tend to attract disadvantaged, nontraditional students.

When choosing a higher education program, students sort into SCPs and bachelor's programs depending on multiple personal factors, such as socioeconomic background, preferences, residential location, and family commitments. Sorting also depends on the availability of bachelor's programs and SCPs in their area of residence and on their ability to move to another location. As a result of sorting, SCP students are, on average, different from bachelor's students. SCP students are more likely to be female, are slightly older, and are less likely to reside in urban locations (table 1.1).[9] They are also more likely to be married and to work while studying, although those who work are less likely to be full-time workers. Further, SCP students are more likely than bachelor's students to be in the bottom 80 percent of the income distribution and substantially less likely to be in the top 20 percent. In a word, SCP students are more disadvantaged that students at bachelor's programs.

Figure 1.5 Higher Education Students in Short-Cycle Programs, circa 2004 and 2018

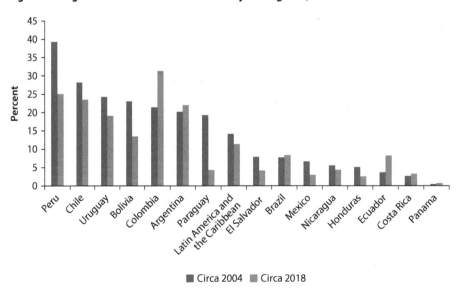

■ Circa 2004 ■ Circa 2018

Source: World Bank calculations based on the Socio-Economic Database for Latin America and the Caribbean (SEDLAC) and administrative data for Brazil and Colombia (see annex 1A).
Note: Blue (orange) bars show the percentage of individuals ages 18–24 years who are enrolled in an SCP relative to all individuals ages 18–24 years enrolled in higher education in 2004 (2018). The data are for the following years: Argentina (2003, 2018), Bolivia (2005, 2018), Brazil (2004, 2018), Chile (2006, 2017), Colombia (2004, 2018), Costa Rica (2004, 2018), Ecuador (2008, 2018), El Salvador (2003, 2018), Honduras (2005, 2016), Mexico (2004, 2018), Nicaragua (2001, 2014), Panama (2004, 2016), Paraguay (2004, 2018), Peru (2003, 2018), and Uruguay (2006, 2018).

Table 1.1 Characteristics of Bachelor's and Short-Cycle Program Students and of High School Graduates, circa 2018

	Bachelor's students	Short-cycle students	HS graduates, never enrolled
Female (%)	54.4	63.1	50.1
Age (years)	24.0	24.9	35.9
Urban (%)	90.3	80.8	81.1
Married (%)	14.5	22.6	57.2
Employed (%)	41.8	43.6	70.6
Full time (%)	56.7	54.4	73.9
Income Q1 (%)	8.9	14.4	16.8
Income Q2 (%)	13.1	17.0	21.1
Income Q3 (%)	19.0	23.5	22.3
Income Q4 (%)	23.9	25.9	22.2
Income Q5 (%)	35.0	19.3	17.6

Source: World Bank calculations based on the Socio-Economic Database for Latin America and the Caribbean.
Note: The table shows averages of characteristics of students enrolled in bachelor's and short-cycle programs, and for high school graduates who have never enrolled in higher education, regardless of age. Simple averages over LAC countries are shown. "Urban" denotes the percentage of students residing in urban areas. "Employed" denotes whether the student works, full or part time. A part-time (full-time) worker works less than (at least) 40 hours a week. "Full time" denotes the percentage of students who work full time, conditional on working. "Income Q1" denotes the percentage of students in quintile 1 of the income distribution (bottom 20 percent), and similarly for the remaining quintiles. The quintiles of the income distribution correspond to total household income (ingreso total familiar). All differences in average characteristics between students in short-cycle programs (SCPs) and bachelor's programs are significantly different from zero. Differences in average characteristics between students in SCPs and high school graduates are significantly different from zero, with the exception of urban and income Q1, Q3, Q4, and Q5.

The comparison with high school graduates who do not enroll in higher education reveals that women are more likely than men to enroll in higher education, and individuals pursue higher education when they are relatively young. High school graduates are more likely than higher education students to be married, employed, and work full time. High school graduates are also more likely to be in the bottom 40 percent of the income distribution.[10] In other words, they are even more disadvantaged than SCP students.

The fact that SCPs attract students of lower economic background compared with bachelor's students may have contributed to SCPs' prevailing stigma in the region, as they might be viewed as less challenging and rewarding than bachelor's programs. At the same time, SCPs' ability to attract more disadvantaged, nontraditional students indicates an ability to serve a qualitatively different market segment—a segment in need of flexible, fast, and practical training.

Stylized fact 4. Completion rates are higher for SCPs than for bachelor's programs.

On average, completion rates in SCPs are higher than in bachelor's programs (57 and 46 percent, respectively). SCPs have higher completion rates in all the countries in the region except Mexico, Panama, and Honduras (figure 1.6).[11] This contrasts with the United States, where SCPs have lower completion rates than bachelor's programs (33 versus 62 percent, respectively).[12] Several

Figure 1.6 Completion Rates, circa 2018

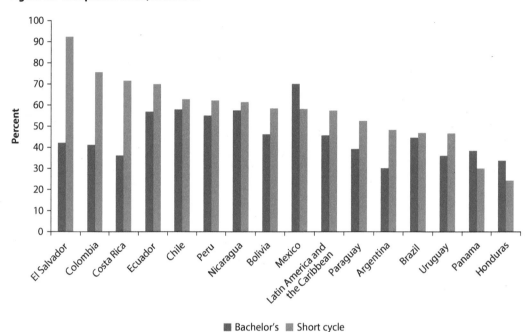

■ Bachelor's   ■ Short cycle

Source: World Bank calculations based on the Socio-Economic Database for Latin America and the Caribbean (SEDLAC) and administrative data for Brazil and Colombia.
Note: The data are for the following years: Argentina (2018), Bolivia (2018), Chile (2017), Costa Rica (2018), Ecuador (2018), El Salvador (2018), Honduras (2016), Mexico (2018), Nicaragua (2014), Panama (2016), Paraguay (2018), Peru (2018), and Uruguay (2018). Completion rates are estimated as the ratio of the number of individuals ages 25–29 years who have completed a higher education program to the number of individuals ages 25–29 years who have ever started a higher education program. For each country, the difference between the two graduation rates is significantly different from zero. For Colombia and Brazil, completion rates for bachelor's programs are the ratio of the average number of graduates in 2014, 2015, and 2016 to the number of incoming students in 2010. The completion rates for short-cycle programs (SCPs) are the ratio of the average number of graduates in 2012, 2013, and 2014 to the number of incoming students in 2010.

factors might explain this contrast. First, since LAC has a higher proportion of higher education students enrolled in bachelor's programs compared with the United States, many such students may have poor completion prospects.[13] Second, students in bachelor's programs in LAC must choose a program (major) in their first year rather than taking general education classes as in the United States. This means that, should students want to switch programs, they would need to start the new program from scratch, a rigidity that may lead students interested in switching programs to drop out of higher education altogether. Third, student support and advising services might be weaker in LAC than in the United States, complicating the identification of struggling students and their assistance. Fourth, bachelor's programs are longer in LAC than in the United States (nominally lasting at least five years), which might induce relatively high dropout rates.

Of course, the fact that SCPs have higher completion rates than bachelor's programs in LAC might also indicate that SCPs have lower graduation standards, perhaps to accommodate a more disadvantaged student body. Yet, as the next stylized fact shows, SCP graduates in LAC accomplish better labor market outcomes than many bachelor's students, suggesting that, even if they have low standards, SCPs do increase students' human capital.

Stylized fact 5. In the labor market, SCP graduates do better than high school graduates and dropouts from bachelor's programs.

Figure 1.7, panel a, shows the unemployment rate for members of the WAP with at least a high school diploma. SCP graduates experience the lowest unemployment rate (3.7 percent) of all five educational attainment levels.[14]

In LAC, on average, 48 percent of the WAP consists of informal workers. These include salaried workers at firms with up to five employees, self-employed workers with at most a high school diploma, and workers with unreported income. While, on average, 52 percent of high school graduates work in the formal sector (figure 1.7, panel b), 82 percent of SCP graduates do. Formal employment for SCP graduates is lower than for bachelor's graduates, yet substantially higher than for bachelor's dropouts.

On average, the hourly wages of SCP graduates are 45 percent higher than those of high school graduates (figure 1.7, panel c). This premium is certainly lower than that of bachelor's graduates, for whom it equals 124 percent. However, it is higher than the premium for bachelor's dropouts.[15]

Figure 1.7 Labor Market Outcomes, by Educational Attainment, circa 2018

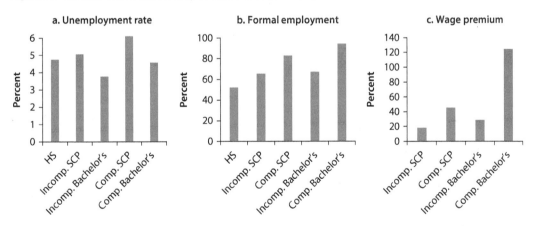

Source: World Bank calculations based on the Socio-Economic Database for Latin America and the Caribbean (SEDLAC).
Note: The figures depict average labor market outcomes for the working-age population, defined as individuals between ages 25 and 65, based on their educational attainment. Complete bachelor's includes individuals with graduate degrees. For each educational attainment, the corresponding bar shows the simple average outcome over countries. Panel a shows the unemployment rate (percentage of unemployed individuals relative to the labor force). Panel b shows the percentage of individuals who have formal employment. Informal workers include salaried workers in firms with up to five employees, self-employed workers with at most a high school diploma, and workers with no reported income. In panel c, the premium in each category reflects the percent by which the average (hourly) wage in the category exceeds the average (hourly) wage for high school graduates. The difference between complete SCP and incomplete bachelor's is significantly different from zero in panels a, b, and c. The difference between complete SCP and complete bachelor's is significantly different from zero in panel c, but not in panel a or b. Comp. = complete; HS = high school; Incomp. = incomplete; SCP = short-cycle programs.

Although figure 1.7 indicates that bachelor's graduates obtain, on average, the best labor market outcomes among individuals who have at least completed high school, it also indicates that the individual must actually graduate from a bachelor's program to attain those outcomes. If the individual does not graduate, then her outcomes are worse, on average, than those of an SCP graduate. In other words, an SCP might be a better option for a student with a high chance of dropping out of a bachelor's program. Given that about half of the higher education students in the region drop out of a bachelor's program,[16] this conclusion is particularly important.

To summarize, on average, LAC has few students enrolled in SCPs. The recent expansion of higher education, far from addressing this issue, may have aggravated it by expanding enrollment in bachelor's programs at a higher rate than in SCPs. Although SCPs tend to attract, on average, disadvantaged and nontraditional students, they have higher completion rates than bachelor's programs, perhaps indicating the appeal of short, flexible, and practical higher education programs. Labor market outcomes for SCP graduates not only surpass those of high school graduates, but also those of bachelor's dropouts, perhaps indicating a mismatch between the skills produced by higher education and those demanded by today's labor markets.

Critical Institutional Aspect: Funding

Given the positive outcomes for SCPs, the question is why more students are not pursuing them. Several answers are possible, including the social stigma of SCPs relative to the prestige of bachelor's programs and the lack of information on SCP outcomes vis-à-vis bachelor's outcomes. Still, another possibility is that SCPs are less affordable than bachelor's programs.

Figure 1.8, panel a, depicts the average tuition for SCPs and bachelor's programs in public and private HEIs in several countries in LAC. Since public HEIs receive funding from public sources, they can charge lower tuition than private HEIs, for bachelor's programs and SCPs. Private HEIs charge more for bachelor's programs than SCPs, likely reflecting the higher cost of the former. In contrast, public HEIs charge the same, or almost the same, for both program types.

The similar tuition charged by public HEIs for both program types might suggest that governments subsidize SCPs and bachelor's programs at the same rate—but this is not the case. Assuming that private HEIs charge tuition equal to their cost, the difference between average public and private tuition can be viewed as a proxy for the average per-student subsidy provided by the government to each program type.

Figure 1.8, panel b, shows that the subsidies for public HEIs are much higher for bachelor's programs than SCPs—by a factor of factor of 3.6 in Peru, 3 in Colombia, and 1.50 in Brazil. In other words, even when public HEI tuition is similar for both program types, the fact that the cost of bachelor's programs is higher implies that governments provide a greater per-student subsidy, in absolute terms, to bachelor's programs.[17]

Figure 1.8 Average Tuition and Per-Student Subsidy, by Program Type, circa 2019

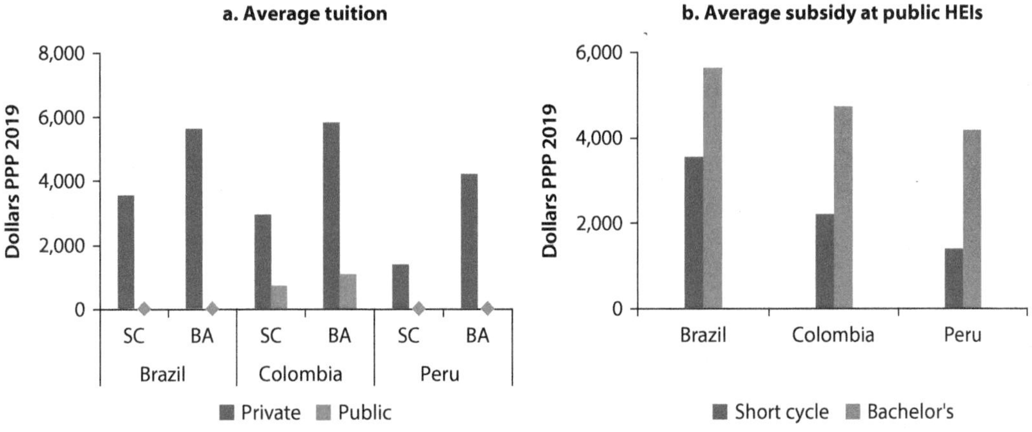

Sources: Countries' administrative information (see annex 1A).
Note: All averages are simple averages over programs. In panel a, the orange diamonds indicate zero average tuition. For Colombia, average tuition at public institutions includes *Servicio Nacional de Aprendizaje* (SENA) programs, which charge zero tuition. In panel b, for a given country, the average subsidy at public HEIs for bachelor's programs equals average tuition in private HEIs – average tuition in public HEIs, and similarly for SCPs. The figure includes all states in Brazil and all programs (licensed and non-licensed) in Peru. All monetary values are in dollars (PPP 2019). BA = bachelor's; HEI = higher education institution; PPP = purchasing power parity; SC = short cycle; SCP = short-cycle program.

Given that SCP students are, on average, more disadvantaged than bachelor's students, this subsidy scheme is regressive. The almost equal tuition for bachelor's programs and SCPs at public HEIs might induce many students to choose bachelor's programs to avoid the SCP stigma even though an SCP might fit them better. Finally, the social stigma itself might be a consequence of the subsidy scheme, as the greater per-student subsidy for bachelor's programs might signal that bachelor's programs have greater social value than SCPs.

Institutions and Students in Five Countries

A unique and novel survey of directors of SCPs was conducted in five countries in LAC: Brazil, Colombia, the Dominican Republic, Ecuador, and Peru. These countries account for 54 percent of all SCP enrollment in LAC. The survey in Brazil focused on two states, São Paulo and Ceará. As a result, the survey data from Brazil correspond to those two states. In Peru, the survey focused on licensed programs. Part of the survey asked the directors about their student body, admission requirements, tuition, and funding. Before reporting on these, this section provides context by characterizing the SCP landscape in these countries.

SCP Landscape

Annex 1B describes the SCP landscape in these countries. The enrollment share of SCPs is above the LAC average of 9 percent in all the countries except the Dominican Republic. The number of HEIs offering these programs ranges from 28 in the Dominican Republic to 1,700 in Brazil. While the SCP enrollment share in LAC has declined since the early 2000s in 10 of 15 countries (see the section titled "Five Stylized Facts") it rose in all the survey countries except Peru.

The presence of the private sector varies widely among countries. In Brazil, 86 percent of HEIs are private and these capture 84 percent of SCP enrollment. In Colombia, 67 percent of the HEIs are private, but these capture only 21 percent of enrollment. This is because SENA, the large public institution providing SCPs in multiple locations, captures 65 percent of enrollment, while other public institutions capture the remaining 17 percent. For-profit HEIs are allowed in Brazil (36 percent of all SCPs) and Peru (77 percent of licensed SCPs).

A variety of HEIs provide SCPs in these countries. Universities participate in the provision of SCPs in Brazil, Colombia, and the Dominican Republic. Meanwhile, SCPs are provided exclusively by non-university HEIs in Peru. In all five countries, SCPs are under the purview of the Ministry of Education, usually through a specific secretariat or agency. Different HEI types have played different roles in the recent expansion of SCP enrollment in our survey countries (box 1.3).

Tuition is free at public HEIs. Colombia is somewhat different, as tuition is free at SENA but not at public HEIs—which, nonetheless, subsidize their tuition. Although tuition is not free at private HEIs, governments offer some scholarships in Brazil, Colombia, the Dominican Republic, and Peru. In addition, they provide student loans in Colombia, the Dominican Republic, Ecuador, and Peru, and a government guarantee for private student loans in Brazil. Importantly, only Brazil offers state-guaranteed loans; in the other countries, students need a guarantor to take a loan. Students can also obtain loans from commercial banks. To enable zero or subsidized tuition at public HEIs, governments provide them with financial support. In contrast, they generally do not provide financial support to private HEIs. [18]

Although SCPs are not selective in the conventional sense, they apply some entry requirements. One requirement at some HEIs is a minimum score on the mandatory national high school exit exam (Brazil, Colombia, and Ecuador) or higher education entry exam (the Dominican Republic and Brazil). In addition, Brazil and Colombia have a mandatory higher education exit exam.

In every country, HEIs need an operating license to open a program. To continue operating, the programs must undergo a license renewal (Colombia and Peru), periodic evaluation (Brazil and the Dominican Republic), or mandatory accreditation (Brazil and Ecuador). In addition, HEIs and programs in Peru and Colombia can pursue voluntary accreditation or high-quality accreditation, respectively, to signal their quality. In the Dominican Republic, which lacks an accreditation agency, HEIs can pursue accreditation from an international agency. The process followed for the periodic evaluations, and for the mandatory or voluntary accreditations, typically involves a self-evaluation and an external or peer evaluation; it can also include the consideration of elements such as students' average scores on the higher education exit exams (Brazil). Brazil, in particular, has a national assessment system to evaluate HEIs annually and assign them a grade; evaluation results and grades are public.

Box 1.3 Which Institutions Have Driven Enrollment Growth?

Among the survey countries, Colombia and Brazil have experienced the greatest short-cycle program (SCP) enrollment growth over the past decade. However, the growth has been driven by different types of higher education institutions (HEIs) in each country. In Colombia, the main driver has been the National Learning Service (SENA, *Servicio Nacional de Aprendizaje*), a public institution that enrolls 65 percent of SCP students (annex 1B). SENA is not an HEI but rather a provider of vocational training that falls under the purview of the Ministry of Labor. However, SENA's SCPs are regulated by the Ministry of Education. Painting a stark contrast, growth in Brazil has been driven by private HEIs (figure B1.3.1).

Figure B1.3.1 Growth in Enrollment in Short-Cycle Programs, by Type of Higher Education Institution

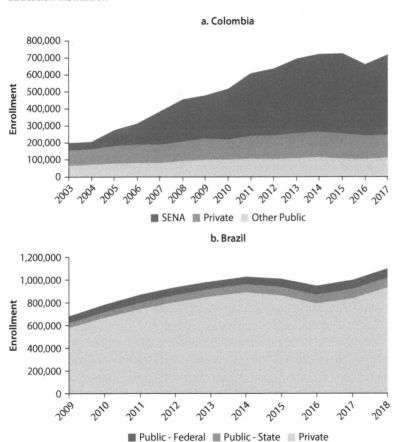

Source: World Bank calculations using *Sistema Nacional de Información de la Educación Superior* (Colombia) and *Instituto Nacional de Estudos e Pesquisas Educacionais Anísio Teixeira* (Brazil). Brazil enrollment refers to the whole country and includes online programs.

box continues next page

Remarkably, SENA's market share in Colombia grew from approximately 20 percent in the early 2000s to 65 percent in 2017 as the outcome of a deliberate expansionary policy. Total enrollment in non-SENA institutions has also risen, but at a much lower rate. In Brazil, SCP enrollment grew rapidly until 2014. Growth slowed in 2012–16 but regained steam after 2016. These changes were mainly due to enrollment fluctuations in private HEIs, as total enrollment in public institutions has changed relatively little over time.

Student Body Characteristics

Figure 1.10, panel a, shows some characteristics of the student body in the sample's average program. The share of part-time students ranges from 25 percent in Peru to 77 percent in Brazil. Female students account for about 40 percent of the student body in all the countries except Peru, where they represent slightly more than 50 percent.[19]

Consistent with attracting more part-time students, programs in Brazil attract a relatively high share of older, nontraditional students (ages 25+), who account for only 20–30 percent of enrollment in the other countries. Programs with a large share (40 percent or more) of nontraditional students are most prevalent in private HEIs, in the field of Economics, Accounting, and Business.

Admission and Academic Readiness

About 95 percent of the programs apply some kind of admission requirement. These requirements have the goal of securing a minimum level of student preparedness as well as a good fit of the student to the program and are particularly important when programs have more applicants than slots. Admission tests of general knowledge are highly popular in all the countries except Colombia (figure 1.9). Although 61 percent of programs give a test of general or specific knowledge, this does not imply that they require a minimum score for admission. In addition, 71 percent of programs require a minimum high school grade point average (GPA) or score in the national entry test (see annex 1B on national entry and exit exams). Given the serious cognitive deficits of students at entry (as discussed below), these admission thresholds are likely quite low. Except in Colombia, where interviews are the most popular admission requirement, more than 80 percent of the programs requires at least a test or minimum GPA/national entry test score for admission purposes.

The existence of admission requirements does not mean that the programs are selective in the conventional sense. Indeed, first-year students bring serious skill deficits (figure 1.10, panel b). More than 75 percent of the programs in each country report a math deficit among their incoming students, and about half of the programs view this deficit as the main one. The deficits are not

Figure 1.9 Admission Requirements

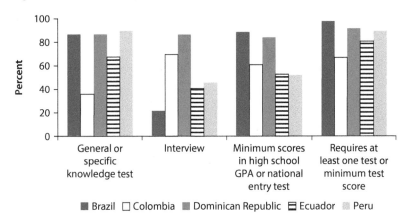

Source: World Bank Short-Cycle Program Survey (WBSCPS).
Note: For each country, the figure shows the percent of programs that apply a given admission requirement. Programs may apply more than one admission requirement. For Brazil, both *Exame Nacional do Ensino Médio* and *Vestibular* are counted as national entry tests. The "Requires at least one test or minimum test score" category includes general or specific tests as well as minimum scores in high school grade point average (GPA) or national entry test (and is hence a composite of the first and third categories). WBSCPS includes only São Paulo and Ceará for Brazil, and licensed programs for Peru.

Figure 1.10 Student Body Characteristics

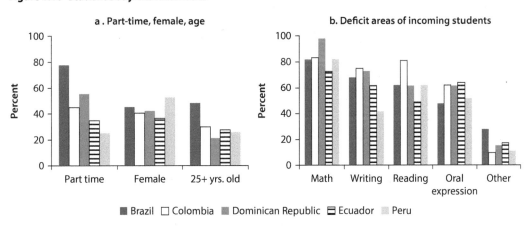

Source: World Bank Short-Cycle Program Survey (WBSCPS).
Note: For each country, panel a shows the program-level (simple) average percentage of part-time, female, and age 25+ students. Panel b shows the percentage of programs reporting that incoming students have deficits in particular areas. Students may have deficits in multiple areas. WBSCPS includes only São Paulo and Ceará for Brazil, and licensed programs for Peru.

limited to mathematics, as more than half of the programs in every country also report deficits in writing, reading, and oral expression.

To mitigate these deficits, more than 85 percent of the programs offer remedial activities. Programs in the Dominican Republic, Ecuador, and Peru are more likely to offer remedial activities before than during the program, while the reverse is true in Brazil.

Figure 1.11 Annual Tuition

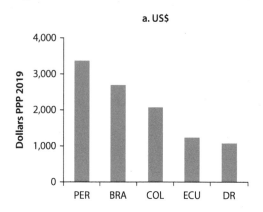

a. US$

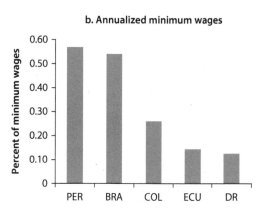

b. Annualized minimum wages

Source: Administrative data for each country (see annex 1A).
Note: For each country, the figure shows the program-level (simple) average tuition, expressed in 2019 PPP dollars or as a proportion of the country's annual minimum wage (equal to 12 times the monthly minimum wage). World Bank Short-Cycle Programs Survey (WBSCPS) includes only São Paulo and Ceará for Brazil, and licensed programs for Peru. BRA = Brazil; COL = Colombia; DR = Dominican Republic; ECU = Ecuador; PER = Peru; PPP = purchasing power parity.

Tuition and Funding

The average annual tuition varies widely across countries, ranging from US$1,100 in the Dominican Republic to US$3,400 in Peru (figure 1.11, panel a). For an individual who earns the monthly minimum wage, the average tuition is below 15 percent of annual wages in the Dominican Republic and Ecuador, but it is about 60 percent in Peru and Brazil (figure 1.11, panel b). Hence, although SCPs are relatively affordable in some countries, they are less so in others.

Public HEIs receive operational funding from public sources that allows them to subsidize tuition, but private HEIs typically do not. Public and private HEIs receive some additional funding from public and private sources for projects related to capital expenditures (for example, equipment purchases) or new projects. Programs at public HEIs are more likely to receive this additional funding, particularly from public sources. Programs at private HEIs, in contrast, depend almost entirely on tuition revenue.

To finance their studies, students rely on their own resources as well as other, external funding mechanisms (see annex 1B for student public funding in the survey countries). Since these mechanisms are not mutually exclusive, a student might have, for example, a scholarship and a loan. Regardless of the mechanisms used in each country, the common denominator is that a relatively small fraction of students receives external funding (figure 1.12, panel a). The lack of it is particularly acute in Peru and, to a lesser extent, Ecuador.

Scholarships (from the government or the institution) are the most common form of external funding. The average program in the Dominican Republic stands out for having 52 and 62 percent of students with a scholarship from the HEI and the government, respectively. Based on government reports, in Brazil, about 7 percent of all higher education students (in bachelor's programs and SCPs) receive the ProUni federal government scholarship,[20] and state governments provide scholarships as well. State and local governments similarly provide scholarships in Colombia.

HEIs provide their own loans, typically in the form of tuition payment plans. Less common are loans from governments and commercial banks. They are most popular in Colombia, where 15 to 20 percent of the students in the average program use them—still a low usage rate. Program directors in Colombia seem to overestimate the percentage of students who receive government loans, as government reports state that only 1.25 percent of SCP students have received a government loan (from *Instituto Colombiano de Crédito Educativo y Estudios Técnicos en el Exterior* [ICETEX]).[21] In contrast, the average program director in Brazil seems to report a more accurate share of students receiving government loans (about 1.7 percent), which is consistent with the approximately 1.3 percent of SCP students who receive loans through the state guaranteed student loan program, known as FIES.[22]

Just because some students have access to external funding mechanisms does not mean that these provide much relief. In the five countries, the clear majority of programs report that the most important reason for student dropout is financial hardship (figure 1.12, panel b). This might be in part because the supply of government or HEI scholarships is limited, in number and magnitude, as is the supply of government loans. And although commercial bank loans for higher education are available in all the countries, students do not tend to use them.

Figure 1.12 Student Funding

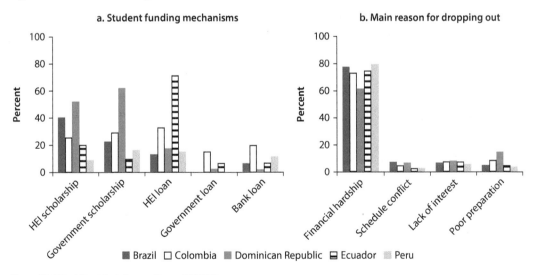

a. Student funding mechanisms

b. Main reason for dropping out

■ Brazil □ Colombia ■ Dominican Republic ⊟ Ecuador ▨ Peru

Source: World Bank Short-Cycle Program Survey (WBSCPS).
Note: For each country, panel a shows the program-level (simple) average percentage of students who use each of the following funding mechanisms: HEI scholarships, government scholarships, HEI loans, government loans, and commercial bank loans. Students might use multiple funding mechanisms. In Brazil, FIES is a state guaranteed loan from commercial banks. Since FIES involves a subsidy (for example, through a subsidized interest rate), program directors may have reported it as a government scholarship. For each country, panel b shows the percentage of programs that report each reason as the main one to explain student dropout ("other reasons" are omitted from the figure). For a given country, percentages add up to 100. WBSCPS includes only São Paulo and Ceará for Brazil, and licensed programs for Peru. HEI = higher education institution.

According to the program directors, students are typically wary of taking a loan at a commercial bank, often because of lack of familiarity with the financial system. Hence, even when external funding is available, students do not seem to use it.

Pathways to a Bachelor's Degree

If students view an SCP as a "dead end" because it does not allow them to pursue a bachelor's degree afterward, then allowing the SCP classes to count as credit toward a longer degree might enhance their attractiveness. Indeed, the vast majority of programs (more than 95 percent in Brazil, Colombia, and the Dominican Republic, and 80–85 percent in Ecuador and Peru) report that their classes provide credits toward a bachelor's program. Nonetheless, few students from SCP programs seem to go on to bachelor's programs. Administrative data from Colombia show that, among the students who began their SCP in 2006, only 7 percent continued to a bachelor's program, and only 3.15 percent earned a bachelor's degree. [23] For comparison, in the United States, the latter proportion is 14 percent.[24]

In other words, although SCPs claim to provide credits for longer credentials, in practice, this might not be the case. Anecdotal evidence indicates that credits do not transfer seamlessly even among bachelor's programs, from the same or different institutions. Bachelor's programs, then, might be even less likely to accept credits from SCPs, as they might view these as having lower or unverifiable quality.

Conclusions

In LAC, finishing an SCP delivers better labor market outcomes than starting but not finishing a bachelor's program. Since about half of the students in bachelor's programs in LAC drop out, SCPs emerge as an attractive alternative—not only for those students, but also for others. Importantly, SCPs deliver better outcomes, although they take in more disadvantaged students than those in bachelor's programs. Not only are SCPs' labor market outcomes better, they also graduate students at higher rates.

It is surprising, then, that SCPs are less widespread in LAC than in other regions. Although social stigma might partly explain this, there are two other potential explanations. The first is the lack of affordability of SCPs for some students. Indeed, governments provide greater per-student subsidies for bachelor's programs than for SCPs—although students in the latter are more disadvantaged and hence in greater need of the subsidy. As a result, financial hardship is the main reason why students drop out of SCPs, although they are relatively affordable. The second explanation is the lack of pathways from an SCP toward a longer degree. Although programs claim to provide these pathways, administrative and anecdotal evidence indicates that these pathways are rare. These two elements—less favorable funding for SCPs than for bachelor's degrees and lack of pathways from an SCP to a bachelor's degree—might in turn exacerbate the original stigma and deter students from pursuing SCPs.

Annex 1A. Country Administrative Information

Table 1A.1 Country Administrative Information

Country	Institution	Source
Brazil	National Institute of Educational Studies and Research "Anísio Teixeira," INEP. Synopses of Higher Education Statistics 2018. Ministry of Education, 2019. Association of Higher Education Institutions in the State of São Paulo, SEMESP. Higher Education Map, 2019.	*Instituto Nacional de Estudos e Pesquisas Educacionais "Anísio Teixeira," (INEP).* *Sinopses Estatísticas da Educação Superior 2018.* http://inep.gov.br/sinopses-estatisticas-da-educacao-superior *Fundo de Financiamento Estudantil* (FIES), 2019. http://portalfies.mec.gov.br/ *Sindicato das Entidades Mantenedoras de Estabelecimentos de Ensino Superior no Estado de São Paulo* (SEMESP). Mapa do Ensino Superior, 2019. https://www.semesp.org.br/pesquisas/mapa-do-ensino-superior-no-brasil-2019/
Chile	Higher Education Information Service, SIES, Ministry of Education. Office of Higher Education. Research Center, Ministry of Education. Office of Higher Education.	*Servicio de Información de Educación Superior (SIES), Ministerio de Educación. Subsecretaría de Educación Superior.* https://www.mifuturo.cl/instituciones-de-educacion-superior-en-chile/ *Centro de estudios. Ministerio de Educación. Subsecretaría de Educación Superior.* http://datos.mineduc.cl/dashboards/20209/descarga-base-de-datos-asignaciones-de-becas-y-creditos-en-educacion-superior/
Colombia	National Information System of Higher Education, SNIES, Ministry of Education. Statistical summary, 2019.	*Ministerio de Educación* *Sistema Nacional de Información de la Educación Superior* (SNIES). *Resumen estadístico*, 2019. https://snies.mineducacion.gov.co/portal/
Ecuador	Secretariat of Higher Education, Science, Technology and Innovation, SENESCYT. Statistics on higher education, science, technology and innovation.	*Secretaría de Educación Superior, Ciencia, Tecnología e Innovación* (SENESCYT). *Estadísticas de educación superior, ciencia, tecnología e innovación.* https://siau.senescyt.gob.ec/estadisticas-de-educacion-superior-ciencia-tecnologia-e-innovacion/?doing_wp_cron=1606556190.6860320568084716796875 Various web sites for tuition information.
Peru	Secretariat of Technical, Technological and Artistic Education, Ministry of Education	*Dirección General de Educacion Técnico-Productiva y Superior Tecnológica y Artística, Ministerio de Educación, Ponte en Carrera:* https://www.ponteencarrera.pe/pec-portal-web/inicio/donde-estudiar Tuition: https://estudiaperu.pe/ and https://logrosperu.com/

Annex 1B. Institutional Framework for WBSCPS Countries

Table 1B.1 Institutional Frameworks for WBSCPS

Indicator	Brazil	Colombia	Dominican Republic	Ecuador	Peru
1. SCP enrollment share (%)	12	32	4	14	25
2. Program types	Technological (2–3 yrs)	Technical (2 yrs) Technological (3 yrs)	Technical (2 yrs) Prof. technical (técnico superior; 2-3 years)	Technical Technological (mostly 2 yrs)	Technical (2 yrs) Prof. technical (3-4) Tech. bachelors (3-4)
3. Number of HEIs offering SCPs	1,700 São Paolo + Ceará: 467	217	28	182	HEIs w/ licensed prog.: 75 Other HEIs: 747
4. Private enrollment (%)	84 São Paolo + Ceará: 77	21	49	53	HEIs w/ licensed prog.: 97 Other HEIs: 50
5. HEI types and enrollment shares (%)	São Paolo + Ceará: Universities 41 Universities Centers 17 Schools 38 IF and CEFET 3	Universities 9 University Institutes 13 Technol. Institutes 7 Technical Institutes 6 SENA 65	Universities 47 Tech. Institutes 53	Tech. & Technol. Institutes 95 Univ. and Polytechnic Schools 5	HEIs w/ licensed programs: Higher education institutes 100
6. Public funding to students at public HEIs	Zero tuition	Zero tuition at SENA Public HEIs: government scholarships; loans from public institution (ICETEX)	Zero tuition, but "academic fees."	Zero tuition	Zero tuition
7. Funding for students at private HEIs	ProUni (government scholarship for low-income, high ability students) FIES (government and state-guaranteed student loans banks) FUNDACRED (loans)	Government scholarships Loans from public institution (ICETEX)	Government scholarships Loans from public institution (FUNDAPEC)	Loans from public bank (Banco del Pacífico)	Public loans and scholarships (PRONABEC) for low-income, high-ability students

table continues next page

Annex 1B Institutional Framework for WBSCPS Countries *(continued)*

Indicator	Brazil	Colombia	Dominican Republic	Ecuador	Peru
8. Public funding to public HEIs	Yes. Sources: federal, state, municipality	For SENA: yes (dedicated taxes) / For other public HEIs: yes	Yes	Yes	Yes
9. Public funding to private HEIs	No	No	n/a	Partial for some private HEIs (*cofinanciadas*)	No
10. National mandatory entry exam	ENEM (high school graduation exam) required by public HEIs / *Vestibular* (HE entry exam) required by some HEIs	SABER 11 (mandatory for high school graduation)	POMA or PAA (mandatory for HE entry)	*Ser Bachiller* (mandatory for high school graduation)	Only for students applying to PRONABEC scholarship
11. National mandatory exit exam	ENADE (mandatory for HE graduation; only some majors tested in a given year)	SABER T&T (mandatory for SCP graduation)	n/a	No	No
12. Operating license	Mandatory (initial accreditation) by HEI and program.	Mandatory by HEI and program; must be renewed periodically	Mandatory; evaluation required to renew license every 5 years.	Mandatory by HEI	Mandatory by HEI and program; lasts 5 years.
13. Accreditation	At private HEIs, accreditation must be renewed, generally every 3 years.	High-quality accreditation is voluntary for HEIs and programs; mandatory for teaching programs. Lasts 4 years.	HEIs can voluntarily pursue international accreditation.	Periodic mandatory accreditation is needed to remain open.	Voluntary for HEIs and programs; mandatory for education, law and health programs.
14. For-profit HEIs	Allowed (36% of SCPs in Brazil; 39% in São Paolo + Ceará)	Not allowed	Not allowed	Not allowed	Allowed (77% of licensed SCPs)

Sources: Brazil: INEP 2017; Colombia: SNIES 2017; Dominican Republic: General Report on Higher Education Statistics 2018 and Historical Report and Historical Summary (2018), SENESCYT; Peru: Ministry of Education data for 2019; 2020 for licensed programs. Other sources: Brazil: WBSCPS for (3). DR: WBSCPS for (3), (4) and (5). Peru: SEDLAC for (1); WBSCPS for licensed programs in (3), (4), (5). "WBSCPS" refers to the WBSCPS universe when data are available, and to effective surveys otherwise.

Note: Some figures for (1) and (4) differ from those in figures 1.5 and 1.2, respectively, because this table is based on administrative data rather than Socio-Economic Database for Latin America and the Caribbean (SEDLAC) and pertains to slightly different years. For Brazil, S-System HEIs count as university centers or schools. For Colombia, *Servicio Nacional de Aprendizaje* (SENA) is not counted as an HEI in (3) but its students are counted as part of public enrollment in (4). For Ecuador, private share includes enrollment in private institutions with public funding (*cofinanciadas*). When an HEI has branches in multiple cities, each branch is counted separately. CEFET = Federal Centers for Technological Education (*Centros Federais de Educação Tecnológica*) (Brazil); ENADE = National Exam of Student Achievement (*Exame Nacional de Desempenho dos Estudantes*) (Brazil); ENEM = National Assessment of Secondary Education (*Exame Nacional de Ensino Médio*) (Brazil); FIES = Student Financing Fund (*Fundo de Financiamento Estudantil*) (Brazil); FUNDAPEC = Pro-Education and Culture Action Educational Credit Foundation (*Fundación Acción Pro Educación y Cultura* [APEC] *de Crédito Educativo*) (Dominican Republic); HEI = higher education institution; IF = Federal institute (*Instituto Federal*) (Brazil); ICETEX = Colombian Institute of Educational Credit and Technical Training Abroad (*Instituto Colombiano de Crédito Educativo y Estudios Técnicos en el Exterior*) (Colombia); PAA = Academic Aptitude Test (*Prueba de Aptitud Académica*) (Dominican Republic); POMA = (*Prueba de Orientación y Medición Académica*) (Dominican Republic); PRONABEC = National Program of Scholarships and Educational Credit (*Programa Nacional de Becas y Crédito Educativo*) (Peru); SABER = Systems Approach for Better Education Results; Prof. = professional; SCP = short-cycle progam; Tech. = technical. WBSCPS = data from the World Bank Short-Cycle Program Survey.

Notes

For their excellent research assistance, Andrea Franco, Manuela Granda, Angélica Sánchez, and Gabriel Suárez are gratefully acknowledged.

1. The objectives of SCPs have also been established in the Dublin Descriptors as part of the Bologna process among European Union countries. These descriptors are used for the European Higher Education Area and are reflected in the European Qualifications Framework for Lifelong Learning. According to them, an SCP degree prepares the student for employment, while also providing preparation for, and access to, a bachelor's program. For further details, see https://core.ac.uk/download /pdf/35319995.pdf and http://ecahe.eu/assets/uploads/2016/01/Joint-Quality -Initiative-the-origin-of-the-Dublin-descriptors-short-history.pdf.

2. UNESCO establishes that the ISCED 5 level has a minimum duration of two years and, for the case of higher education systems where credentials are based on the accumulation of credits, a comparable time period and intensity are required to complete the ISCED 5 level. See http://uis.unesco.org/sites/default/files/documents/isced -2011-sp.pdf.

3. Similar to nursing, teaching is an SCP in some countries but a bachelor's program in others.

4. In the survey countries, 98.16 of the programs last two or three years.

5. Sevilla (2017) provides a list of the types of HEI that are authorized to provide SCPs in each country.

6. Colombia, Brazil, and Peru have institutions with national coverage that provide vocational and technical training and, in some cases, also teach SCPs. In Colombia, SENA is a public institution overseen by the Ministry of Labor. Founded in 1957 with the purpose of providing vocational and technical education, SENA added SCPs in 2003. In Brazil, the S System is a set of organizations whose names begin with "S" and that provide services to workers (for example, vocational training or social assistance) or firms (for example, consulting or technical assistance). The organizations have common roots and similar characteristics, each representing a business sector, including, for instance, the National Industrial Learning Service, the Social Service of Commerce, and the Industry Social Service. While these organizations are focused on vocational training, some of them also teach SCPs. In Peru, SENATI is a private organization that was founded in 1961 by manufacturing firms to provide technical training, including SCPs. It teaches in dual mode—in the classroom and through work practices in companies.

7. Strictly speaking, some of these individuals might still be enrolled in their bachelor's program. The qualitative findings remain when individuals ages 35–65 are considered.

8. Complete bachelor's includes individuals with a postgraduate degree. In LAC, 13 percent of the individuals with a bachelor's degree also have a postgraduate degree.

9. Since SCP programs include teaching (a traditionally female field), the report also calculates the percentage of females only for the countries where SCP programs do not include teaching. In those countries, on average, female students make up 53.8, 59.7, and 50.8 percent of the bachelor's students, SCP students, and high school

graduates. In other words, the qualitative patterns shown in table 1.1 do not result from the inclusion of teaching among SCPs.

10. Most of the qualitative patterns in table 1.1 remain when the sample is restricted to ages 17–30.

11. Mexico, Panama, and Honduras have very low SCP shares (below 3 percent), as shown in figure 1.5.

12. Source: National Center of Education Statistics, https://nces.ed.gov/programs/coe /indicator_ctr.asp.

13. Bachelor's programs absorb 91 of higher education enrollment in LAC (figure 1.4), but only 65 percent in the United States (National Center of Education Statistics, https://nces.ed.gov/programs/coe/indicator_cha.asp#:~:text=2000%20through%20 2029.-,See%20Digest%20of%20Education%20Statistics%202019%2C%20table%20 303.70.,enrolled%20in%202%2Dyear%20institutions.

14. For comparison, in the United States, the unemployment rates of bachelor's graduates, SCP (associate degree) graduates, bachelor's or SCP dropouts, and high school graduates are 2.2, 2.7, 3.3, and 3.7 percent, respectively. Source: https://www.bls.gov /emp/tables/unemployment-earnings-education.htm.

15. For comparison, in the United States, the wage premiums for bachelor's graduates, SCP (associate degree) graduates, and bachelor's or SCP dropouts are 67, 19, and 12 percent, respectively. Source: https://www.bls.gov/emp/tables/unemployment-earnings -education.htm.

16. The exact share of students in the region who drop out of bachelor's programs, 48.6 percent, equals the product of the bachelor's enrollment share (approximately 0.90, per figure 1.4) and the bachelor's dropout rate (100-46 = 54 percent.)

17. For comparison, in the United States, this ratio is 1.56. Source: staff calculations based on grant aid and tax benefits per student at public two- and four-year institutions, from https://research.collegeboard.org/pdf/trends-college-pricing-2019-full-report.pdf.

18. The only private HEIs in the survey countries with public funding are Ecuador's *instituciones cofinanciadas*.

19. The percentage of female students enrolled in SCPs is lower in the survey countries than the average for LAC.

20. Source for *ProUni* information: http://dadosabertos.mec.gov.br/fies . Also see http:// dadosabertos.mec.gov.br/prouni.

21. This estimate is the product of the percentage of ICETEX loans given to SCP students (2.3 percent in 2018), the percentage of higher education students covered by an ICETEX loan (8.7 percent in 2018), and the inverse of the SCP share outside SENA (16 percent in 2018). Sources: https://snies.mineducacion.gov.co/1778 /articles-391288_recurso_1.pdf and https://portal.icetex.gov.co/Portal/Home/el -icetex/plan-estrategico/resultado-por-indicadores.

22. This estimate is the product of the percentage of FIES loans given to SCP students (1.7 percent in 2018), the percentage of higher education students covered by a FIES loan (9.8 percent in 2018), and the inverse of the percentage of the SCP share (13 percent in 2018). Source: http://dadosabertos.mec.gov.br.

23. Staff calculations, based on data from the Ministry of National Education of Colombia for the entry cohort of the first semester of 2006.

24. Source: CCRC, https://ccrc.tc.columbia.edu/Community-College-FAQs.html.

References

Bailey, T., S. Jaggars, and D. Jenkins. 2015. *Redesigning America's Community Colleges: A Clearer Path to Student Success.* Cambridge, MA: Harvard University Press.

Brunner, J., and A. D. Miranda. 2016. *Educación Superior en Iberoamérica: Informe 2016.* Santiago de Chile: Centro Interuniversitario de Desarrollo.

CEDLAS (Center for Distributive, Labor and Social Studies) and World Bank. 2014. *A Guide to SEDLAC—Socio-Economic Database for Latin America and the Caribbean.* Washington, DC: World Bank.

Ferreyra, M., C. Avitabile, J. Botero, F. Haimovich, and S. Urzúa. 2017. *At a Crossroads: Higher Education in Latin America and the Caribbean.* Washington, DC: World Bank.

Sevilla, M. P. 2017. "Panorama de la educación técnica profesional en América Latina y el Caribe." *Serie Políticas Sociales,* Economic Commission for Latin America and the Caribbean, Santiago, Chile.

CHAPTER 2

Are Short-Cycle Programs Worthwhile?

Sergio Urzúa

Introduction

Latin America and the Caribbean (LAC) requires new engines of growth. The region's low productivity levels and fiscally constrained environment have negatively impacted competitiveness and raise questions about its ability to secure equal opportunities. More recently, the extraordinary circumstances and socioeconomic impact associated with the COVID-19 pandemic, as well as the changing world of work where the demand for skills evolves rapidly, are reshuffling labor markets. In this complex context, skilled human capital can be a formidable engine of economic and social progress (Ferreyra et al. 2017), and well-designed short-cycle programs (SCPs) can serve as a building block of the recovery.

By design, SCPs hold the promise to adapt to technological changes. They should foster skills fast, as they have a clear goal of training students for work in a relatively short time. In this way, SCPs tend to be more connected to labor markets than other higher education alternatives. However, the region's coverage of this level of education is low. As was mentioned in chapter 1, only 9 percent of higher education students are enrolled in SCPs in LAC, compared with about 30 percent in North America or East Asia and Pacific.

However, and despite the potential of SCPs, little is known about whether they boost students' future careers. The objective of this chapter is to fill this gap by presenting new evidence on the impact of short-term programs in LAC. The analysis focuses on two key labor market outcomes: employment and earnings after graduation. To this end, this chapter first presents a cross-country comparison of the recent trends in the economic returns to bachelor's and short-cycle degrees. The empirical strategy follows a long-standing literature and reports the average salary premiums for SCP and bachelor's graduates relative to high school graduates (Mincerian returns).

To provide a more meaningful estimation of the economic impact of SCPs relative to the alternatives, the chapter further compares net lifetime earnings for graduates of bachelor's programs and SCPs. This analysis is carried out using administrative data from higher education programs in Chile and Colombia, accounting for tuition costs as well as forgone earnings. In this way, the text assesses the relative disparities in net returns from a long-term perspective. The rich dataset used to conduct this exercise as well as others in this chapter is described in box 2.1.

Of course, any analysis of the economic benefits associated with different higher education degrees would be incomplete without an examination of the decision that leads students to enroll in (and eventually graduate from) different higher education programs. For example, students could choose between SCPs and bachelor's programs, taking into account their characteristics, local labor

---

Box 2.1 Sources of Information

The analysis in this chapter uses several sources of information. The estimation of the economic returns to higher education programs in the region uses the unharmonized household surveys from the Socio-Economic Database for Latin America and the Caribbean (the Center for Distributive, Labor and Social Studies and the World Bank), which are described in chapter 1.

In addition, the analysis takes advantage of administrative sources of information. Data from the Ministry of Education containing student-level records for cohorts of graduates from higher education institutions (HEIs) (age, gender, degree and HEI, graduation date, and duration). A second source is the Higher Education Information Service data set, which contains information on 46,893 academic programs in 208 HEIs from 2010 to 2020, including the formal duration of the program, tuition costs, and location (municipality). The third source is www.mifuturo.cl, a website of the Ministry of Education that provides information on average labor income four years after graduation for 1,574 higher education programs including short-cycle programs.

For Colombia, the primary data source is the Labor Observatory for Education (Observatorio Laboral para la Educación) of the Ministry of Education. This is a longitudinal, individual-level data set containing information on higher education graduates. The data set includes graduation year, higher education degree earned, HEI attended, location (municipality) of work, and base income used for contributions for employees in the formal sector. This is further augmented with information at the program level from the National Higher Education Information System (Sistema Nacional de Informacion de Educacion Superior), which includes duration and tuition costs for approximately 5,400 higher education programs. On top of this, information was gathered from the Observatorio de la Universidad Colombiana, an independent organization that collects tuition from individual HEIs in the country. Thus, unlike previous studies, this chapter does not rely on tuition

box continues next page

Box 2.1 Sources of Information *(continued)*

aggregated by institution type. Finally, the Ministry of National Education (*Sistema de Prevención y Atención de la Deserción en las Instituciones de Educación Superior*) records student-level higher education trajectories.

Despite the advantages of using large administrative data sets, it is important to acknowledge that the analysis is subject to data limitations. First, the timing of outcomes (earnings observed 1, 2, 4, or 10 years after graduation) can alter the conclusions. Specifically, programs with high returns in the short run might look worse over longer time horizons. Further, academic and labor market outcomes often paint quite different pictures (MacLeod et al. 2017). Thus, future efforts should complement this analysis.

---

market conditions, and the availability of higher education institutions (HEIs) offering these programs, among other factors. This self-selection might limit the scope and interpretation of conventional returns, particularly those obtained from the direct comparison of labor market outcomes across groups of individuals with different degrees. Formally, the simple contrast of averages (for example, average earnings or employment levels) cannot be interpreted as the causal impact of education on a specific outcome.

By exploiting the variation in local availability of SCPs in Colombia and using a conceptual framework grounded in individuals' rational responses, this chapter addresses these concerns and estimates the treatment effect of SCPs on employment and salary. The effect is not the same for all students who pursue an SCP, but rather varies depending on their fallback option—namely, what they would have chosen (whether not enrolling in higher education, or enrolling in a bachelor's program) had they not enrolled in the SCP.

The chapter also presents new evidence on the contribution of SCPs to graduates' initial earnings. In other words, it quantifies program-level (institution-degree-major) contributions to early labor market outcomes. This is done using rich data from Colombia and value-added models. As such, the text provides a different perspective on the economic benefits of SCPs.

Finally, the chapter characterizes the labor demand for individuals with higher education degrees. To this end, it exploits information on online vacancies in Argentina, Chile, Colombia, Mexico, and Peru. Each posting records job characteristics including the required educational qualifications, firm location, and economic sector.

The chapter's main findings can be summarized as follows:

- On average, the Mincerian returns to bachelor's programs are substantially higher than those to SCPs. However, while the returns to bachelor's degrees in LAC have been decreasing over time, the returns to SCPs have risen for more than half of LAC countries. Relative to the alternative of an incomplete bachelor's degree, SCPs emerge as a superior alternative in most of the countries.

- Beyond the average Mincerian returns, all the other metrics of returns utilized in the chapter tell a consistent story of great heterogeneity in the returns to higher education programs in general and SCPs in particular. Returns to bachelor's programs and SCPs vary greatly depending on the field of study and HEI type; returns to SCPs vary greatly depending on student characteristics and their municipalities; SCPs' value-added varies greatly even among programs within the same field; and job opportunities for SCP graduates vary greatly by location.
- In Chile and Colombia, net lifetime returns to individual SCPs vary widely across fields of study and institution types. Although the average net returns to SCP degrees are below those for bachelor's programs, there is large dispersion. In specific fields, SCPs can offer larger net returns than some bachelor's degrees.
- Local availability of SCPs makes students more likely to enroll in them. Empirical exercises indicate that, when SCPs become available, SCP enrollment increases mostly because some students *divert* from bachelor's programs onto an SCP. Those students are mostly male and from middle-income households. The exercises also indicate that those students would benefit from the SCP expansion because the SCP degree would give them higher labor market participation and salaries than a bachelor's degree. Hence, a local expansion in SCP supply can allow for better, more productive matches for some students.
- Program-level value-added varies across fields, but it varies even more within fields—depending, for instance, on the characteristics of the institution and the program itself (beyond the field). For instance, three-year programs contribute more; that is, they have more value added, than two-year programs to formal employment and wages.
- SCP graduates are in high demand relative to graduates from bachelor's programs. For each degree type, most vacancies are posted in science, technology, engineering, and mathematics (STEM) and business. Although vacancies and SCP graduates (representing the labor market demand and supply of SCPs, respectively) are concentrated in the most populated areas of each country, supply is more concentrated than demand. This indicates a possible mismatch between where the jobs are located and where the job candidates reside. In particular, many SCP graduates in less populated areas might not be able to find a local job suited to their skills, whereas firms seeking to hire SCP graduates in more populated areas might not be able to find suitable local candidates.

What Do We Know?

Multiple studies have attempted to quantify the effects of SCPs in a variety of countries. However, the nature of these programs varies significantly across countries, a feature reinforced by both country-specific dynamics in demographic and economic development. This might explain the limited availability of robust and comparable evidence.

One piece of evidence comes from Europe. In several European countries, vocational education lasting from three to four years represents an important step in school-to-work transitions.[1] This particular configuration is known as the dual system. It is typically organized as part of the formal educational structure and involves an employment relationship in addition to formal secondary and tertiary education. It often includes technical and vocational education and training (TVET) programs, some of which span just a few months and, as a result, do not constitute SCPs. The literature has documented that countries with dual systems such as Austria, Denmark, Germany, and Switzerland experience lower youth unemployment and larger employment in skilled occupations and high-wage sectors.[2] This effect may come through better matching of training to labor market demand that results from the human capital accumulation process being contingent on employers offering positions.[3]

Researchers have also conducted more direct comparisons between "vocational" education at the upper secondary or higher education level (the latter including SCPs), and "general" education such as a bachelor's program or a college-prepatory, nontechnical high school diploma.[4] They have analyzed employment profiles over time for graduates from these various educational options. Using data for 18 countries from the International Adult Literacy Survey studies have found that, after accounting for total years of education, graduates from general programs obtain worse employment outcomes than vocational program graduates at the beginning of their careers but better later on. This pattern is particularly pronounced in countries that are known for their extensive dual systems. The skills generated by vocational programs may facilitate transitions into the labor market but may become obsolete faster than those taught at general education programs. Other studies have found similar patterns for vocational relative to general education,[5] including studies for Europe and Central Asian and African countries.[6]

For LAC countries, evidence from the Skills and Trajectory Survey conducted by the Inter-American Development Bank (IDB) in Argentina and Chile suggests that secondary and postsecondary technical education offers high returns and should therefore receive more attention given its potential to improve labor market outcomes.[7] Yet, studies using administrative data for Chile and Colombia estimate the returns to bachelor's programs and SCPs and find that for a substantial proportion of young people, SCPs bring economic losses.[8]

There have been efforts to estimate the labor market returns to certificates and associate degrees in community colleges in the United States.[9] These studies generally find that such credentials provide higher formal employment and/or earnings than the option of not enrolling in community college. They also find that associate degrees yield larger earnings gains than long-term certificates, with the evidence on short-term certificates being less clear.[10] Although this literature quantifies the gains from attending community college relative to not doing so, for data-related reasons, this chapter focuses on a comparison of the relative gains from attending different SCPs, as discussed in the section entitled "Contribution (Value Added) of SCPs."

Some of the literature cited above also suggest that, while SCPs have better short-term impacts than bachelor's programs, the reverse might happen in the long term. To properly understand SCPs' short- and long-term impact, one must refer to the growing literature documenting skills' critical role and their development.[11] Education, of course, is an essential channel for skills development. Nonetheless, whether education develops general or specific skills is debatable, particularly in the case of higher education. This depends on the specific characteristics of programs and degrees, which vary across and within countries. SCPs are known for providing occupation- and career-specific human capital. In LAC, however, the same is true of bachelor's programs given their heavy focus on the specific study area since the freshman year (see chapter 5). Moreover, both SCPs and bachelor's programs in LAC provide general skills because, by providing higher education that lasts at least two years as opposed to mere short-term training, both program types stimulate the development of multiple skills such as critical thinking and problem solving, and of team work and communication. As a result, it becomes extremely difficult—if not impossible—to differentiate between the skill mix fostered by SCPs and bachelor's programs in LAC.

The skill mix is a critical determinant of the short- and long-term effects of SCPs and bachelor's programs. While a detailed analysis of the skill mix of specific programs is beyond the scope of this book, two pieces of evidence are worth noting. First, the SCP directors interviewed for the World Bank Short-Cycle Program Survey (WBSCPS) report that their programs aim to develop not only specific but also general skills, including cognitive and interpersonal (chapter 3). Second, other studies have found that graduates from postsecondary programs with a strong labor market orientation exhibit higher socioemotional and interpersonal skills than others.[12]

Further, general statements about the relative skills and returns of bachelor's and SCPs must be made subject to qualifications. On the one hand, as the next section shows, there is tremendous variation both among bachelor's programs and SCPs in their net lifetime returns, with some SCPs surpassing some bachelor's programs. Looking forward, LAC countries should view higher education as a piece to promote lifelong learning, whereby an individual continues to acquire skills throughout her lifetime (chapter 5). The option of returning to school as needed lessens the emphasis on the skills acquired in any given program as it enables the individual to flexibly acquire the desired mix of skills over time.

On the other hand, the empirical analysis may not adequately account for self-election. In other words, it is not obvious that the same student who self-selects into an SCP would obtain the same average employment profile of a student who self-selects into a bachelor's program. As the section entitled, "Expanding the Supply of SCPs: Who Would Benefit and Why?" shows, when self-selection is adequately accounted for (a task that is admittedly difficult in cross-country analyses), the finding is that SCPs are a better match for students who are poorly prepared for a bachelor's program, at least in the short run. The reason is that those students would most likely attend a nonselective bachelor's program. Their graduation probability would be lower than that of well-prepared students (Ferreyra et al. 2017), and, if they graduated, their labor market outcomes would be below average. Thus, comparing the average labor market trajectory of SCP and bachelor's graduates masks tremendous heterogeneity among students and programs.

Of course, higher education cannot be expected to fully compensate for a deficit in the foundational skills that the student should have acquired in primary and secondary education.[13] Almost all the SCP directors interviewed in the WBSCPS report providing remedial education given the serious deficits of their incoming students (chapter 1). As they design a higher education system for the future, LAC countries must continue to improve the quality of their basic education systems.

Economic Value of SCPs in LAC

For decades, economists have explored ways to assess the economic value[14] of human capital investments (Becker and Chiswick 1966). On conceptual grounds, the empirical challenge behind these efforts is simple: how to come up with the best possible comparison of average earnings across groups of individuals with different schooling levels but identical characteristics otherwise. To illustrate the idea, let W^{SCP} and W^{HS} be the average earnings of two groups: workers reporting an SCP degree and a high school diploma as the final schooling level, respectively. Thus, the return to an SCP degree relative to a high school diploma can be approximated by the ratio between W^{SCP} and W^{HS}. To understand the concept, consider, for example, a ratio equal to 1.25, equivalent to a 25 percent return. This would mean that, on average, workers with an SCP degree earn 25 percent more than workers with a high school diploma. Of course, a fair comparison would involve groups that are observationally equivalent (with the exception of the highest grade completed). To take this into account, the analysis adjusts for worker characteristics. Box 2.2 briefly describes the Mincer equation (Mincer 1974), which is the conventional econometric model used to estimate returns to education.

Table 2.1 displays the Mincerian returns to SCPs in the early 2000s, early 2010s, and late 2010s. For the sake of completeness and comparison, the table also reports returns to any higher education degree (bachelor's or short cycle) and to a bachelor's degree.[15] These returns are relative to a high school diploma.

The table shows several interesting findings. First, regardless of the period of analysis, in most countries, the Mincerian returns to bachelor's degrees are higher than those to SCPs. The returns to a bachelor's degree range from 70 percent (early 2010s in Argentina) to 178 percent (late 2010s in Chile). Second, returns to higher education degrees have been characterized by a steady decline between the early 2000s and the late 2010s. This pattern is mostly driven by a decrease

---

Box 2.2 Estimating Mincerian Returns

The pioneer analysis of Jacob Mincer (1974) laid the foundations for one of the most popular econometric models in applied labor economics: the Mincer model. In a nutshell, the strategy seeks to compare the earnings of individuals reporting different schooling levels after controlling for other observed characteristics (X). The outcome of this comparison is known as the Mincerian return to education. Formally, consider the following regression model (individual i subscripts omitted for simplicity):

$$ln\, W\,(S,X) = \alpha + \beta S + X'\gamma + \varepsilon,$$

where typically W denotes adult earnings, S denotes years of education, and X is a set of variables, including labor market experience, and its square, urban area, and region indicators, among other controls. Since $ln\, W\,(S, X) - ln\, W\,(S - 1, X)$ is approximately equal to $(W\,(S, W) - W\,(S - 1, X))/W(S - 1, X)$ for any S, the coefficient β is interpreted as the economic return to an extra year of education. The setting can be extended to allow for nonlinear effects of education. To see this, let D_s be a binary variable taking the value 1 if the worker reports schooling level s as her final educational attainment, 0 otherwise; and such that $\sum_{s=0}^{s} D_s = 1$. Thus, a more flexible version of the Mincer model is

$$ln W\,(S, X) = \alpha + \sum_{s=1}^{s} \beta_s D_s + X'\gamma + \varepsilon , \qquad (B2.2.1)$$

where β_s with $s = 1,...,S$ is the economic return to schooling level D_s relative to D_0 (baseline). In the empirical application described in this section, the set of schooling levels considered includes (a) primary education, (b) secondary education (high school diploma), (c) SCP dropout (higher education without a degree from an SCP), (d) SCP graduate, (e) bachelor's dropout, and (f) bachelor's degree graduate. For most of the analysis, "high school diploma" is the baseline category, so the parameters of interest (that is, those corresponding to options (c) to (f)) must be interpreted relative to that schooling level. The estimation of equation (B2.2.1) also considers the potential impact of self-selection into employment. For this purpose, the equation is estimated using a self-selection model à la Heckman, using family background characteristics as exclusion restrictions.

---

in the return to bachelor's degrees, which went from 139 percent in the early 2000s to 109 percent almost two decades later. The evolution of the returns to SCPs offers a less pessimistic view. On average, over the course of two decades, those obtaining SCP degrees received earnings approximately 60 percent greater than those of high school graduates. During this period, for half of the countries, the Mincerian returns to SCPs increased.

Figures 2.1 and 2.2 present these findings graphically. Figure 2.1 displays the changes in returns between the early 2000s and the late 2010s for bachelor's and SCP degrees. The figure shows that, while most countries experienced a reduction in the returns of bachelor's degrees, 7 of the 12 countries experienced an

Table 2.1 Mincerian Returns to Higher Education Degrees in LAC Countries, 2000 to 2010s

Country	Any higher education degree			Bachelor's degree			Short-cycle program degree		
	Early 2000s	Early 2010s	Late 2010s	Early 2000s	Early 2010s	Late 2010s	Early 2000s	Early 2010s	Late 2010s
Argentina	56	60	58	72	70	70	32	48	42
Bolivia	196	84	106	236	78	108	152	92	100
Chile	150	142	118	216	198	178	64	62	48
Costa Rica	106	112	126	114	114	142	46	92	36
Ecuador	132	98	88	136	100	96	26	52	44
El Salvador	98	134	102	120	142	98	66	106	110
Honduras	106	128	104	110	132	106	54	46	76
LAC	111	98	93	139	112	109	57	63	60
Mexico	80	84	86	80	82	90	70	46	44
Nicaragua	120	110	100	148	114	104	18	62	74
Paraguay	128	94	116	182	124	134	74	60	80
Peru	80	56	62	126	94	110	42	30	32
Uruguay	82	74	60	122	92	72	38	56	46

Source: Kutscher and Urzúa (2020), background paper for this book, based on Socio-Economic Database for Latin America and the Caribbean.
Note: The table reports the returns to higher education degrees relative to the alternative of a high school diploma. The estimation of the Mincer model also considers the potential impact of self-selection into employment. The set of controls includes labor market experience, age and its square, urban area indicators, and region indicators. Argentina (2003), Argentina (2010), Argentina (2016), Bolivia (2000), Bolivia (2011), Bolivia (2016), Chile (2000), Chile (2011), Chile (2015), Costa Rica (2001), Costa Rica (2010), Costa Rica (2016), Ecuador (2003), Ecuador (2010), Ecuador (2016), El Salvador (2000), El Salvador (2010), El Salvador (2016), Honduras (2002), Honduras (2010), Honduras (2016), Mexico (2004), Mexico (2010), Mexico (2016), Nicaragua (2001), Nicaragua (2009), Nicaragua (2014; no later data were available), Panama (2001), Panama (2010), Panama (2016), Paraguay (2003), Paraguay (2010), Paraguay (2016), Peru (2000), Peru (2010), Peru (2016), Uruguay (2000), Uruguay (2011), Uruguay (2016). LAC = Latin America and the Caribbean.

increase in the returns of short-term programs, with gains ranging from 5 to 45 percentage points. Figure 2.2 displays the returns to SCP degrees across the 12 countries and for the most recent period of analysis (late 2010s), which are also shown in table 2.1. For El Salvador and Bolivia, the Mincer model delivers estimates above 100 percent; the range is between 40 and 80 percent for Argentina, Chile, Ecuador, Honduras, Paraguay, and Uruguay; and it is between 20 and 40 percent for Costa Rica and Peru. Overall, these results suggest an advantage of SCP degrees over the alternative of a high school diploma.

At first glance, the advantages of SCP degrees relative to a high school diploma reported in figure 2.2 might not be surprising, as they ultimately reflect the economic return to new skills and capabilities. A more exigent comparison group would be those who start bachelor's programs but leave before obtaining the degree, that is, bachelor's dropouts. Figure 2.3 reports the results. They indicate that in most countries, the returns are higher for SCP degrees than for incomplete bachelor's programs. Thus, relative to dropping out of a bachelor's program, SCPs emerge as a financially superior alternative (with the exception of Chile and Peru, where the difference between returns is not significantly different from zero).[16]

Figure 2.1 Changes in Mincerian Returns to Bachelor's and SCP Degrees, between the Early 2000s and Late 2010s

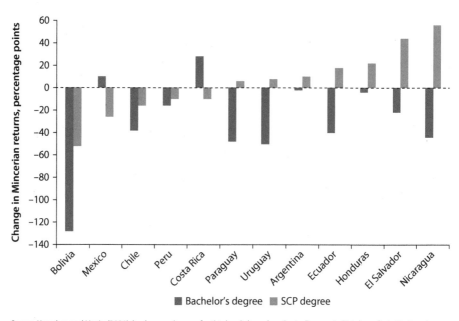

Source: Kutscher and Urzúa (2020), background paper for this book, based on Socio-Economic Database for Latin America and the Caribbean.
Note: This figure uses results obtained from estimation of the Mincer model described in box 2.2. It displays the difference between the estimated coefficients associated with the relevant schooling categories (bachelor's and SCP degrees) between the early 2000s and the late 2010s. The results are reported as percentage point differences. SCP = short-cycle program.

Figure 2.2 Mincerian Returns to a SCP Degree in Latin America and the Caribbean, by Country, Late 2010s

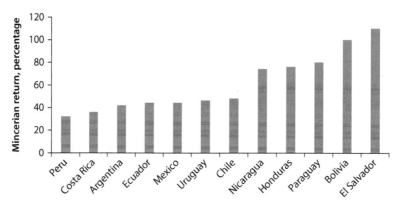

Source: Kutscher and Urzúa (2020), background paper for this book, based on Socio-Economic Database for Latin America and the Caribbean.
Note: The figure reports the returns to an SCP degree relative to the alternative of a high school diploma in the late 2010s. The coefficients represent the average difference of (ln) monthly earnings between workers with an SCP degree and workers with a high school diploma, controlling for gender, age and its square, urban area indicators, and regional indicators by country. The returns are computed as the exponential function of the coefficient minus 1. The estimation of the Mincer model also considers the potential impact of self-selection into employment. SCP = short-cycle program.

Although this analysis is informative, it does not fully capture some critical elements, such as the tuition and opportunity costs of attending higher education. And the results might mask considerable heterogeneity in the returns of bachelor and SCP degrees, for instance, across institutions and fields.[17] The next section further investigates to understand how heterogeneous the returns to higher education are.

Costs, Duration, and Economic Returns: Chile and Colombia

Although they are informative on earnings premia, Mincerian returns do not take into account some of the critical aspects molding the overall impact of higher education degrees on individuals' labor market outcomes. For example, Mincerian returns do not account for direct costs such as tuition and fees, or the indirect opportunity costs of forgone earnings. As such, they might mischaracterize the relative benefits and/or costs associated with different types of higher education degrees.

Recent studies have documented negative returns to some higher education programs in Chile and Colombia after taking into account direct and indirect costs. This section builds the analysis on the studies of Espinoza and Urzúa (2018) and González-Velosa et al. (2015) and uses student-level administrative data from Chile and Colombia to estimate the net economic returns to higher

Figure 2.3 Short-Cycle Program Degree Relative to College Dropouts (Bachelor's Program): Mincerian Returns, Late 2010s

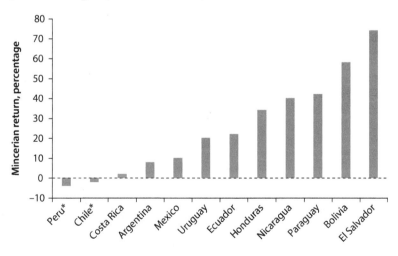

Source: Kutscher and Urzúa (2020), background paper for this book, based on Socio-Economic Database for Latin America and the Caribbean.
Note: This figure uses results obtained from estimation of the Mincer model described in box 2.2. It displays the ratio (minus one) between the estimated coefficients corresponding to an SCP degree and an incomplete bachelor's program.
* The coefficient is not statistically different from zero.

Box 2.3 Value of a Higher Education Degree over the Life Cycle

Estimation of the net economic returns in lifetime earnings to higher education can provide
evidence on the overall long-term effects of the human capital accumulation process. Consider
the schooling decision problem of an individual who, after completing secondary education,
is deciding whether to pursue a higher education degree. Assume that she is weighing the
alternatives of enrolling in a higher education program versus entering the labor force right
after graduating from high school. The ex-post returns to program j, defined by the combination of an institution, type of degree, and major, can be written as:

$$r_{HS}(j) = \frac{NPV(j) - NPV_{HS}}{NPV_{HS}},$$

where $NPV(j)$ is the net present value of earnings of pursuing degree j and NPV_{HS} is the present
value of not pursuing higher education after graduating from high school. Formally,

$$NPV(j) = \sum_{t=d_{j}+1}^{R} \frac{Y_j(t)}{(1+r)^t} - \sum_{t=1}^{d_j} \frac{C_j}{(1+r)^t} \text{ and } NPV_{HS} = \sum_{t=1}^{R} \frac{Y_{HS}(t)}{(1+r)^t},$$

where $Y_j(t)$ is the income associated with program j at age t, C_j represents tuition fees, d_j is the
program's theoretical duration, r is the discount rate, R denotes retirement age, and $Y_{HS}(t)$ represents the counterfactual income received under the alternative of a high school degree (and
no higher education). Exploiting individual-level data, Espinoza and Urzúa (2017) posit a strategy for doing this. The results reported in this chapter follow their approach. A key assumption
is that the average individual obtaining a higher education degree would have received counterfactual earnings comparable to those of the 75th percentile of the earnings distribution of
high school graduates.

Ex-post returns accrue to students who graduate from their programs—that is, they are
conditional on graduation. In contrast, ex-ante returns would take into account the likelihood
of graduating and weigh ex-post returns accordingly. The calculations outlined above can be
extended to obtain ex-ante, unconditional expected returns. For clarity of presentation, this
chapter focuses on ex-post returns.

---

education programs taking these aspects into account. Box 2.3 describes the
approach.

Chile and Colombia have complex higher education systems. Chile has three
types of HEIs: universities (which offer bachelor's and SCP degrees), professional institutes (which offer four-year SCPs), and technical training centers
(only authorized to offer two-year SCPs). In Colombia, there are four types of
HEIs: universities, university institutes, technological institutes, and technical
professional institutes. In undergraduate education, there are three levels:
technical-professional (SCP), technological (SCP), and professional (bachelor's).
While universities and university institutes can offer any of the three

undergraduate types of qualification, technological institutes and technical professional institutes can only offer SCP degrees. And despite the fact that the National Training Service (SENA, *Servicio Nacional de Aprendizaje)* mostly focuses on vocational training and professional apprenticeship programs, this public institution also offers SCP degrees that are comparable to those granted by technical institutes (see chapter 1).

In principle, these intricate structures might prevent a clear identification of SCPs, but administrative data allow a precise categorization. Table 2.2 presents basic statistics on the higher education systems in Chile and Colombia.

A large number of HEIs and programs emerges as a distinctive characteristic of the higher education systems in both countries, with average tuition costs in the range of US$3,500 to US$6,500. These figures represent a significant fraction of per capita gross domestic product—US$14,450 for Colombia in 2018 and US$24,000 for Chile in 2019 (in purchasing power parity dollars).

Table 2.2 Descriptive Statistics, Higher Education in Chile and Colombia

	Types of HEI		
A. Chile (2019)	*Technical training centers (2-yr SCP)*	*Professional institutes (4-yr SCP)*	*Universities (bachelor's and SCPs)*
Demand side			
Total enrollment (number)	137,940	379,456	676,915
First-year enrollment (number)	60,927	122,616	152,153
Supply side			
Number of HEIs	48	41	61
Number of programs	3,185	7,313	6,864
Duration (years)	2.3	2.9	4.0
Tuition costs (PPP dollars of 2019, annual)	$3,562	$3,667	$6,224

	Types of HEI			
B. Colombia (2018)	*Technical professional institutes (SCP)*	*Technological institutes (SCP)*	*University institutes (bachelor's and SCPs)*	*Universities (bachelor's and SCPs)*
Demand side				
Enrollment (number)	1,983	10,129	11,230	40,043
First-year enrollment (number)	1,327	5,647	8,155	26,410
Supply side				
Number of HEIs	34	49	133	132
Number of programs	964	2,152	4,174	6,840
Duration (years)	2.7	2.6	3.6	4.4
Tuition costs (PPP dollars 2019, annual)	$3,829	$4,477	$4,555	$6,522

Sources: Kutscher and Urzúa (2020), background paper for this book. Calculations based on *Mi Futuro,* from the Ministry of Education of Chile, and *Sistema Nacional de Infórmacion de la Educación Superior* from the Ministry of Education of Colombia.
Note: SCPs offered by *Servicio Nacional de Aprendizaje* are not included. HEI = higher education institution; PPP = purchasing power parity; SCP = short-cycle program.

The variation in tuition across programs, as the literature shows, contributes to the large disparities in their net returns (Espinoza and Urzúa 2018; Ferreyra et al. 2017). This section revisits this evidence but, unlike previous studies, it focuses on SCPs.

To start, consider the following question: When it comes to HEI returns, is a bachelor's degree the most profitable alternative? Based on the Mincerian returns reported in table 2.1, the answer to this question would be a firm yes. However, this view omits two central facts reflected in table 2.2. First, on average, SCPs are shorter than bachelor's programs. And second, on average, they command a lower tuition. Accounting for these, the response to the question might change, as SCPs might compete well with bachelor's programs.

To explore these issues, figure 2.4 examines the case of Chile and compares, across fields, the average net returns to SCP and bachelor's degrees granted by universities. The focus on universities secures a meaningful comparison that is unaffected by the heterogeneity of HEI types. Notably, SCP degrees in arts and social sciences granted by universities deliver, on average, higher average net returns than bachelor's degrees granted by the same institutions. Hence, even among university-granted degrees, SCPs are sometimes the superior alternative.

A similar finding emerges for Colombia. Focusing on degrees granted by universities in Colombia, Kutscher and Urzúa (2020) show that, despite a general advantage of bachelor's degrees, SCP degrees in social sciences have higher average returns (60 percent) than bachelor's degrees in the same field (40 percent). In addition, Colombia's rich administrative data allow for the

Figure 2.4 Average Net Returns to SCP and Bachelor's Degrees Granted by Chilean Universities, by Field

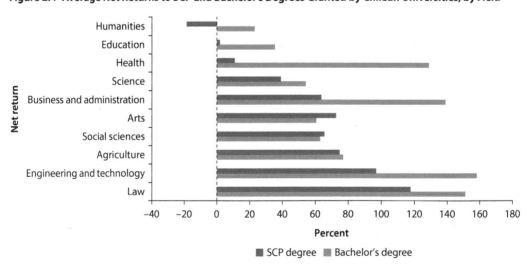

Source: Kutscher and Urzúa (2020), background paper for this book. Calculations based on individual-level data from the Ministry of Education of Chile, Higher Education Information Service, and *Mi Futuro.*
Note: Net returns are relative to the alternative of a high school diploma. The figure shows averages over individual returns. SCP = short cycle program.

separate estimation of net returns for males and females. The authors find that net returns to bachelor's and SCP degrees are higher for males than females regardless of HEI type—although with some exceptions. For instance, among degrees in health granted by universities, net returns to SCPs are 18 percent higher for females than males (in contrast, net returns to bachelor's degrees are 71 percent higher for males than females).

Are the returns to SCP degrees higher when granted by a university relative to other HEIs? Figure 2.5 focuses on Chile and compares, across fields, the average net returns to SCP degrees granted by different HEI types. Students who obtained these degrees from universities in fields such as law and social sciences experience higher net returns than those obtaining the same SCP degrees from non-university HEIs. Nonetheless, in the field of science, some SCP degrees from non-university HEIs yield higher returns than those from universities.

Figure 2.6 conducts a similar comparison for Colombia. In all fields but arts, the returns are higher at some type of non-university HEI than at universities. For instance, the average net return to a health degree from a technological institute is above 60 percent, whereas it is below 4 percent from a university. Thus, in Chile and Colombia, SCPs granted by non-university HEIs often deliver higher returns than those from universities, and this is particularly true for Colombia.

Can we go beyond a comparison of average returns by field and type of institution? Yes, because individual-level data for Chile and Colombia allow for

Figure 2.5 Average Net Returns to SCPs, by Field and Type of Institution, Chile

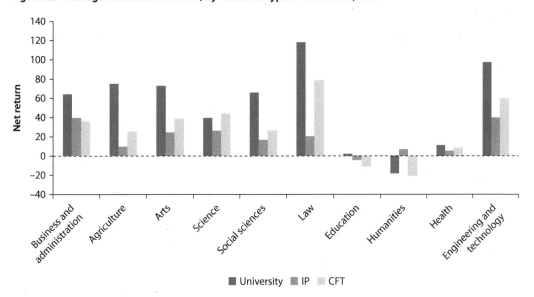

Source: Kutscher and Urzúa (2020), background paper for this book. Calculations based on individual-level data from the Ministry of Education of Chile, Higher Education Information Service, and *Mi Futuro.*
Note: Net returns are relative to the alternative of a high school diploma. The figure shows averages over individual returns. CFT = technical training centers (*centros de formacion tecnica*); IP = professional institutes (*institutos profesionales*); SCP = short-cycle program.

Figure 2.6 Average Net Returns to SCPs, by Field and Type of Institution, Colombia

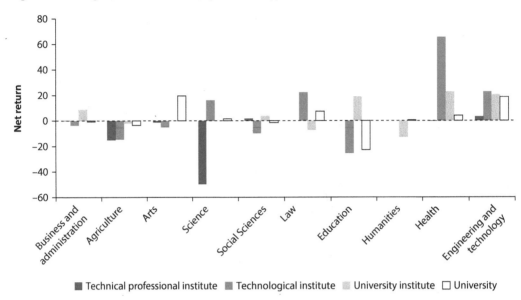

Source: Kutscher and Urzúa (2020), background paper for this book. Calculations based on data from the Ministry of National Education of Colombia, National Education Information System, and *Observatorio Laboral para la Educación* from Colombia.
Note: Net returns are relative to the alternative of a high school diploma. The figure shows averages over individual returns. For Colombia, SCPs offered by *Servicio Nacional de Aprendizaje* are not included. SCP = short-cycle program.

constructing the distribution of program-level average returns by field. Figure 2.7 displays net returns from the 25th (circle) and 75th (square) percentiles of these distributions for bachelor's (in blue) and SCP degrees (in orange). Panel a shows Chile, and panel b shows Colombia. For the sake of completeness, the figure also presents the averages (diamonds) of the corresponding distributions. For simplicity, the terms "worst" and "best" are used to refer to the 25th and 75th percentiles, respectively.

In both countries, the variation in program-level returns across fields is striking, as it ranges from −30 to 180 percent. In every field, the average bachelor's program provides higher net returns than the average SCP, yet in some fields, the average SCP provides higher net returns than the "worst" bachelor's programs. Further, in most fields, the "best" SCP provides higher net returns than the "worst" bachelor's program. In Chile, the average SCP in fields such as engineering and technology or law provides higher net returns than the average bachelor's program in fields such as arts, education, or humanities. In Colombia, the average SCP in engineering and technology provides higher net returns than the "worst" bachelor's programs in almost all other fields. In other words, a variety of SCPs provide higher returns than many bachelor's programs.

An important caveat regarding the preceding analysis on returns is in order. A program's negative returns do not necessarily indicate that it is not worth

Figure 2.7 Heterogeneity in Average Returns to Higher Education Programs, by Field and Type of Degree

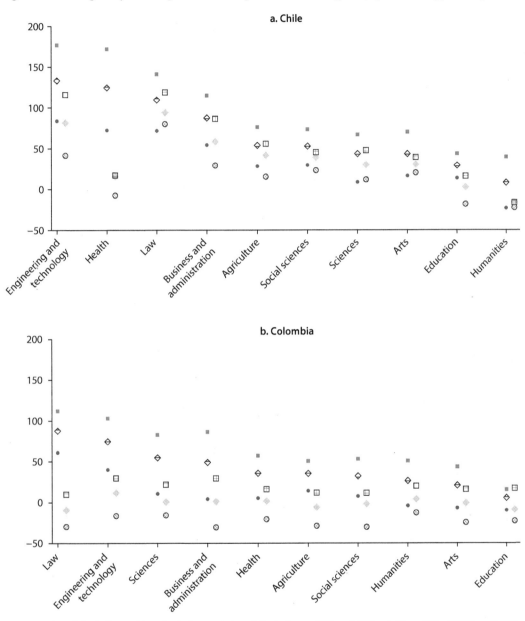

Sources: World Bank calculations based on individual-level data from the Ministry of Education of Chile, Higher Education Information Service, and *Mi Futuro*; the Ministry of National Education, National Education Information System, and *Observatorio Laboral para la Educación* from Colombia. *Note:* Net returns are relative to the alternative of a high school diploma. For each country and program type, the figure shows the average, 25th percentile, and 75th percentile of the distribution of (average) program returns by field. For Colombia, SCPs offered by *Servicio Nacional de Aprendizaje* are not included. SCP = short-cycle program.

pursuing. The program might be socially valuable, as is the case of elementary school teaching and social work, or provide the student with nonpecuniary returns. Rather, the analysis seeks to show that, for students interested in raising their lifetime income, some programs are clearly better than others. It also seeks to alert the regulator of the great variation in SCP returns, and to provide him with data to make decisions (chapter 5).

All in all, despite the large disparities across HEI types and fields, the estimates of net returns in Chile and Colombia indicate that SCPs can offer larger economic benefits relative to bachelor's degrees. Among the institutions granting SCP degrees, universities are not always the highest return option, as other HEI types offer higher returns depending on the field. In light of the SCP stigma in the region and the funding differences between bachelor's programs and SCPs (see chapter 1), these findings suggest that families, students, and policy makers might be overlooking the economic benefits of SCPs.

Expanding the Supply of SCPs: Who Would Benefit and Why?

LAC has witnessed efforts to expand SCP supply over the past two decades.[18] For instance, the number of SCPs in Colombia and Chile grew by approximately 3 and 2 percent a year, respectively, between the early 2000s and the late 2010s (see chapter 3).[19] Are students more likely to pursue SCPs when their supply is expanded? Do students benefit from an SCP relative to not pursuing higher education at all? Do they benefit from an SCP relative to a bachelor's program? Answering these questions is critical for policy makers interested in expanding the supply of SCPs.

As it turns out, the answer to these questions largely depends on students' fallback options—what they would choose if SCPs were not available. When SCPs become available, there are two types of students: (a) students *diverting* from enrolling in a bachelor's program and instead enrolling in an SCP, and (b) students *entering* the higher education system by enrolling in an SCP. Students in these groups likely differ in their characteristics, preferences, and previous skills, as well as in the gains or losses they would obtain from the SCP. Identifying students in categories (a) and (b) is ultimately a conceptual and policy relevant challenge.

High school graduates face an important decision: whether to enroll in higher education and, in the case of enrolling, whether to choose a bachelor's program or an SCP. Although some students might have strong preferences for one option, there is no prior reason to think that one alternative is better than the other for *all* students. While students who do not attend higher education enter the labor market earlier than those who pursue higher education, some of them might benefit from delaying work and enrolling in an SCP. For others, choosing a bachelor's program rather than an SCP might harm their labor market trajectories if they are more suited to acquiring practical skills in an SCP rather than traditional, academic skills in a bachelor's program.

Colombia provides a unique setting to analyze these higher education choices and their labor market effects. As described in box 2.1, administrative data allow the researcher to follow high school graduates, observe their higher education trajectories,[20] and, for those who graduate from higher education, observe their formal market employment and earnings. Exploiting these data, Ferreyra, Galindo, and Urzúa (2020) determine the effect of the enrollment choices made by the 2005 cohort of high school graduates on their formal employment probability and average earnings in 2013. Estimating this effect is not straightforward because of *self-selection*: high school graduates choosing to enroll in an SCP might be different from those making other choices, in observed (for example, family income) and unobserved (for example, perseverance) characteristics. A meaningful comparison must take these differences into account.

To gain traction on the problem, the authors focus on a variable that does not pertain to the student herself but can help explain her choices—namely, the availability of SCPs in her municipality. This is because having an SCP in her municipality makes it easier—less costly—for her to enroll in one. Figure 2.8 confirms this intuition. It examines the average choices of students from the 2005 high school cohort who lived in a municipality with an SCP relative to the choices of students living in municipalities without an SCP. As expected, the former group was more likely to enroll in these programs (10.4 versus 7.3 percent; see the orange bars in figure 2.8). In other words, SCP availability is one of the determinants of students' enrollment choices.

Equipped with this evidence, consider the following question: Which students would respond to the opening of an institution offering SCPs within a 10-kilometer radius from their home municipality? To answer it, consider first the baseline scenario, when such institution is not available. In this case, students can select among the following three options: not enrolling in higher education, enrolling in an SCP (outside the 10-kilometer radius), or enrolling in a bachelor's program. After the institution offering SCPs opens within a 10-kilometer radius, students can select the same options as before but can also enroll in an SCP at the new institution. What will they do? By addressing the self-selection issue through SCP availability and modeling student responses as grounded on basic economic principles, Ferreyra, Galindo, and Urzúa (2020) show that SCP enrollment would increase, mostly as a result of students *diverging* from bachelor's degrees as opposed to students *entering* higher education. In other words, SCP availability would make some students (the "switchers") switch from a bachelor's program to an SCP. Moreover, the switchers would be mostly males poorly prepared for higher education, coming from disadvantaged households in small or medium-size municipalities. More important for this chapter, had the switchers persisted in their choice of a bachelor's program rather than switching to an SCP, their formal employment rate and salaries would have been lower than with the SCP. In other words, SCPs are a better match for those students—formally, they experience a positive SCP treatment effect—as the availability of SCPs gives them access to better, more productive labor market matches.

Figure 2.8 Enrollment in Higher Education, by Availability of Short-Cycle Institutions

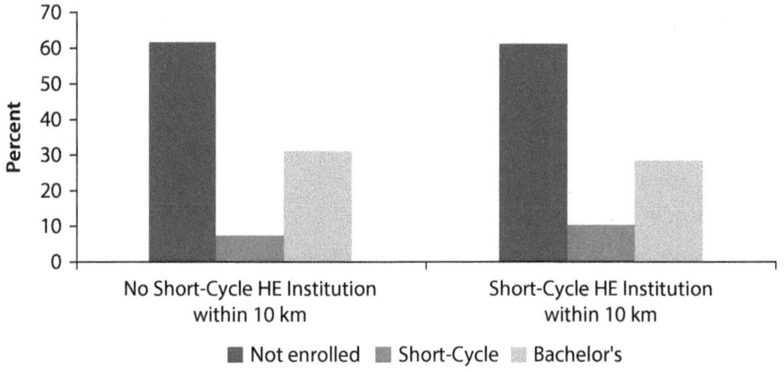

Source: Ferreyra, Galindo, and Urzúa 2020, background paper for this book, based on data from the National Education Information System and the Ministry of National Education of Colombia.
Note: The figure shows the percentage of students choosing each option (not enrolled in higher education, enrolled in an SCP, and enrolled in a bachelor's program) by availability of short-cycle higher education institutions in a 10-kilometer radius from the student's high school municipality. Percentages account for differences in students' socioeconomic background, test scores in the high school exit exam, and local (municipality) characteristics. HE = higher education; km = kilometer; SCP = short-cycle program.

The finding that changes in SCP availability would not lead many high school graduates to enter higher education may indicate that what prevents their entry is not supply-side constraints but rather long-run credit constraints. Indeed, Ferreyra et al. (2017) document these constraints have a larger role on higher education access than short-term credit constraints. Nonetheless, there is a group of high school students that would enter higher education if the local labor market conditions for SCP graduates improved. These students are mostly females from disadvantaged and large households. An SCP degree would give a higher formal employment rate and salaries than a high school diploma. This finding speaks to the gender disparities in the region. To attract these female high school graduates into higher education, an SCP expansion might not be enough.

To summarize, this section illustrates that an SCP expansion could have different impacts on different students as the effects vary among students, depending on what they would choose if they did not enroll in an SCP (their fallback or second-best option) and on their background characteristics. For male students with poor academic preparation, who come from disadvantaged families in small or medium-size municipalities, SCPs provide better employment and salary prospects than the fallback option of a bachelor's program. For female students from disadvantaged, large families but who are not necessarily poorly prepared, SCPs provide better labor market outcomes than the fallback option of not enrolling in higher education. Thus, a variety of high-quality offerings in the higher education system, including SCPs as well as bachelor's programs, should allow individuals to find their best, most productive match. This is consistent with the chapter's previous finding that SCP returns are far from homogeneous.

Contribution (Value Added) of SCPs

This section turns to how much SCPs contribute to student outcomes—namely, how much value they add.[21] To distinguish a program's contributions from its outcomes, consider, for instance, the salary earned by the graduate of one such program immediately upon graduation. This salary is the *outcome* of inputs coming from herself (for example, ability and effort), her peers, and the program (for example, faculty and facilities). The goal, then, is to quantify the program's value-added contribution, net of the contribution made by the student herself and her peers, to early labor market outcomes (employment in the formal sector and wages). The focus is on Colombia, whose rich administrative data allow for this estimation. Box 2.4 presents the estimation approach used in the background paper by Ferreyra et al. (2020), written for this book.

Table 2.3 presents statistics for program outcomes and program contributions to formal employment and monthly wages. In particular, the table shows the number of programs, the mean of actual outcomes, and statistics from the distribution of program-level contributions (the mean and 25th, 50th, and 75th percentiles). The statistics are provided for all programs and for programs in specific fields.

In the average program, 76 percent of the graduates find employment in the formal sector (in contrast, only 36 percent of individuals ages 25–65 attain formal employment in Colombia). Among SCP graduates employed in the formal sector, the average monthly salary is Col$891,000 (approximately US$450 in 2013), which is greater than the 2013 monthly minimum wage of Col$590,000 (or US$315.)

Echoing the section entitled, "Economic Value of SCPs in LAC," table 2.3 shows that outcomes and contributions vary across fields. On average, math and natural sciences deliver the greatest contributions to formal employment, and health makes the greatest contribution to wages. The table also shows very large ranges of contributions for every field of study—namely, there is large *within-field* variation. Overall, contributions to labor market outcomes vary greatly among programs. Going from the 25th to the 75th percentile of contributions to formal employment implies a 20-percentage point increase in formal employment probability, or about one-fourth of the average program's outcome (76 percent). In terms of wages, going from the 25th to the 75th percentile of the value-added distribution entails an increase of Col$143,000, which is larger than the standard deviation of actual wages and equals 17 percent of the mean program's wage. Taken together, these results suggest that programs differ widely in their average outcomes and in their contributions to student outcomes. Thus, students and policy makers would benefit from knowing how specific programs fare in average outcomes and contributions.

Box 2.4 Estimating Value Added

Consider outcome Y_{ijt}^k, where k refers to the outcomes of interest, i to the student, j to the program, and t to the cohort. Thus, the following can be posited:

$$Y_{ijt}^k = X_i{'}\alpha^k + Z_{ijt}{'}\beta^k + u_j^k + \delta_t^k + \in_{ijt}^k,$$

where X_i contains student Systems Approach for Better Education Results (SABER) 11 scores as well as gender, age, parental socioeconomic status, and mother's education; Z represents peer characteristics (average SABER 11 and proportion of peers' mothers with at least a bachelor's degree) in the student's cohort; u_j is a program fixed effect; δ_t is a cohort fixed effect; and $\in_{ijt}$ represents unobserved individual-level characteristics that affect the outcome of interest. Thus, the vector X contains "individual characteristics," and Z contains "peer characteristics." The main parameter of interest is the set of program-level fixed effects, u_j, which estimate the program-level contributions to student outcomes. X determines not only student outcomes, but also selection into programs. This is particularly true of SABER 11, which measures students' academic readiness for higher education. Although many short-cycle programs are open access, others use SABER 11 as an admission criterion. Further, SABER 11 provides the student information on her abilities that she may use when choosing a program.

For wages, figure 2.9 further illustrates the variation in program contributions across and within fields. Most programs in engineering and architecture, health, and math and natural sciences make above-average contributions. In contrast, most programs in economics and business, agronomy, social science, and arts make below-average contributions. Once again, although some fields are more likely to deliver an above-average contribution than others, all of them—health in particular—display large within-field variation.

To summarize, program value-added contributions vary across and within fields. The large within-field variation in program contributions implies that for a student seeking a program that will add much value to her human capital, it is not enough to choose a field with a high *average* contribution, as low-contribution programs exist even within seemingly "good" fields. From the point of view of the policy maker, the large within-field variation means she may need to monitor value-added contributions closely to identify programs throughout the distribution, especially at the lower end.

What are the characteristics of institutions associated with high value-added contributions to wages? Correlations between program-level contributions and a set of institution- and program-level characteristics help to address this question. These suggest that three-year programs contribute more than two-year programs.[22] And, consistent with some of the findings reported in the previous sections, technological institutes deliver higher wage contributions than universities.

Table 2.3 Program-Level Average Outcomes and Value Added: Overall and by Field of Study

	Outcomes		Value added			
Outcome and field	N	Mean	Mean	P25	P50	P75
Employment						
Agronomy and veterinary	31	0.61	−0.14	−0.29	−0.21	−0.09
Arts	79	0.65	−0.11	−0.20	−0.09	−0.02
Health	48	0.74	−0.01	−0.12	0.02	0.12
Social sciences	39	0.62	−0.15	−0.24	−0.15	−0.08
Economics and business	325	0.79	0.03	−0.04	0.06	0.13
Engineering and architecture	311	0.78	0.01	−0.07	0.02	0.10
Math and natural sciences	18	0.82	0.05	0.03	0.07	0.09
Total programs	851	0.76	0.00	−0.10	0.02	0.10
Monthly wages						
Agronomy and veterinary	31	762.18	−122.41	−157.57	−124.94	−102.06
Arts	79	841.96	−53.58	−130.28	−80.59	30.21
Health	48	952.17	78.35	−66.39	10.28	230.28
Social sciences	39	790.76	−85.13	−164.30	−102.92	6.92
Economics and business	325	860.48	−19.99	−84.19	−39.04	29.40
Engineering and architecture	311	935.57	31.08	−59.38	18.24	102.60
Math and natural sciences	18	939.52	30.46	−41.60	2.29	91.26
Total programs	851	891.03	0.00	−86.42	−19.51	57.04

Source: Ferreyra et al.(2020), background paper for this book.
Note: In this table, a program is the unit of observation. Statistics are weighted by the number of students in the program. Value added is estimated with fixed-effects models (see box 2.4); it averages zero for each outcome. Wages are expressed in thousands of 2013 Colombian pesos. SCPs taught by *Servicio Nacional de Aprendizaje* are included. N = number of programs; P = percentile; SCP = short-cycle program.

More selective or specialized institutions also deliver higher wage contributions, as well as programs taught in large cities. Finally, distance programs make lower (but only marginally significant) contributions than face-to-face programs.

From a policy standpoint, the wide variation in program-level outcomes and contributions is concerning. It suggests the need for stronger monitoring on the part of the policy maker—particularly to identify programs in the lower tails of outcomes and contributions—as well as the importance of making information on program-level outcomes and contributions available to students who are choosing a program. At the same time, Ferreyra et al. (2020) caution against using this information to build rankings, since these are highly sensitive to the underlying metric. In other words, the ranking of programs based on average outcomes is different from that based on value-added contributions, and rankings based on outcomes (or contributions) for formal employment are different from those for salaries.[23] Chapter 5 returns to these issues.

Figure 2.9 Distribution of Program-Level Contributions to Wages, by Field

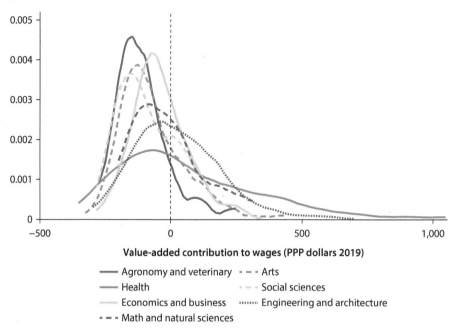

Value-added contribution to wages (PPP dollars 2019)

—— Agronomy and veterinary   – – · Arts
—— Health   ·· — · Social sciences
~~~ Economics and business   ········ Engineering and architecture
– – – Math and natural sciences

Source: Ferreyra et al. (2020) background paper for this book.
Note: The figure shows the distribution of program-level value-added to wages, by field of study. Wages are expressed in thousands of 2013 Colombian pesos. Program-level contributions are estimated in the regression reported in box 2.4. Their overall average is zero. For Colombia, SCPs taught by *Servicio Nacional de Aprendizaje* are included. PPP = purchasing power parity; SCP = short-cycle program.

Demand for SCP Graduates: Exploiting Data on Vacancies

The expansion of internet access across countries and socioeconomic groups has transformed the job search process.[24] Nowadays, internet-based recruitment exists in almost every country in LAC. This section exploits this innovation to characterize the demand for SCP graduates. The analysis is carried out using data on vacancies posted on job portals between February 2017 and February 2018 in Argentina, Chile, Colombia, Mexico, and Peru.[25] As online job portals reach more and more people, and with the increasing use of electronic platforms due to the COVID-19 pandemic, the importance of studying online vacancies increases considerably.

Most of the existing research using online vacancies has focused on developed countries.[26] However, one study focuses on LAC countries using the Latin American and Caribbean Economic Association–IDB Job Vacancy Project data set.[27] It finds that online portals capture an important demand for low-skilled jobs involving routine tasks in occupations at high risk of being automated. Using the same data set, this section builds on that study to provide a detailed characterization of the types of jobs available to SCP graduates on online portals.

A key concern when using online vacancies is that the socioeconomic and demographic characteristics of internet users might differ from those of the general population. This bias is likely lower among SCP graduates because they are likely to have regular internet access. Assessing whether the online vacancies are representative of labor demand in the market is difficult because there are no data on the universe of vacancies. Still, in a background paper for this book, Galindo, Kutscher, and Urzúa (2021) compare the distributions of online job postings with those obtained from representative samples of jobs in each country, showing that they are not too far apart. Thus, to some extent, the data on vacancies are informative of the overall job opportunities in these economies.

Table 2.4 documents the strong demand for SCPs on online portals. Across countries, the fraction of vacancies that require at least an SCP degree is higher than (or very similar to) the fraction of vacancies explicitly demanding a bachelor's degree. The overrepresentation of jobs in the service sectors in these samples might be a factor behind this result. Nonetheless, since an applicant with an SCP degree could also fill vacancies that require at least primary or secondary education, SCP graduates are qualified to fill about 75 percent of the total vacancies.

The information from job vacancies allows a detailed analysis by occupation. Figure 2.10 presents the most demanded occupations by educational level in Chile and Mexico. The high demand in the business and STEM fields, for bachelor's and SCP graduates (and to some extent high school graduates) is striking. Similar patterns can be found for the other countries in the sample.

Two nonexclusive characterizations of the labor markets emerge from this result. The first is that individuals with different degrees compete for the same positions, which would suggest an unraveling of the job ladder (for instance, individuals with bachelor's degrees competing for vacancies requiring an SCP degree, and those with an SCP degree competing for vacancies requiring a high school diploma). The second is that competition might not exist because different degrees carry different, specific skills, suggesting the existence of segmented labor markets by degree type. For instance, an SCP graduate could be

Table 2.4 Minimum Educational Level Required as Posted Online, by Country

Minimum level of education required	Argentina	Chile	Colombia	Mexico	Peru
Primary education	0.03	0.02	0.03	0.04	0.01
High school degree	0.40	0.60	0.56	0.58	0.53
SCP degree	0.20	0.14	0.26	0.08	0.25
Bachelor's degree	0.12	0.07	0.04	0.09	0.04
Graduate degree	0	0	0.01	0.01	0.01
No information	0.25	0.15	0.11	0.20	0.16
Number of vacancies	580,820	1,148,359	1,896,277	2,032,132	1,290,437

Source: Galindo , Kutscher, and Úrzua (2021), background paper for this book, based on the Latin American and Caribbean Economic Association–Inter-American Development Bank Job Vacancy Project data set.
Note: For each country, the table shows the proportion of total vacancies posted online by minimum level of education required. For each country, the proportions sum to 1 (100 percent). SCP = short-cycle program.

Figure 2.10 Most Demanded Occupations, by Educational Level, Chile and Mexico

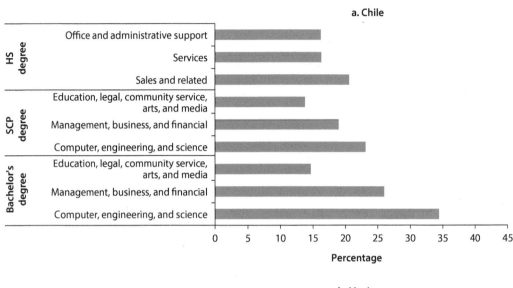

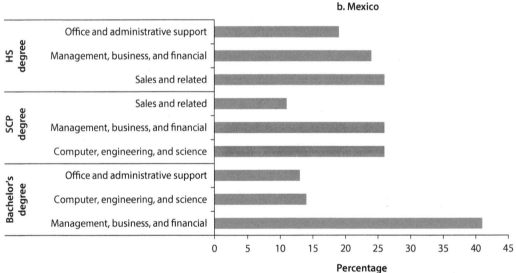

Source: Galindo, Kutscher, and Urzúa (2021), background paper for this book, based on the Latin American and Caribbean Economic Association–
Inter-American Development Bank Job Vacancy Project data set.
Note: For each country and degree type, the figure shows the percentage of vacancies for the three sectors with the greatest numbers of
vacancies for each degree type. HS = high school; SCP = short-cycle program.

doing network maintenance while a bachelor's graduate does information system design. In other words, individuals with different skill levels would be
demanded within similar fields. It will be interesting to assess which view pre-
vails in the postpandemic labor markets.

Map 2.1 Geographic Distribution of SCP Vacancies and SCP Graduates

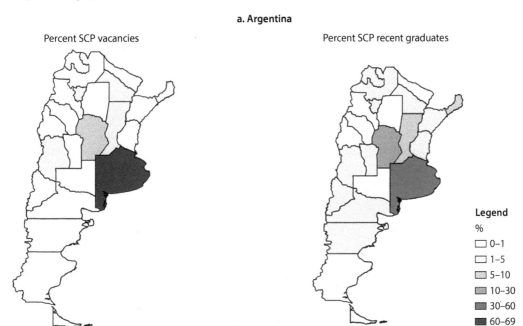

a. Argentina

Percent SCP vacancies   Percent SCP recent graduates

Legend
%
☐ 0–1
☐ 1–5
◻ 5–10
◼ 10–30
◼ 30–60
■ 60–69

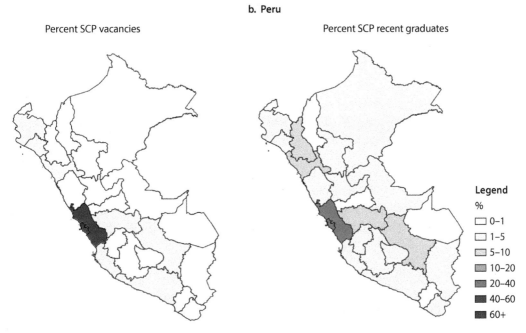

b. Peru

Percent SCP vacancies   Percent SCP recent graduates

Legend
%
☐ 0–1
☐ 1–5
◻ 5–10
◼ 10–20
◼ 20–40
◼ 40–60
■ 60+

Sources: Galindo, Kutscher, and Urzúa (2021), background paper for this book, based on the Latin American and Caribbean Economic Association–Inter-American Development Bank Job Vacancy Project data set, Argentina's Statistical Annals of Higher Education (2018) and Peru's Database of Registered Degrees (2019), *Sistema de Gestión de Títulos* (SIGETI).
Note: For each country, the figure shows the percentage of vacancies requesting SCP degrees posted by firms from each location (panel a) and the percentage of individuals who graduated from an SCP in 2017–18 (panel b). Both percentages are relative to the whole country. The location is the level-1 administrative division. SCP = short-cycle program.

The data on online vacancies also help to contrast the geographic distribution of the vacancies requiring an SCP degree (the labor market demand for SCPs) and the individuals who graduated from SCP programs over the same time period (the labor market supply of SCPs). Map 2.1 displays the distributions for Argentina and Peru across each country's first-level administrative divisions. Demand for and supply of SCP graduates are concentrated in the main locations. However, the supply of SCP graduates is less geographically concentrated than the demand, suggesting a possible geographic mismatch that should alert policy makers. A disorganized expansion of SCPs throughout a country might not meet the demand for those skills in the places where they are needed, and it might give degrees to individuals living in places where there are no jobs requiring their skills. By preventing some SCP graduates from finding local jobs, this mismatch might contribute to the SCP social stigma.

Conclusions

SCPs can form a skilled labor force quickly and efficiently in response to market demands. Despite this promise, LAC has few SCP graduates and students relative to other regions. This chapter has studied the economic returns to SCPs in LAC by using various metrics—Mincerian returns, net lifetime returns, treatment effects, program average outcomes and value-added contributions, and labor market demand. Although the Mincerian returns to higher education relative to a high school diploma have declined since the early 2000s, this has been mostly driven by bachelor's degrees. Trends for SCP returns are less clear, with more than half of the countries reporting an increase. Even more interestingly, relative to the alternative of incomplete bachelor's programs, SCPs emerge as a superior alternative.

Although Mincerian returns provide information on average returns, the other metrics speak more to the variation or heterogeneity of returns to higher education programs in general and SCPs in particular—and they all show great variation. Using administrative data from higher education programs in Chile and Colombia, the chapter estimated the net-of-cost lifetime value of SCPs and bachelor's programs. The findings reveal that economic returns vary greatly depending on program type, HEI type, and field of study. For an uninformed student, this high variation translates into high risk.

The analysis of who benefits from expanding SCP supply in Colombia provided yet another angle to the heterogeneous returns—this time among students. The research findings show that making SCPs available would indeed increase SCP enrollment, largely as a result of disadvantaged male students *diverging* from bachelor's degrees. If these students chose a bachelor's program rather than an SCP, their labor market outcomes would be worse. On the contrary, female students from low-income households would not respond to SCP availability, but they would respond to greater local demand for SCP graduates by *entering* higher education and enrolling in an SCP. In other words, SCP treatment effects vary across students depending on what they would choose if they did not enroll in an SCP.

Complementary conclusions emerged from the value-added analysis performed for Colombia. Although program-level contributions vary across fields, they vary even more within fields due to the variation in institution- and program-level characteristics. Moreover, the analysis of job vacancies indicated that there is not only a large demand for SCPs, but also a possible geographic mismatch between the demand for and supply of SCP graduates, as the firms demanding them are more geographically concentrated than the new SCP graduates. In other words, labor markets for SCP graduates are also heterogeneous across locations.

Although the wide variation in program-level outcomes and value-added contributions is concerning, it also gives policy makers the opportunity to understand what makes a program "good" or "pertinent." The institution- and program-level characteristics that are available in administrative data sets are associated with a program's value-added contribution. But *other* program characteristics—usually not measured in administrative data sets—may have an even stronger association. These characteristics include whether the program features internships, how it connects with the local labor market, how it relates to the private sector, and whether it offers a flexible class schedule. The World Bank Short-Cycle Program Survey collected data on these characteristics, which are used in chapter 4 to investigate their relationships with program outcomes and value added. Together with the evidence presented here and the evidence in chapter 3 on SCP supply, those results should provide rich and useful information to policy makers interested in understanding what makes an SCP "good," and in expanding the supply of "good" programs.

Notes

1. Cedefop (2018).

2. Ryan (2001); Quintini and Manfredi (2009); Quintini, Martin, and Martin (2007).

3. Ryan (2001).

4. Hanushek et al. (2017).

5. Golsteyn and Stenberg (2017); Verhaest et al. (2018).

6. Arias et al. (2014); Arias, Evans, and Santos (2019).

7. Bassi et al. (2012).

8. Gonzalez-Velosa et al. (2015).

9. Bahr (2016); Liu, Belfield, and Trimble (2015); Dadgar and Trimble (2015); Dynarski, Jacob, and Kreisman (2016); Bettinger and Soliz (2016); Jepsen, Troske, and Coomes (2014); Minaya and Scott-Clayton (2017); Stevens, Kurlaender, and Grosz (2015); Xu and Trimble (2016).

10. In the United States, a full-time student can earn an associate degree in two years. This requires general education courses. A certificate usually involves two or fewer years of

courses in a professional/technical field only. A bachelor's degree lasts at least four years.

11. See, for instance, Heckman, Stixrud, and Urzúa (2006).

12. Bassi et al. (2012).

13. Ferreyra et al. (2017)

14. This section draws on the background paper by Kutscher and Urzúa (2020), written for this book.

15. The analysis was carried out only for countries where it was possible to distinguish between graduates of bachelor's programs and SCPs.

16. Interestingly, the comparison of the Mincerian returns to SCP degrees relative to the alternative of bachelor's dropouts over time suggests a general upward trend. In Ecuador, El Salvador, and Paraguay, the estimated returns increased more than 30 percentage points between the early 2000s and the late 2010s; in Bolivia, Honduras, and Uruguay, they increased between 10 and 30 percentage points; whereas in Argentina and Chile, the increase was less than 10 percentage points. Costa Rica and Mexico are the only countries with decreasing returns during this period.

17. Other characteristics might contribute to the heterogeneity in returns. For example, there might be two groups of SCP graduates: "first-time learners," working toward their first higher education degree, and "further learners," seeking to add specific, technical skills via SCPs to their skills portfolio. One would expect these groups to have different profiles in terms of labor market outcomes, socioeconomic characteristics, and even the types of HEIs they attend. Given current data limitations, it is not possible to investigate this issue further. It remains an important topic for future research.

18. This section draws on the background paper by Ferreyra, Galindo, and Urzúa (2020) written for this book. This paper extends and generalizes the methodology used by Mountjoy (2019).

19. These growth rates correspond to the net number of programs. The rates are calculated as the difference between the entry and exit rates reported in table 3.1, in chapter 3.

20. An important limitation is that enrollment data for SENA, which accounts for a large share of secondary enrollment in Colombia, is not available. Hence, "not enrolled" includes students who effectively obtain a high school diploma and do not enter the higher education system, plus those who enroll in SENA.

21. This section draws on the background paper by Ferreyra et al. (2020), written for this book.

22. Evidence for the United States also finds that longer programs make higher contributions (Jepsen, Troske, and Coomes 2014; Liu, Belfield, and Trimble 2015; Xu and Trimble 2016; Bahr 2016).

23. These findings are similar to those of Minaya and Scott-Clayton (2019) for the United States.

24. This section draws on the background paper by Galindo, Kutscher, and Urzúa (2021), written for this book.

25. A challenge in using online job vacancies is that the sample of online job vacancies is not representative of all job vacancies. However, as a greater share of the population becomes connected to the internet, this bias is progressively eliminated. In Latin America, 65 percent of individuals use the internet. However, the fraction varies among countries. Chile has the largest share, at 82 percent, and Peru has the smallest, at 53 percent (Word Telecommunication/ICT Development data set).

26. Several authors have analyzed online job vacancies in the United States and the variation in skill requirements. Deming and Kahn (2018) find substantial variation in skill requirements, even within occupations, over 2010–15. They argue that higher paying labor markets and firms demand higher levels of cognitive skills and social skills from their employees. Hershbein and Kahn (2018) show that skill requirements in job vacancy postings differentially increased in areas that were hit hard by the Great Recession, relative to less hard-hit areas. They also find that the effects are most pronounced in routine-cognitive occupations, which exhibit relative wage growth as well.

27. González-Velosa and Peña (2019).

References

Arias, O. S., C. Sánchez-Páramo, M. E. Dávalos, I. Santos, E. R. Tiongson, C. Gruen, N. de Andrade Falcão, G. Saiovici, and C. A. Cancho. 2014. *Back to Work: Growing with Jobs in Europe and Central Asia.* Europe and Central Asia Reports. Washington, DC: World Bank.

Arias, O., D. K. Evans, and I. Santos. 2019. *The Skills Balancing Act in Sub-Saharan Africa: Investing in Skills for Productivity, Inclusivity, and Adaptability.* Africa Development Forum. Washington, DC: World Bank and Agence française de développement.

Bahr, P. R. 2016. "The Earnings of Community College Graduates in California." A CAPSEE Working Paper, Center for Analysis of Postsecondary Education and Employment, New York.

Bassi, M., M. Busso, S. Urzúa, and J. Vargas. 2012. *Disconnected: Skills, Education, and Employment in Latin America.* Washington, DC: Inter-American Development Bank.

Becker, G. S., and B. R. Chiswick. 1966. Education and the Distribution of Earnings. *The American Economic Review* 56 (1/2): 358–69.

Bettinger, E., and A. Soliz. 2016. "Returns to Vocational Credentials: Evidence from Ohio's Community and Technical Colleges." A CAPSEE Working Paper, Center for Analysis of Postsecondary Education and Employment, New York.

Cedefop (European Centre for the Development of Vocational Training). 2018. "Apprenticeship Schemes in European Countries: A Cross-Nation Overview." Cedefop, Thessaloniki, Greece

Dadgar, M., and M. J. Trimble. 2015. "Labor Market Returns to Sub-Baccalaureate Credentials: How Much Does a Community College Degree or Certificate Pay?" *Educational Evaluation and Policy Analysis* 37 (4): 399–418.

Deming, D., and L. B. Kahn. 2018. Skill Requirements across Firms and Labor Markets: Evidence from Job Postings for Professionals. *Journal of Labor Economics* 36 (S1): S337–69.

Dynarski, S., B. Jacob, and D. Kreisman. 2016. "The Fixed-Effects Model in Returns to Schooling and Its Application to Community Colleges: A Methodological Note." Center for Analysis of Postsecondary Education and Employment, New York.

Espinoza, R., and S. Urzúa. 2018. "The (Un)expected Economic Consequences of the Recent Expansion of Higher Education in Latin America." *Latin American Policy Journal* 7 (spring).

Ferreyra, M., C. Avitabile, J. Botero, F. Haimovich, and S. Urzúa. 2017. *At a Crossroads: Higher Education in Latin America and the Caribbean.* Washington, DC: World Bank Group.

Ferreyra, M., T. Melguizo, A. Franco, and A. Sanchez. 2020. "Estimating the Contribution of Short-Cycle Programs to Student Outcomes in Colombia." Policy Research Working Paper 9424, World Bank, Washington, DC.

Ferreyra, M., C. Galindo, and S. Urzúa. 2020. "Labor Market Effects of Short-Cycle Programs: Challenges and Evidence from Colombia." World Bank, Washington, DC.

Galindo, C., M. Kutscher, and S. Urzúa. 2021. "Online Job Vacancies and Short-Cycle Programs in Latin America." Background paper for this book, World Bank, Washington, DC.

Golsteyn, B. H., and A. Stenberg. 2017. "Earnings over the Life Course: General versus Vocational Education." *Journal of Human Capital* 11 (2): 167–212.

González-Velosa, C., and N. Peña. 2019. "Demanda de Trabajo en América Latina: ¿Qué podemos aprender de los portales de vacantes online?" División de Mercados Laborales, Nota Técnica N. IDB-TN-1769. Inter-American Development Bank, Washington, D.C.

González-Velosa, C., G. Rucci, M. Sarzosa, and S. Urzúa. 2015. "Returns to Higher Education in Chile and Colombia." No. IDB-WP-587, IDB Working Paper Series, Inter-American Development Bank, Washington, DC.

Hanushek, E. A., G. Schwerdt, L. Woessmann, and L. Zhang. 2017. "General Education, Vocational Education, and Labor-Market Outcomes over the Lifecycle." *Journal of Human Resources* 52 (1): 48–87.

Heckman, J., J. Stixrud, and S. Urzúa. 2006. "The Effects of Cognitive and Non-cognitive Abilities on Labor Market Outcomes and Social Behavior." *Journal of Labor Economics* 24(3): 411–82.

Hershbein, B., and L. B. Kahn. 2018. "Do Recessions Accelerate Routine-Biased Technological Change? Evidence from Vacancy Postings." *American Economic Review* 108 (7): 1737–72.

Jepsen, C., K. Troske, and P. Coomes. 2014. "The Labor-Market Returns to Community College Degrees, Diplomas, and Certificates." *Journal of Labor Economics* 32 (1): 95–121.

Kutscher, M., and S. Urzúa. 2020. "An Economic Argument for Short-Cycle Programs in Latin America and the Caribbean." World Bank, Washington, DC.

Liu, V., C. Belfield, and M. Trimble. 2015. "The Medium-Term Labor Market Returns to Community College Awards: Evidence from North Carolina." *Economics of Education Review* 44 (C): 42–55.

MacLeod, W. B., E. Riehl, J. E. Saavedra, and M. Urquiola. 2017. "The Big Sort: College Reputation and Labor Market Outcomes." *American Economic Journal: Applied Economics* 9 (3): 223–61.

Minaya, V., and J. Scott-Clayton. 2017. "Labor Market Trajectories for Community College Graduates: New Evidence Spanning the Great Recession." A CAPSEE Working Paper. Center for Analysis of Postsecondary Education and Employment, New York.

Minaya, V., and J. Scott-Clayton. 2019. "Labor Market Outcomes and Postsecondary Accountability: Are Imperfect Metrics Better than None?" In *Productivity in Higher Education*, edited by C. Hoxby, and K. Stange. University of Chicago Press.

Mincer, J. 1974. "Schooling, Experience, and Earnings." National Bureau of Economic Research, Cambridge, MA.

Mountjoy, J. 2019. "Community Colleges and Upward Mobility." Unpublished manuscript. University of Chicago.

Quintini, G., and T. Manfredi. 2009. "Going Separate Ways? School-to-Work Transitions in the United States and Europe." Working Papers, No. 90, OECD Social, Employment and Migration, OECD Publishing, Paris, https://doi.org/10.1787/221717700447.

Quintini, G., J. P. Martin, and S. Martin. 2007. "The Changing Nature of the School-to-Work Transition Process in OECD Countries." IZA DP No. 2582, Institute of Labor Economics, Bonn, Germany.

Ryan, P. 2001. "The School-to-Work Transition: A Cross-National Perspective." *Journal of Economic Literature* 39 (1): 34–92.

Stevens, A., M. Kurlaender, and M. Grosz. 2015. "Career-Technical Education and Labor Market Outcomes: Evidence from California Community Colleges." A CAPSEE Working Paper. Center for Analysis of Postsecondary Education and Employment, New York.

Verhaest, D., J. Lavrijsen, W. Van Trier, I. Nicaise, and E. Omey. 2018. "General Education, Vocational Education and Skill Mismatches: Short-Run versus Long-Run Effects." *Oxford Economic Papers* 70 (4): 974–93.

Xu, D., and M. Trimble. 2016. "What about Certificates? Evidence on the Labor Market Returns to Nondegree Community College Awards in Two States." *Educational Evaluation and Policy Analysis* 38 (2): 272–92.

CHAPTER 3

Supply of Short-Cycle Programs

María Marta Ferreyra

Introduction

Short-cycle programs (SCPs) hold the promise of skilling individuals in a relatively short time while responding to the needs of the local economy. This is because, in an ideal scenario, institutions open SCPs in response to market needs, compete with one another to deliver a variety of high-quality programs, and fashion their products to provide not only good training, but also good labor market outcomes. When their supply behaves in this way, SCPs can realize their economic and social promise.

To assess whether SCPs in Latin America and the Caribbean (LAC) have the capacity to fulfill this promise, this chapter investigates the supply of SCPs in the region. The chapter starts by comparing market dynamics between bachelor's programs and SCPs, analyzing the entry of SCPs—namely, what factors guide institutions as they decide whether to open a new program—and comparing SCP supply across cities of different sizes. The chapter then turns to the survey countries (Brazil, Colombia, the Dominican Republic, Ecuador, and Peru) to examine a rich set of program characteristics that describe the "products" offered by the institutions.

Little is typically known about the supply side in higher education, such as why institutions open or close programs, or how they compete.[1] Even with some quantitative indicators, such as faculty size and the number of labs, almost nothing is known about SCP practices—for instance, how they hire and evaluate faculty, how they engage with the private sector, and how they assist students' job searches. Nonetheless, institutions choose these practices for a reason and use them to differentiate their "product." And, as chapter 4 demonstrates, some characteristics of SCPs are clearly associated with student academic and labor market outcomes.

The main findings of this chapter are as follows:

- The market for SCPs is highly dynamic—more so than that of bachelor's programs. SCPs enter and exit ("churn") more frequently than bachelor's programs.
- When deciding whether to open a new program in a particular location and knowledge field, an institution considers the potential demand for the field's graduates as given by economic activity at the local level for the corresponding sector and the relative employment of the field's recent graduates. Private higher education institutions (HEIs) and non-university HEIs are the institutions that respond most to local economic conditions.
- Institutions also factor in their costs when deciding whether to open new programs, adding programs in fields where they already have a presence or offering low-cost programs. Cost is particularly relevant for private HEIs since they rely mostly on tuition revenue.
- Program enrollment suffers when there are more direct competitors. Nonetheless, institutions seek to attract students by differentiating their product in terms of tuition, field, or geographic coverage. Tuition is an especially important factor determining the sorting of students across HEIs. A critical determinant of market structure is the presence of public, subsidized institutions, particularly when these are large and widespread across the country.
- SCPs are not equally distributed across space, as the supply of higher education programs is much larger in large and medium-size cities than small ones. However, distance and online programs mitigate this inequality, by expanding students' options beyond face-to-face programs.
- In the World Bank Short-Cycle Program Survey (WBSCPS) countries, the HEIs with SCPs are young, and the programs are young and frequently updated. SCPs teach mostly a fixed curriculum, with substantial emphasis on practical training. On average, they have good infrastructure in terms of workshops and labs and good student-faculty ratios. The instructors are mostly part time, male, relatively young, with good academic qualifications, and who often work in the field. Almost all of them are evaluated at least once a year, and student evaluations are the most common input for faculty evaluation. Prior to the COVID-19 pandemic, online teaching was rare, which suggests that these programs must have faced a severe challenge to provide it.
- On average, SCPs in the WBSCPS countries engage closely with the private sector, whose representatives often sit on the HEIs' governing boards. The programs tend to have internship agreements with private companies, which often participate in curriculum design and student evaluation. While the programs offer students multiple supports to their job search, the most common support is a relatively passive one—the provision of job market information. Services that would be more immediately useful, such as arranging job interviews or preparing students for the practical aspects of a job search, are

less common. And, although the programs usually evaluate student and faculty performance more than once a year, they engage less frequently in activities related to students' labor market outcomes, such as eliciting firms' opinions of their graduates, inquiring about firms' needs, or collecting graduates' employment data.

- SCPs in our survey countries tend to believe that students care mostly about training quality, which might explain why they seem more attentive to the curriculum, faculty, and practical training than to students' job search and labor market outcomes. Perhaps for this reason, the SCPs tend to view themselves as better than their competitors in training quality but not in employment outcomes. This finding suggests that, although these programs are responsive to the local economy and attempt to provide good training, they might need to place greater emphasis on students' labor market outcomes.

Dynamics and Competition in SCP Markets

The market for SCPs is extremely dynamic, as programs open and close frequently.[2] This section analyzes the market dynamics by focusing on two countries, Colombia and Chile.

The market for SCPs is more dynamic than the market for bachelor's programs, as the former exhibits greater turnover or "churn" of programs. Table 3.1 shows that the average life of an SCP is shorter than that of the average bachelor's program in both countries. Among the SCPs offered in a given year in Colombia, on average, 20.8 percent of the programs are newly opened that year, whereas only 7.2 percent of the bachelor's programs are new in a given year. Not only do SCPs enter at a higher rate than bachelor's programs, they also exit at a higher rate. In Colombia, 18 percent of the SCPs close in a given year, relative to 5.5 percent of the bachelor's programs. Similar patterns hold in Chile.

Entry of SCPs

An important question, then, is what leads institutions to open new programs—that is, what leads to program entry? Colombia and Chile are interesting case studies because they represent two very different market paradigms (table 3.2).

Table 3.1 Average Turnover of Short-Cycle versus Bachelor's Programs

	Colombia		Chile	
	SCPs	Bachelor's programs	SCPs	Bachelor's programs
Average program life (years)	7.5	13.7	11.3	19.6
New programs per year (%)	20.8	7.2	12.0	5.9
Programs exiting per year (%)	18.0	5.5	10.3	4.7

Sources: Carranza et al. (2021), background paper for this book, based on Higher Education Information Service (SIES), from 2005 to 2018 for Chile, and National Higher Education Information System (SNIES), from 2003 to 2017 for Colombia.
Note: The table shows country-level averages for the variables listed in the rows; averages are taken over programs and years. SCP = short-cycle program.

Table 3.2 Two Market Paradigms: Colombia and Chile

Indicator	Colombia	Chile
SCP share in higher education (%)	32	48
Enrollment in public institutions (%)	81	0
Largest provider(s) (with market share)	SENA (public–65%)	• Duoc (private–16%) • INACAP (private–16%) • AIEP (private–16%) • Santo Tomás (private–12%)

Sources: Carranza et al. (2021), background paper for this book, based on Higher Education Information Service (SIES) for 2018 in Chile, and National Higher Education Information System (SNIES) for 2017 in Colombia.
Note: For Colombia, public enrollment includes SENA. Figures are rounded to the nearest integer. AIEP = Apex International Education Partners; INACAP = *Instituto Nacional de Capacitacion Profesional*; SCP = short-cycle program; SENA = *Servicio Nacional de Aprendizaje.*

SCPs capture almost half of higher education enrollment in Chile, whereas they capture about a third in Colombia. A large public institution, the National Learning Service (SENA, *Servicio Nacional de Aprendizaje*), captures 65 percent of total SCP enrollment in Colombia as of 2017. It has branches throughout the country and charges zero tuition. The remaining 35 percent of SCP enrollment is split almost equally among non-SENA public institutions (henceforth, public institutions), which receive public subsidies but still charge tuition, and private institutions. In contrast, all the SCP enrollment in Chile is in private institutions,[3] four of which—Duoc, INACAP, AIEP, and Santo Tomás—capture 60 percent of the SCP enrollment and have branches throughout the country.

Thus, the SCP market is an oligopoly with concentrated supply in both countries. Yet, the patterns of SCP entry and competition differ between the two countries, due to the presence of a large, widespread public provider in Colombia (SENA), which charges zero tuition, and the absence of such an institution in Chile.[4] In Colombia, SENA's size, reach, and resources make it extremely difficult for a private institution to grow large and have branches throughout the country. As a result, HEIs are mostly local and small in Colombia. The absence of such an institution in Chile has allowed some private HEIs to grow large and open branches throughout the country, also concentrating the market, but in the hands of a few private providers.

Most higher education students in LAC attend a local institution (Ferreyra et al. 2017), and that is particularly true of SCP students. As a result, SCP providers mostly serve local students and compete locally. SCP markets vary not only by location, but also by field. For instance, four distinct markets in Chile are health in Santiago, health in Valparaíso, business in Santiago, and business in Valparaíso. A particular institution in Santiago, for example, might be a strong competitor in health but not in business. And even if that institution has a branch in Valparaíso as well, it might be a strong health competitor in Santiago but a weak one in Valparaíso.

Consider an institution that operates in a given location (a department in Colombia, or a region in Chile) and is pondering whether to open a new program in a certain field (for instance, nursing).[5] The statistical analysis conducted in the background paper by Carranza et al. (2021) suggests that the institution will be more likely to open the new program in at least one of the following cases: [6]

- *Labor demand is high for the field.*
  Labor demand is high for the field when the local economic activity in the relevant sector (health care, in this case) is high relative to that in other sectors, or when recent graduates in the field are highly likely to find employment relative to those in other fields. In this example, the institution will be more likely to open the nursing program if local hospitals and health care facilities are doing well, or if nurses find employment easily in the local economy.

  Figure 3.1 illustrates that new programs open in response to the local economy. SCPs are more responsive than bachelor's programs to labor demand (panel a), which explains the greater entry rate of SCPs in table 3.1. Among SCP providers, private institutions are more responsive than public ones (figure 3.1, panel b), perhaps because their main revenue source is tuition, and attracting students is easier when offering programs that are relevant to the local labor market. Among private SCP providers, non-university HEIs are more responsive than universities (panel c), perhaps because they

Figure 3.1 Entry into the Higher Education Market and Local Economic Conditions

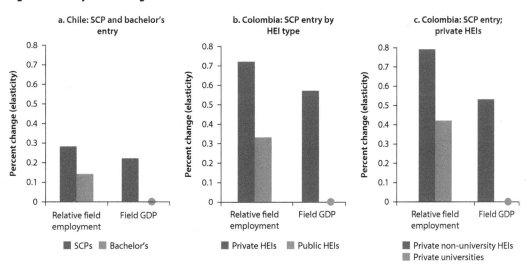

Source: World Bank calculations based on Carranza et al. (2021), background paper for this book.
Note: The figure shows the average percentage change in the probability that an HEI opens at least one new program in its geographic location (department for Colombia, region for Chile) in a given field. Probability is associated with a 1-percent increase in the (lagged) field GDP or relative field employment for that location and field. A dot on the horizontal axis indicates that the corresponding estimate is not significantly different from zero. Panel a compares entry on the part of SCPs and bachelor's programs in Chile. Panel b compares SCP entry on the part of public and private HEIs in Colombia (public HEIs do not include *Servicio Nacional de Aprendizaje* [SENA]). Panel c compares SCP entry among private HEIs (universities and non-university HEIs). Field GDP is the portion of the location's GDP that can be associated to the field; association is based on the share of SCP graduates working in each sector of the economy in the location with a degree in the field. Relative field employment is the share of employed SCP graduates who completed a program in the field. GDP = gross domestic product; HEI = higher education institution; SCP = short-cycle program.

have a leaner cost structure and are, in most cases, fully specialized in SCP provision.

As discussed in this chapter, SCPs in the WBSCPS engage with the private sector in multiple ways. These interactions might be one reason behind their responsiveness to local economic conditions.

- *The cost of opening the program is low.*
  The cost of opening the program is low, for instance, when the institution already offers programs in the field, perhaps specializing in it. In this case, the institution has already paid the fixed cost of offering programs in the field. For example, it may have already hired the relevant faculty and acquired the relevant equipment. Although the marginal cost of opening an additional program in an existing field is relatively low, entering a new field altogether can be quite costly. This consideration is particularly important for private institutions, which rely mostly on tuition revenues and do not receive public funds to cover the fixed costs of entering a new field.

  In Colombia and Chile, HEIs are indeed more likely to open a program in a given field when the field captures a larger share of their enrollment, which means that they are relatively specialized in it (figure 3.2, panel a). And, as expected, the higher bar for private HEIs in Colombia indicates that they are more sensitive to costs than their public counterparts.[7]

- *The institution has market power.*
  An institution is more likely to open a program in a given field when it faces less competition in it. In Colombia and Chile, entry in a given field is more likely when the institution captures a higher share of the total market enrollment in the field (figure 3.2, panel b), or when there are fewer competing institutions offering programs in it—namely, when the HEI enjoys a certain amount of market power in the location and field.

  SENA's presence shapes SCP entry in Colombia. When opening new programs, private HEIs only respond to competition from other private HEIs, while public HEIs respond to competition from all HEIs and from SENA. This is related to how Colombian HEIs compete, an issue that is discussed later in this chapter. In Chile, the presence of the largest institution, Duoc, in a given field and geographic area deters the entry of other institutions in that market.

Exit of SCPs

In Colombia and Chile, HEIs that close programs in a given field are also more likely to open new ones in it.[8] For about 90 percent of the program closings since the early 2000s, there has been a simultaneous program opening on the part of the same HEI, in the same location and field. Simultaneous openings and closings might happen in several cases. The first is when an HEI reviews a program's curriculum and changes it substantially, effectively creating a new program. The second is when an HEI removes an outdated program in a given field (for instance, administration of adventure tourism) and replaces it with a new one

Figure 3.2 Entry, Fixed Costs, and Market Power

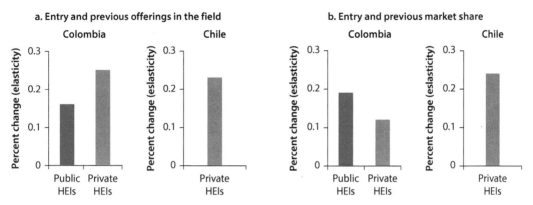

Source: World Bank calculations based on Carranza et al. (2021), background paper for this book.

Note: Panel a shows the average percentage change in the probability that an HEI opens at least one new program in its geographic location (department for Colombia, region for Chile) in a given field. Probability is associated with a 1 percent increase in the (lagged) proportion of HEI students enrolled in the field (relative to total enrollment in the HEI). A high share indicates that the HEI is specialized in the field. Panel b shows the average percentage change in the probability that an HEI opens at least one new program in its geographic location (department for Colombia, region for Chile) in a given field. Probability is associated with a 1 percent increase in the HEI's (lagged) enrollment share (relative to all institutions) in that location and field. A high share indicates that the HEI has market power. For Colombia, public HEIs do not include *Servicio Nacional de Aprendizaje* (SENA). HEI = higher education institution.

that is more general (for example, hospitality management) or qualitatively different (for example, nonprofit management). The third case is when an HEI opens a new program but wants to protect it from the competition of its own programs in the field—namely, to avoid cannibalization among programs. The fourth is when the HEI closes a program that has lost enrollment lately or has not placed graduates well. This is particularly relevant in Chile, where public monitoring of employment outcomes for individual programs incentivizes HEIs to close programs with poor job placement.

Competition among SCPs

Institutions clearly compete for students in the SCP market. In Colombia and Chile, an HEI's enrollment in a given field suffers with an increase in the number of competing institutions offering programs in that field (figure 3.3). In the case of Colombia, an expansion in SENA's enrollment has a strong negative association with enrollment in HEIs, especially public HEIs, which compete more directly with SENA.

Given these competitive pressures, HEIs differentiate their programs from those of other institutions through prices and program offerings.

Colombia

In Colombia, SENA is free, public HEIs charge subsidized tuition, and private HEIs charge even higher tuition (figure 3.4, panel a). As a result, these providers attract different types of students (figure 3.4, panels b and c). On average, SENA attracts students with the lowest income and academic readiness. The remaining students sort between public and private HEIs depending, in part, on their

Figure 3.3 Enrollment and Competition

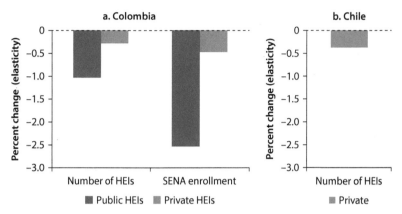

Source: World Bank calculations based on Carranza et al. (2021), background paper for this book.
Note: The figure shows the average percent change in an HEI's enrollment in a (field, location, year) as a function of a 1 percent increase in the number of competing HEIs or in *Servicio Nacional de Aprendizaje* (SENA) (for Colombia) enrollment in that (field, location, year). For Colombia, public HEIs do not include SENA. Blue and orange denote the response of public and private HEIs, respectively. HEI = higher education institution.

Figure 3.4 Tuition and Student Sorting in Colombia

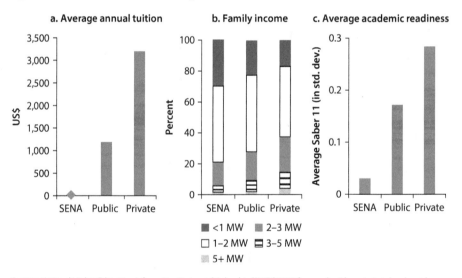

Sources: National Higher Education Information System of Colombia (SNIES) 2019 for panel a; *Obsevatorio Laboral para la Educación* (OLE) 2013 and Systems Approach for Better Education Results (SABER) 11 (several years) for panels b and c.
Note: Panel a shows average annual tuition by HEI type in dollars (PPP 2019). The diamond on the horizontal axis for SENA indicates SENA's zero tuition. Panel b shows, for each HEI type, the percentage of students from each family income level. Panel c shows average Saber 11 (a measure of academic readiness) by HEI type. Panels b and c correspond to the SCP graduates included in OLE in 2013. Public HEIs do not include *Servicio Nacional de Aprendizaje* (SENA). HEI = higher education institution; MW = monthly minimum wage; PPP = purchasing power parity; SCP = short-cycle program.

academic readiness and family income—on average, those with higher readiness but lesser means attend public HEIs, while the reverse is true of students attending private HEIs.

By having a dedicated funding source, SENA is able to offer programs with high production costs such as those in engineering (figure 3.5), which encompasses technology-related programs. Public HEIs, which also rely on public funding, can finance relatively costly programs as well. Given their lack of public funding, private HEIs tend to specialize in lower-cost areas, such as business, and emphasize the provision of cognitive and social skills of general applicability. As a result of this differentiation, public providers compete with SENA more closely than private providers, mostly for the lowest income students, while also competing with private providers for higher income students. Private providers, in turn, compete mostly among themselves. These patterns explain why enrollment and entry respond differently to competitors among HEI types.

Chile

In Chile, HEIs differentiate themselves in multiple ways. First, they differentiate by geographic coverage (figure 3.6). For instance, Duoc is only present in the three most populous metropolitan areas (Santiago, Valparaíso, and Concepción, which are located in the Metropolitan, Valparaíso, and Biobío regions, respectively). And, while INACAP dominates the market in the Maule region, the market in Los Lagos is dominated by AIEP. Such geographic coverage is partly related to the HEI's business model. For example, Duoc follows a

Figure 3.5 Distribution of SCP Fields, by Institution Type in Colombia

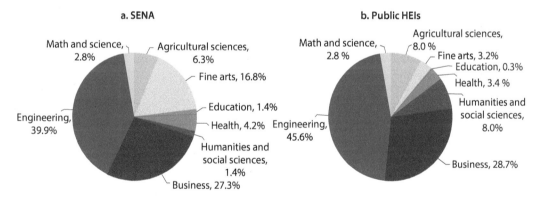

a. SENA

- Math and science, 2.8%
- Agricultural sciences, 6.3%
- Fine arts, 16.8%
- Education, 1.4%
- Health, 4.2%
- Humanities and social sciences, 1.4%
- Business, 27.3%
- Engineering, 39.9%

b. Public HEIs

- Math and science, 2.8%
- Agricultural sciences, 8.0%
- Fine arts, 3.2%
- Education, 0.3%
- Health, 3.4%
- Humanities and social sciences, 8.0%
- Business, 28.7%
- Engineering, 45.6%

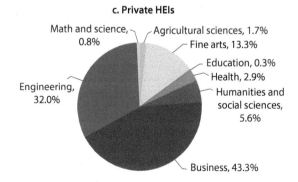

c. Private HEIs

- Math and science, 0.8%
- Agricultural sciences, 1.7%
- Fine arts, 13.3%
- Education, 0.3%
- Health, 2.9%
- Humanities and social sciences, 5.6%
- Business, 43.3%
- Engineering, 32.0%

Source: National Higher Education Information System of Colombia (SNIES) 2017.
Note: The figure shows the percentage of programs corresponding to each field by institution type. Public HEIs do not include SENA. HEI = higher education institution; SCP = short cycle program; SENA = *Servicio Nacional de Aprendizaje.*

Figure 3.6 Regional Market Shares of the Largest HEI in Chile

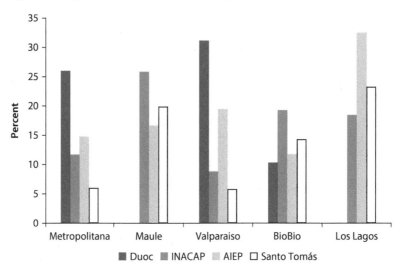

Source: Carranza et al. (2021), background paper for this book. Calculations based on Higher Education Information Service (SIES) for 2018.
Note: For each region, the figure shows the 2018 share of first-year enrollment at Duoc, *Instituto Nacional de Capacitación Profesional* (INACAP), Apex International Education Partners (AIEP), and Santo Tomás.
HEI = higher education institution.

rather centralized model that requires coordination among branches and provides student services and amenities with a high fixed cost. This model would not be viable outside the largest metropolitan areas.

Second, HEIs compete on prices. Among the four largest HEIs, tuitions are similar at Duoc and INACAP and higher than those at AEIP and Santo Tomás (figure 3.7, panel a). Other non-university HEIs charge the lowest tuitions in the market. As a result of this price competition, students sort across HEIs based on income. Here, income is proxied by high school types: public (municipal), subsidized private (private with vouchers), and unsubsidized private (private). The share of students from nonpublic schools is highest at Duoc, which charges the highest tuition (figure 3.7, panel b).

Third, HEIs differentiate their product through other elements such as academic advising, job search assistance, facilities' quality, and student life. More generally, they differentiate by creating a "culture" that is valued by the students and a "brand" or reputation that is valued by employers and students alike.

The ability of HEIs to compete on prices may have changed since 2017, when free higher education for the lowest six deciles of the income distribution (*gratuidad*) was enacted for SCPs. Since the out-of-pocket price is now zero for all programs, price is no longer a differentiating factor among programs. Instead, students choose among programs based on the nonprice elements. Anecdotal evidence indicates that the institutions with the highest reputations have faced excess demand since gratuidad and have implemented some admission requirements, whereas before *gratuidad* they filled their seats on a first-come, first-served basis.

Figure 3.7 Tuition and Student Background in Chile

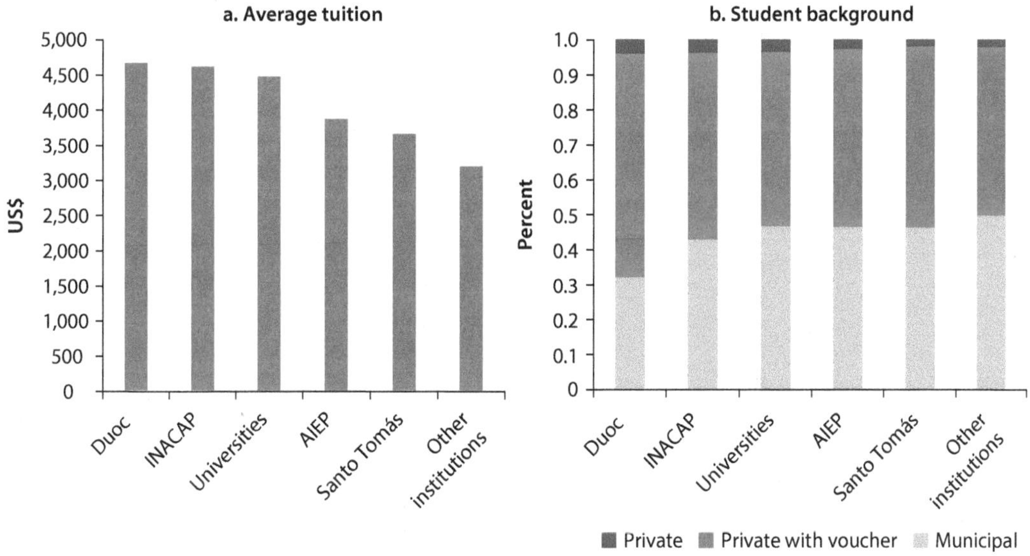

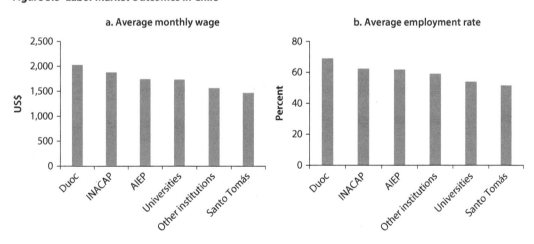

Source: Ministry of Education (Mifuturo.cl) for 2018.
Note: Panel a shows, for each HEI or HEI type, the annual average tuition in 2019 PPP dollars. The statistics shown for universities refer exclusively to SCPs taught at universities. Panel b shows, for each HEI or HEI type, the percentage of students who graduated from each of the following high school types: municipal (public), private with voucher (subsidized private), or private (unsubsidized private). AIEP = Apex International Education Partners; HEI = higher education institution; INACAP = *Instituto Nacional de Capacitación Profesional*; SCP = short-cycle program.

Figure 3.8 Labor Market Outcomes in Chile

a. Average monthly wage

b. Average employment rate

Source: Ministry of Education (Mifuturo.cl) for 2010–20.
Note: For each HEI or HEI type, the figure shows the average wages for graduates four years after graduation, and the average employment rate of graduates in the year after graduation. "Universities" refers exclusively to SCPs taught at universities. AIEP = Apex International Education Partners; HEI = higher education institution; INACAP = *Instituto Nacional de Capacitación Profesional*; SCP = short-cycle program.

Tuitions are related to labor market outcomes (figure 3.8.) On average, graduates from the institutions with the highest levels of tuition have the highest employment rates and wages. Although this does not provide evidence that the institutions with the highest tuition have the highest value added, it suggests that the labor market outcomes of these institutions support or "justify" the tuition they charge.

Role of Location

Not all locations have the same access to SCPs and, more generally, to higher education programs (table 3.3). Relative to small and medium-size cities, larger ones are more likely to have at least one HEI offering SCPs or bachelor's programs and are served by more HEIs. As a result, students in large cities can choose among a higher number of programs, bachelor's and SCPs.

Almost all large cities in Colombia count on SCP provision from SENA, but very few small and medium-size cities do. In other words, as of 2017, SENA covers similar geographic areas as other HEIs, but not necessarily smaller, more remote locations.[9] Data from Colombia also show that while face-to-face programs are less common in small and medium-size cities, distance programs are more common and span a wide variety of arrangements. For instance, an HEI may not have a branch in a particular city, but it may rent space there to teach classes every other weekend. These arrangements give smaller, more remote locations access to higher education options.

Table 3.3 Supply of SCPs, by City Size

Measure	Colombia: City size				Chile: City size			
	Very Large	Large	Medium	Small	Very Large	Large	Medium	Small
Cities with at least one institution offering:								
Bachelor's programs (%)	100	97.4	56.3	15.2	100	87.5	21.5	0
SCPs (%)	100	97.4	40.2	8.1	100	87.5	31.2	0.5
Cities where SENA teaches SCPs (%)	100	89.5	14.2	0.9	n/c	n/c	n/c	n/c
Average number of institutions offering:								
Bachelor's programs	57	9.3	1.1	0.2	127.0	9.2	0.4	0
SCPs	42	5.8	0.7	0.1	82.0	7.4	0.7	0
Average number of programs offered								
Bachelor's	616.4	73.9	4.8	0.4	2,272	143.5	2.1	0
SCPs in HEIs	403.6	56.6	3.6	0.3	1,544	108.8	6.2	0
SCPs in SENA	123.8	27.7	1.6	0.1	n/c	n/c	n/c	n/c
Average proportion of programs								
Face-to-face	0.76	0.55	0.47	0.46	n/a	n/a	n/a	n/a
Distance	0.15	0.35	0.47	0.50	n/a	n/a	n/a	n/a
Online	0.09	0.10	0.06	0.04	n/a	n/a	n/a	n/a
Average Herfindahl Index across institutions								
Bachelor's programs	0.010	0.45	0.83	0.96	0.037	0.280	0.699	n/c
SCPs	0.359	0.623	0.915	0.99	0.122	0.315	0.752	n/c
Number of municipalities	5	38	254	770	1	24	93	182

Sources: World Bank calculations based on data from the National Higher Education Information System (2017) for Colombia and Higher Education Information Service (SIES) (2018) for Chile.
Note: The table shows indicators of availability of bachelor's programs and SCPs by city (municipality) size. City size categories are given by population and are defined as follows: very large (population > 1,000,000); large (between 100,001 and 1,000,000); medium (population between 20,001 and 100,000); and small (up to 20,000). For Colombia, distance programs involve arrangements such as face-to-face classes once every other weekend, and online programs are attributed to the municipalities where their students live. For a given municipality, the Herfindahl index is calculated as the sum of the squared market shares for the institutions in the municipality, where an institution's share is the proportion of its bachelor's (or SCP) students relative to the total number of bachelor's (or SCP) students in the municipality. It is a measure of market concentration and ranges between zero and one. The closer it is to 1, the higher is the market concentration. HEI = higher education institution; n/a = not available; n/c = does not correspond (SENA is located in Colombia); SCP = short-cycle program; SENA = *Servicio Nacional de Aprendizaje.*

The SCP market in Chile is highly concentrated around the four largest providers. The question arises as to whether the concentration abates in smaller cities, where some of these providers might not be present. As the Herfindahl index in table 3.3 shows, market concentration is higher in small and medium-size cities—not just in Chile, but also in Colombia. The reason is that these cities have fewer providers. Thus, not only do small cities have fewer options, they also have less competition. Nonetheless, as distance and online programs continue to expand, the number of options and the extent of competition should continue to rise.

To summarize, SCPs turn over at higher rates than bachelor's programs, with more frequent entry and exit. This is because they are more responsive to the local economy and the needs of the labor market. Private and non-university institutions, in turn, respond the most to the local economy. Institutions factor in their costs when deciding whether to open new programs, adding programs in fields in which they already have a presence, and offering lower-cost programs in the case of private HEIs. Program closing is highly correlated with program entry. While enrollment is sensitive to the number of competitors, institutions differentiate their product by tuition, field coverage, and geographic coverage. In particular, tuition contributes to the sorting of students across institutions. A critical determinant of market structure is the presence of public, subsidized institutions, especially when these are large and widespread throughout the country. Yet, regardless of such institutions, large cities give students more options than smaller cities do, both in bachelor's programs and SCPs, and give rise to less concentrated, more competitive markets.

Programs and Providers in LAC

This section turns to the supply of SCPs—providers and programs—in the surveyed countries: Brazil, Colombia, the Dominican Republic, Ecuador, and Peru. For Brazil, the survey focuses on the states of São Paulo and Ceará, and for Peru, it focuses on programs licensed as of October 2019. The number of SCPs in these countries ranges from 209 in the Dominican Republic to 2,388 in Brazil (table 3.4). Most programs are offered by private HEIs. In Brazil and Peru, where for-profit HEIs are allowed, these account for 36 and 77 percent of all SCPs, respectively.

In each country, business and engineering (including computer-related programs) account for more than half of the offerings (figure 3.9). Business is

Table 3.4 Programs in the WBSCPS Countries

Country	Number of programs	Programs taught at private HEIs (%)
Brazil (São Paulo and Ceará)	2,388	84
Colombia	2,130	60
Dominican Republic	209	54
Ecuador	543	62
Peru (licensed programs)	387	100

Source: Program universes for WBSCPS countries.
Note: HEI = higher education institution; WBSCPS = World Bank Short-Cycle Program Survey.

Figure 3.9 Distribution of Programs across Fields in the WBSCPS Countries

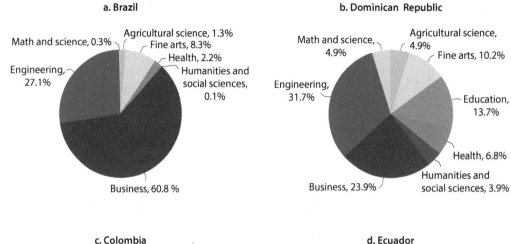

a. Brazil

b. Dominican Republic

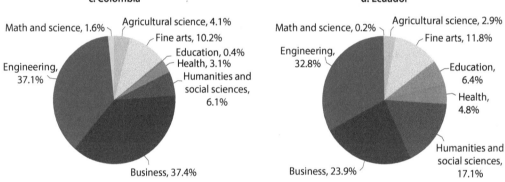

c. Colombia

d. Ecuador

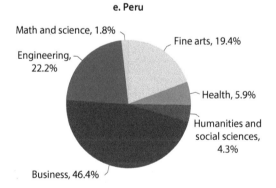

e. Peru

Source: Program universes for WBSCPS countries.
Note: The figure shows the percentage of programs in each field for every WBSCPS country. WBSCPS = data from the World Bank Short-Cycle Program Survey. Only São Paulo and Ceará are included for Brazil, and licensed programs for Peru.

most prevalent in Brazil and Peru, which have the largest fraction of programs taught by private HEIs, consistent with the fact that private institutions typically gravitate toward lower cost fields.

The rest of this section provides a rich description of providers and their products—the programs—based on the WBSCPS. Programs choose their characteristics not by chance but in order to compete most effectively in the market. Chapter 4 discusses how those characteristics relate to student academic and labor market outcomes.

General Characteristics of Providers and Programs

In the countries covered by the WBSCPS, almost all SCPs last two or three years, and most last three years. Some of the HEIs teaching the SCPs have multiple branches throughout the corresponding country, and some programs are offered in multiple cities by the corresponding HEI, particularly in Colombia, the Dominican Republic, and Peru (figure 3.10). In Brazil and Ecuador, in contrast, HEIs operate mostly locally.

The average HEI is relatively young, ranging from 24 to 50 years old in Ecuador and the Dominican Republic, respectively (figure 3.11, panel a).

Figure 3.10 Number of Cities Where the Institution Offers the Program

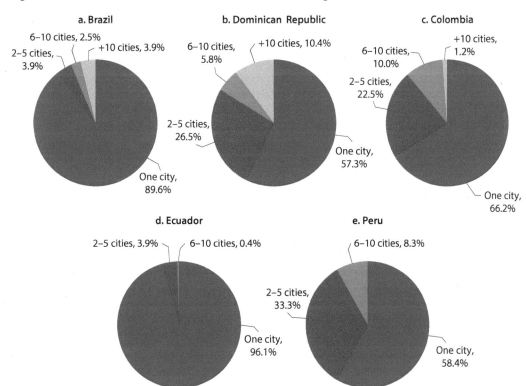

Source: World Bank Short-Cycle Program Survey.
Note: The figure shows the percentage of programs that are taught in one city, 2–5 cities, 6–10 cities, or 10+ cities by the corresponding HEI. Only São Paulo and Ceará are included for Brazil, and licensed programs for Peru. HEI = higher education institution.

Figure 3.11 HEI Age, Program Age, and Program Size

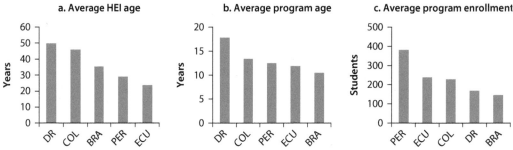

Source: World Bank Short-Cycle Program Survey.
Note: For every country, the figure shows the average HEI age (panel a), average program age (panel b), and average program enrollment (panel c). If multiple programs are taught at the same HEI, each program is counted separately. BRA = Brazil; COL = Colombia; DR = Dominican Republic; ECU = Ecuador; HEI = higher education institution; PER = Peru. Only São Paulo and Ceará are included for Brazil, and licensed programs for Peru.

Not only are HEIs young, the programs are young as well (figure 3.11, panel b). The average program age ranges from 10 to 18 years in Brazil and the Dominican Republic, respectively, and about half of the programs in each country are 10 years old or younger. Average program enrollment ranges between 140 and 240 students in Brazil, the Dominican Republic, Colombia, and Ecuador; it is substantially higher in Peru, at 380 students (figure 3.11, panel c). In the five countries, the most common size is between 101 and 300 students. Peru and Ecuador have the highest share of very large programs with more than 1,000 students.

Curriculum, Training, and Graduation Requirements
In the five countries, most programs offer a fixed curriculum (figure 3.12, panel a). In light of the negative experience with the "cafeteria style" curriculum of most community colleges in the United States (Bailey, Jaggars, and Jenkins 2015), the fixed curriculum is a positive feature. On average, programs spend about half the time in practical training in workshops, labs, or professional practice (figure 3.12, panel b). As mentioned in chapter 1, more than 80 percent of the programs offer remediation activities for underprepared students; these take place before and/or during the program.

As a testament of the work-oriented nature of these programs, many of them include mandatory internships outside the HEI (figure 3.12, panel c). While only 28 percent of the programs in Brazil include internships, almost all the programs in Ecuador require them, and more than half of the programs in Colombia, the Dominican Republic, and Peru do so as well. The mandatory internship can take place during the program, at the end of it, or at both times.

In addition to teaching occupation-specific skills, the programs also aim to train students in a broad set of general competencies. These are grouped into cognitive (reading, writing, and numeracy), technical (computer use for basic tasks, presentations, and advanced tasks), socioemotional (communication, responsibility, teamwork, and adaptability), and work habits (ability to work under hardship or pressure, persistence in complex tasks, and ability to find new

Figure 3.12 Curriculum and Practical Training

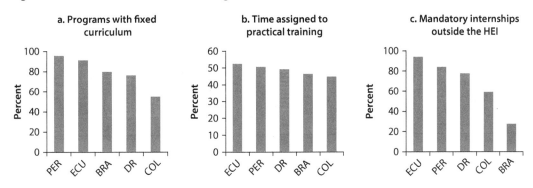

Source: World Bank Short-Cycle Program Survey.
Note: For each country, the figure shows the percentage of programs with a fixed curriculum (panel a), the program-level average percentage of time assigned to practical training (panel b), and the percentage of programs with a mandatory internship outside the HEI (panel c). BRA = Brazil; COL = Colombia; DR = Dominican Republic; ECU = Ecuador; HEI = higher education institution; PER = Peru. Only São Paulo and Ceará are included for Brazil, and licensed programs for Peru.

Figure 3.13 Competencies Taught by the Programs

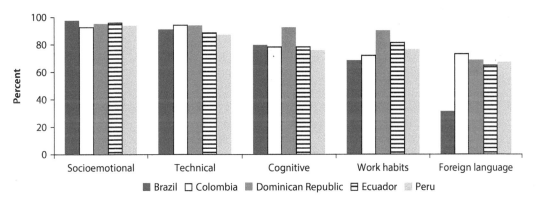

Source: World Bank Short-Cycle Program Survey.
Note: For each type of competency (socioemotional, technical, cognitive, work habits, and foreign language), the figure shows the percentage of programs in each country that claims to teach them. The competencies encompass the following skills: cognitive (reading, writing, and numeracy), technical (computer use for basic tasks, presentations, and advanced tasks), socioemotional (communication, responsibility, teamwork, and adaptability), and work habits (ability to work under hardship or pressure, persistence in complex tasks, and ability to find new and better ways to do things). A program is considered to teach a given set of competencies when it teaches all the skills encompassed by it. Only São Paulo and Ceará are included for Brazil, and licensed programs for Peru.

and better ways to do things). Socioemotional skills, which are key to interpersonal relationships, are the ones most frequently taught (by 90 percent of the programs; see figure 3.13). Technical skills on computer use is the second most taught skill. Although more than 75 percent of the programs claim to teach cognitive skills, these are only the third most taught skills. Work habits come in fourth place. For comparison with these general competencies, the figure shows the percentage of programs that teach reading and writing in a foreign language, which is the least taught skill.

To graduate from an SCP, a student must complete all the required classes and, if required, the mandatory internship. Beyond this, some programs have

Figure 3.14 Additional Graduation Requirements

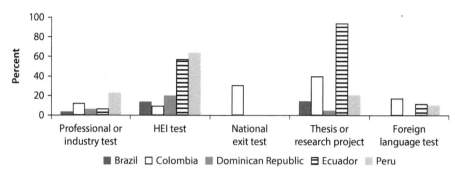

Source: World Bank Short-Cycle Program Survey.
Note: For each country, the figure shows the percentage of programs using each graduation requirement. A program can use more than one requirement. In Colombia, Saber T&T is the national exit test. Only São Paulo and Ceará are included for Brazil, and licensed programs for Peru.

additional graduation requirements (figure 3.14). Programs in all the countries give institution-specific graduation exams; these are particularly prevalent in Ecuador. Professional or industry tests, which often provide professional licensing to graduates in some fields (such as health), are also required in all the countries. A fraction of the programs in all the countries require the completion of a thesis or research project, ranging from 5 percent of the programs in the Dominican Republic to 40 percent in Colombia and 94 percent in Ecuador. While additional graduation requirements might contribute to the "quality" of graduates, some of them might be burdensome for students and require skills that were not developed during the program, as is probably the case of writing a research project or demonstrating foreign language proficiency.

Consistent with their dynamism, on average, programs have been updated very recently—about two years ago in Brazil, the Dominican Republic, Ecuador, and Peru, and four years ago in Colombia (figure 3.15, panel a). Programs are updated for multiple reasons, such as the HEI's perception of the labor market, students' feedback, graduates' labor market outcomes, employers' requests, and government standards—all of which demonstrate the HEIs' interest in responding to labor market needs, just as they do when deciding whether to open a new program.

Programs must have an operating license to function. In addition, they can voluntarily pursue accreditation in Peru, high-quality accreditation in Colombia, and international accreditation in the Dominican Republic (chapter 1). Figure 3.15, panel b, shows the percentage of programs in Peru, Colombia, and the Dominican Republic that have these voluntary accreditations, or that have been deemed of high quality by the regulator in Brazil and Ecuador. To facilitate exposition, we describe all these programs as having "high-quality accreditation." These programs report that its benefits are a reputation boost among employers, greater ability to differentiate themselves from competitors, and greater ability to attract good students and place graduates in the labor market.

Figure 3.15 Curriculum Update and High-Quality Accreditation

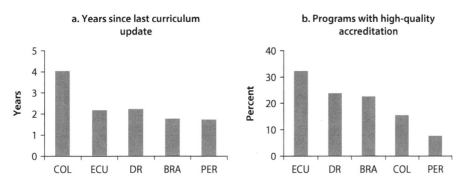

a. Years since last curriculum update

b. Programs with high-quality accreditation

Source: World Bank Short-Cycle Program Survey.
Note: Panel a shows the program-level average number of years since the last update to the program's curriculum. Panel b shows the percentage of programs in each country with high-quality accreditation (HQA). HQA is defined as follows: Brazil (BRA): programs taught at HEIs with an IGC score above the 75th percentile of the joint universe in São Paulo and Ceará; Colombia (COL): HQA granted by Ministry of Education; Dominican Republic (DR): international accreditation; Ecuador (ECU): HQA under pre-2018 accreditation regime; Peru (PER): accreditation granted by Ministry of Education. HEI = higher education institution; IGC = General Index of Programs. Only São Paulo and Ceará are included for Brazil, and licensed programs for Peru.

Figure 3.16 Faculty Size and Hiring

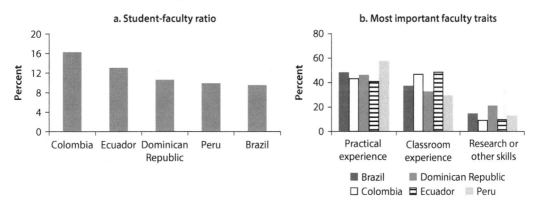

a. Student-faculty ratio

b. Most important faculty traits

■ Brazil   ■ Dominican Republic
□ Colombia   ▤ Ecuador   ▨ Peru

Source: World Bank Short-Cycle Program Survey.
Note: Panel a shows the program-level average student-to-faculty ratio, calculated as the ratio between the program's enrollment and the number of instructors. Neither enrollment nor number of instructors is adjusted by part- or full-time status. Panel b shows the percentage of programs that cite each trait (practical experience in the field, classroom experience, research or other skills) as most important when hiring faculty. For a given country, responses add up to 100. Only São Paulo and Ceará are included for Brazil, and licensed programs for Peru.

Faculty

On average, the programs have adequate quantity and "quality" of instructors. The average student-faculty ratio is low (between 10 and 16), and instructors are mostly hired for their practical experience in the field and classroom experience (figure 3.16, panels a and b).

The proportion of full-time faculty is low in most of the countries, as would be expected from instructors who work in their area of expertise (figure 3.17). Instructors are relatively young; 30 to 40 percent of them (and even more in Ecuador) are younger than age 40. Young instructors may have more up-to-date

Figure 3.17 Faculty Characteristics

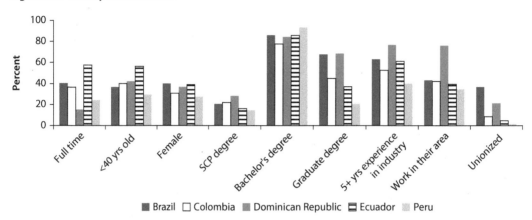

Source: World Bank Short-Cycle Program Survey.
Note: For each country, the figure shows the program-level average percentage of faculty with each characteristic. "yrs" = years;
"Work in their area" = the instructor works in his/her area of expertise outside the higher education institution. Only São Paulo and Ceará
are included for Brazil, and licensed programs for Peru. SCP = short-cycle program.

training, although they might also be less experienced than their older counterparts. The fraction of female instructors is quite low, at about a third, and lower than the fraction of female students (37 to 53 percent, depending on the country), yet this might be expected given the programs' nature. The faculty are academically qualified: more than 78 percent of the instructors have bachelor's degrees. In Brazil and the Dominican Republic, about two-thirds of the instructors have graduate degrees.

Although the share of the faculty with five or more years of experience in industry is high in the Dominican Republic, Brazil, and Ecuador (above 60 percent), it is lower in Colombia and Peru. Similarly, the share of the faculty working in industry in the area of their expertise is particularly high in the Dominican Republic (76 percent), but it ranges between 35 and 45 percent elsewhere. To the extent that students benefit from instructors currently working in industry, this might be a weakness of the programs. Faculty unionization is below 10 percent in Colombia, Ecuador, and Peru but is higher in the Dominican Republic and Brazil (21 and 37 percent, respectively).

Remarkably, almost all the programs evaluate their faculty, and most of them do so more than once a year. Multiple criteria are applied, including student evaluations; review of class syllabi and lesson plans; classroom observation; informal comments from students, other faculty, and staff; and colleagues' peer evaluations (figure 3.18, panel a). Although the program directors view several of these criteria as "very important," the one most frequently cited as such in every country is student evaluations. In contrast, the use of other criteria varies more across the countries. Professional development and training similarly vary across the countries (figure 3.18, panel b). In the previous year, 70 percent or more of the programs in Ecuador, Brazil, and Peru provided or financed professional development and training for all or almost all their faculty, but only 40–50 percent of the programs did so in Colombia and the Dominican Republic.

Infrastructure and Delivery Mode

The infrastructure for practical training includes labs and workshops. It appears to be sufficient, at least in terms of quantity: the average number of students per lab or workshop is low, ranging from three to eight across countries (figure 3.19, panel a), and most programs report having sufficient infrastructure for their needs (figure 3.19, panel b). Nonetheless, infrastructure varies across countries: it is sufficient at 90 percent of the programs in Brazil but only 60 percent in Ecuador. And, while 83 percent of the programs in Brazil conduct annual maintenance of labs and workshops, less than 60 percent do so in Ecuador and the Dominican Republic (figure 3.19, panel c).

Figure 3.18 Faculty Evaluation and Training

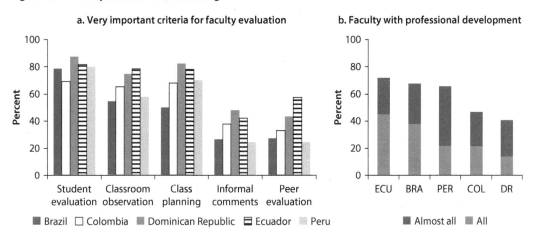

Source: World Bank Short-Cycle Program Survey.
Note: Panel a shows the percentage of programs that view each criterion for faculty evaluation as "very important." A program may have more than one "very important" criterion. Panel b shows the percentage of programs that report having provided or paid for professional development to almost all or all of their faculty during the previous year. Only São Paulo and Ceará are included for Brazil, and licensed programs for Peru.

Figure 3.19 Physical Infrastructure

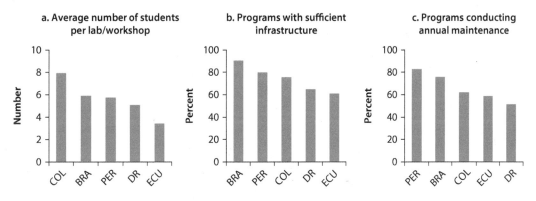

Source: World Bank Short-Cycle Program Survey.
Note: Panel a shows the program-level average number of labs/workshops per student. Panel b shows the percentage of programs that report having sufficient infrastructure for all their students. Panel c shows the percentage of programs that report conducting annual maintenance of their facilities. BRA = Brazil; COL = Colombia; DR = Dominican Republic; ECU = Ecuador; PER = Peru. Only São Paulo and Ceará are included for Brazil, and licensed programs for Peru.

Figure 3.20 Percentage of Classes Offered Online

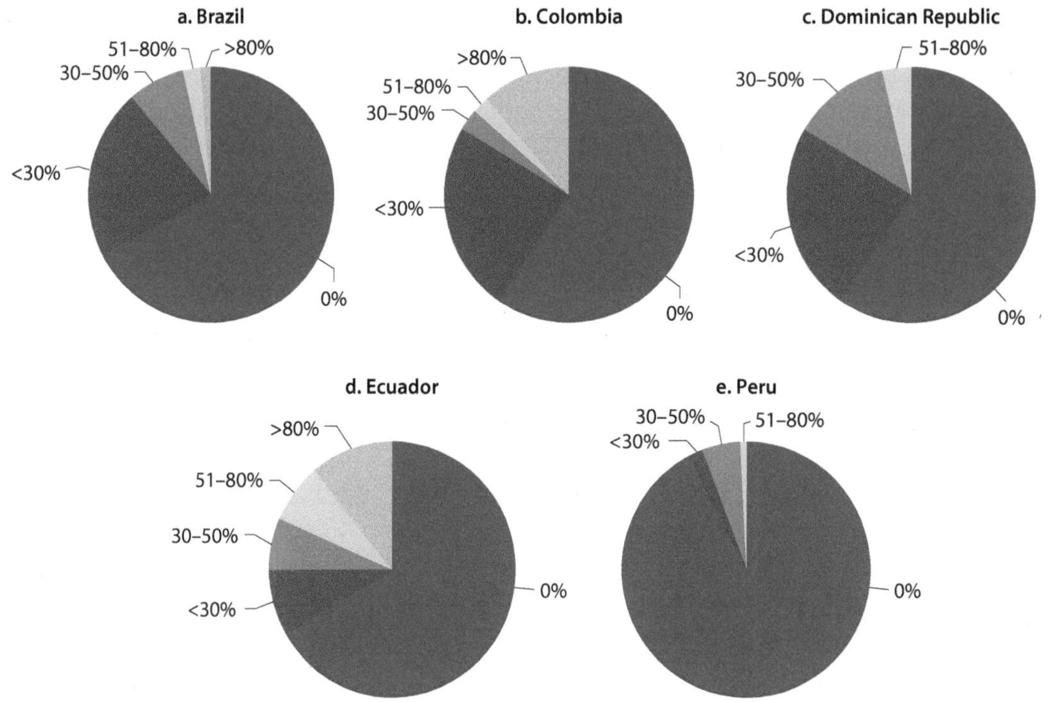

a. Brazil

b. Colombia

c. Dominican Republic

d. Ecuador

e. Peru

Source: World Bank Short-Cycle Program Survey.
Note: The figure shows, for each country, the fraction of programs that fall into each of the following categories for the percentage of classes that they teach online: 0%, less than 30%, 30%–50%, 51%–80%, more than 80%. Only São Paulo and Ceará are included for Brazil, and licensed programs for Peru.

Online teaching was rare before the COVID-19 pandemic. Most of the programs did not offer any class online (figure 3.20). Even in the three countries where online classes were most prevalent (Brazil, Colombia, and the Dominican Republic), most programs offered less than 30 percent of their classes online. Before the pandemic, students took online classes for multiple reasons, including schedule conflict (prevalent in Brazil, Colombia, and Ecuador), preference for online learning (prevalent in the Dominican Republic), and geographic distance to the institution (prevalent in Peru). Because online teaching was so rare before the pandemic, adapting to it might have been particularly challenging for the programs.

Governance and Private Sector Connections

Most of the programs are taught at HEIs that have a governing body aside from the provost (*rector*). This is the case for 69 percent of the programs in Peru and over 87 percent of the programs in the remaining countries. The governing body (or board) may include faculty, students, private firms, government officials, and other individuals. On average, faculty make up the greatest share of the board in all the countries except the Dominican Republic, with a particularly prominent role in Brazil and Ecuador (figure 3.21, panel a). Except in Ecuador, firms are better represented than students. As expected, government officials are more common at public than private HEIs.

In addition to participating in governing boards, the private sector engages with the programs in multiple ways (figure 3.21, panel b). The most common (above 80 percent of the programs) is by having student internship agreements. In more than half of the programs in Colombia, Ecuador, and Peru, the private sector also participates in curriculum design or student evaluation and lends or provides equipment. Further, the private sector participates in faculty training in 45 percent of the Dominican Republic's programs. Some programs have agreements with firms to hire their graduates, particularly in Peru. Interestingly, programs with a higher share of nontraditional students have more private sector engagement but less job search assistance, which is consistent with the notion that these students are particularly interested in programs with strong connections to the local economy but do not need much assistance to find a job—either because they already have a job, or because they have experience finding one. Overall, engagement with the private sector appears quite strong.

Figure 3.21 Private Sector Engagement

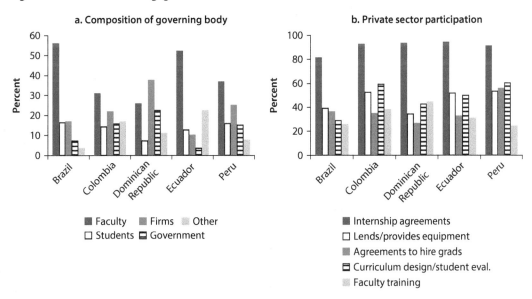

Source: World Bank Short-Cycle Program Survey.
Note: Panel a shows, for each country, the average composition of the governing body of the higher education institution (HEI), namely the average percentage of members that consist of faculty, students, firm representatives, government officials, and others (conditional on the program having a governing body aside from the provost). For a given country, the percentages add up to 100. Panel b shows, for each country, the percentage of programs that engage the private sector through each of the following not mutually exclusive mechanisms: internship agreements, agreements whereby the private sector would hire graduates from the program, faculty training on the part of the private sector, equipment leasing or provision on the part of the private sector, participation in curriculum design or student evaluation. For the latter, the figure shows the average of the percentage of programs with curriculum design participation and the percentage of programs with student evaluation participation. Only São Paulo and Ceará are included for Brazil, and licensed programs for Peru.

Programs entrust their engagement with the private sector to different individuals: the program director, a board member, somebody specifically assigned, or whoever is available for the task (figure 3.22) The programs seem to be intentional about private sector engagement, as only a small fraction report not relating to the private sector or leaving this relationship to "whoever is available."

Figure 3.22 Person in Charge of Relations with the Private Sector

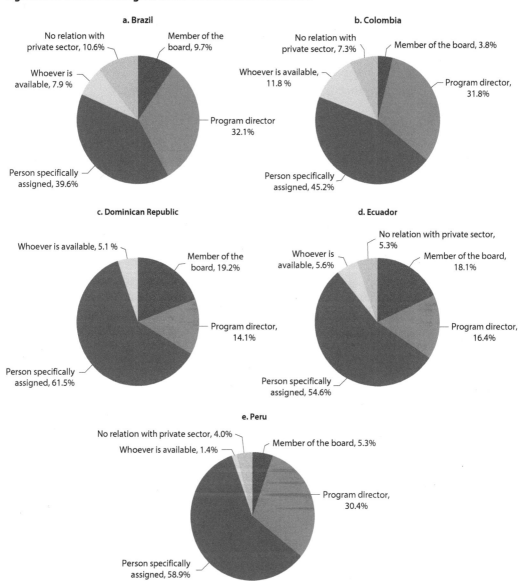

Source: World Bank Short-Cycle Program Survey.
Note: The figure shows, for each country, the percentage of programs in each of the categories defined by the person in charge of relating with the private sector. Only São Paulo and Ceará are included for Brazil, and licensed programs for Peru.

Activities Related to Students' Job Search and Outcomes

To assist students in their job search, the programs conduct various activities, such as providing job market information, training students for job interviews, having an employment center (*bolsa de trabajo*), coordinating job interviews with firms, and having agreements with private firms to hire graduates (figure 3.23). Providing job market information is the main activity in each country. Only in Peru is this activity (slightly) surpassed by training or arranging job interviews. Running employment centers is popular in Colombia, Ecuador, and Peru but not in Brazil or the Dominican Republic.

Given their focus on employment, the programs provide relatively little support to students' job search. Although information provision is useful, students might need more practical, immediate assistance in their job search—such as arranging job interviews or providing assistance through an employment center for resume preparation and job applications.

More than 78 percent of the programs conduct faculty evaluations and analyze student performance more than once a year (figure 3.24, panel a), which allows them to address student- or faculty-related issues quickly. Other activities related to students' labor market outcomes are conducted less frequently. The programs are less likely to collect data on graduates' employment, gauge employers' satisfaction with the program graduates, or inquire about local firms' needs more than once a year. And although some programs collect data on their graduates' initial jobs (regardless of how often), the fraction of such programs varies widely, from 42 percent in Brazil to 97 percent in Peru (figure 3.24, panel b).

Programs and Competitors

In the view of the program directors, the program feature that is most valued by students is training quality, as given by the program's academic quality, faculty

Figure 3.23 Activities to Support Students' Job Search

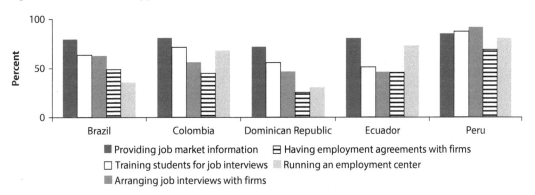

Source: World Bank Short-Cycle Program Survey.
Note: The figure shows, for each country, the percentage of programs that support their students' job search through each of the following mechanisms: provision of job market information, employment agreements whereby firms will hire the program's graduates, training students for job interviews, arranging job interviews, and running an employment center or *bolsa de trabajo*. Only São Paulo and Ceará are included for Brazil, and licensed programs for Peru.

Figure 3.24 Activities to Support Students' Job Market Outcomes

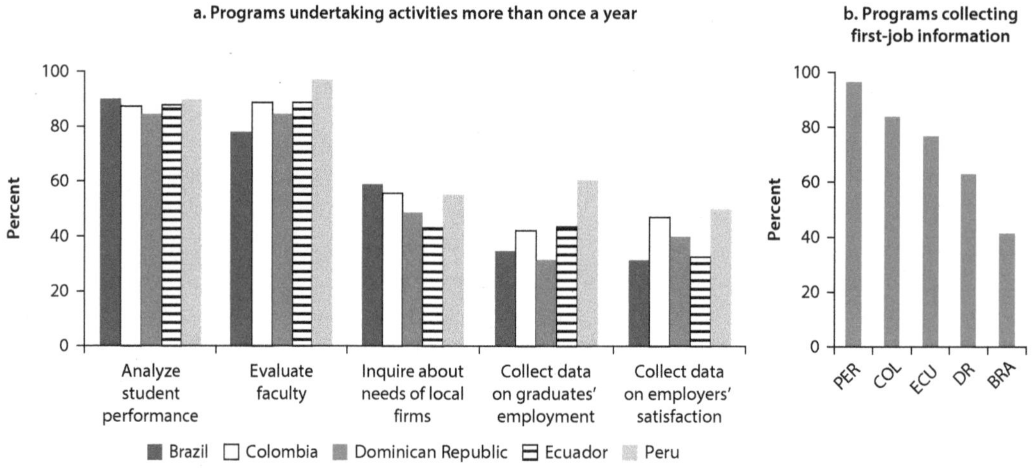

Source: World Bank Short-Cycle Program Survey.

Note: Panel a shows the percentage of programs that report conducting each activity more than once a year; activities are not mutually exclusive. Panel b shows the percentage of programs that collect information on graduates' first employment after completing the program. BRA = Brazil; COL = Colombia; DR = Dominican Republic; ECU = Ecuador; PER = Peru. Only São Paulo and Ceará are included for Brazil, and licensed programs for Peru.

quality, and practical training (figure 3.25, panel a). Indeed, more than half of the program directors reported this as the most valued feature. In contrast, less than a quarter of the program directors reported employment (including job prospects, internships, job search assistance, and HEI connections with employers) as the most valued feature.

In each country, most of the programs view other local SCPs as their main competitors, followed by local bachelor's programs (figure 3.25, panel b). This is consistent with the findings in the section entitled "Dynamics and Competition in the SCP Market," which show the responsiveness of SCPs to local market conditions. Relative to their competitors (figure 3.26), more than 60 percent of the programs believe they are better in training (curriculum plus academic and practical training); between 45 and 65 percent of the programs believe they are better in terms of academic services, materials, and equipment; and between 40 and 60 percent believe they are better in terms of employment (connections with the private sector, employment opportunities, and job search assistance). In addition, between 35 and 55 percent believe they provide better funding options.

This self-perception relative to competitors is interesting for multiple reasons. First, it is mathematically not possible for more than half of the programs to be better than their competitors in training. More importantly, the fact that most programs view themselves as superior in training but not in employment of graduates suggests that they might be emphasizing the former rather than the latter and that they are aware of it. Perhaps they view their role as providing training that is as good as possible, trusting that this alone will give students good employment. This view would be consistent with their perception that training is indeed the most valuable feature to students. Programs might believe that

Figure 3.25 Programs' Main Features and Competitors

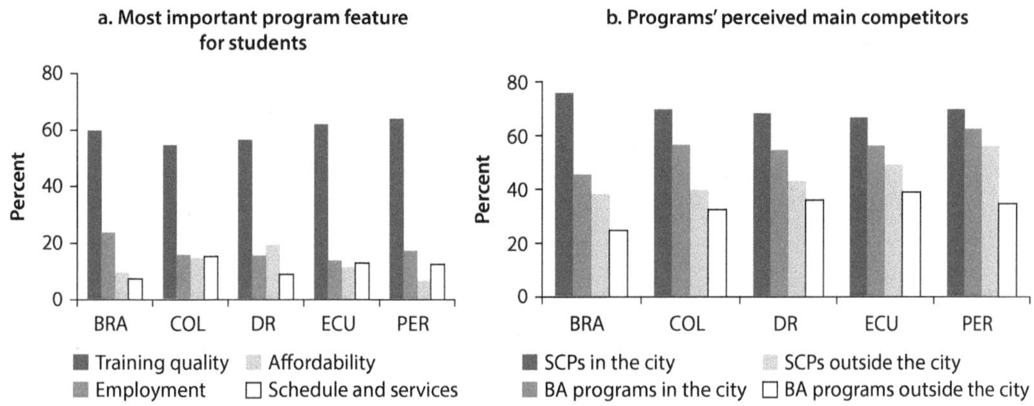

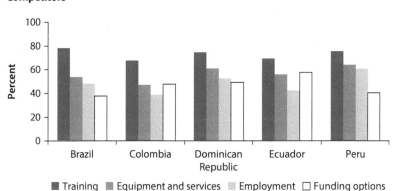

a. Most important program feature for students

b. Programs' perceived main competitors

Panel a legend:
■ Training quality ▨ Affordability
■ Employment □ Schedule and services

Panel b legend:
■ SCPs in the city ▨ SCPs outside the city
■ BA programs in the city □ BA programs outside the city

Source: World Bank Short-Cycle Program Survey.
Note: Panel a shows, for each country, the percentage of programs that report each feature as the most important for their students. Features are training quality, affordability, schedule and student services, and employment. "Training quality" includes faculty quality, practical training, and academic quality; "Affordability" includes program cost and financial aid from the HEI; "Schedule and services" includes class schedule and quality of student services; "Employment" includes employment prospects after graduation, internship opportunities, job search assistance, and HEI connections with potential employers. For training quality, the figure shows the sum of the percentage of programs that mention each of the three components as most important for students, and similarly for the other features. For a given country, the percentages add up to 100. Panel b shows the percentage of programs that view each of the following as a main competitor: SCPs in the program's location; SCPs outside the program's location; BA programs in the program's location; BA programs outside the program's location. Main competitors' categories are not mutually exclusive. BA = bachelor's; BRA = Brazil; COL = Colombia; DR = Dominican Republic; ECU = Ecuador; HEI = higher education institution; PER = Peru; SCP = short-cycle program. Only São Paulo and Ceará are included for Brazil, and licensed programs for Peru.

Figure 3.26 Aspects in Which the Program Believes It Is Better Than Its Competitors

Legend:
■ Training ■ Equipment and services ▨ Employment □ Funding options

Source: World Bank Short-Cycle Program Survey.
Note: The figure shows, for each country, the percentage of programs that view themselves as better than similar short-cycle programs in each of the following categories: training, employment, equipment and services, and financial aid. "Training" includes the following items: curriculum, academic training, and practical training. "Employment" includes job search assistance, employment opportunities, and private sector contacts. "Equipment and services" includes student academic services and materials and equipment. For each program, "training" is the average response over its three items (response equal to one if the program considers itself better than the competitors, 0 otherwise), and similarly for the other categories. Only São Paulo and Ceará are included for Brazil, and licensed programs for Peru.

because students value training the most, they must provide better training than their competitors. Alternatively, they might believe that because their training surpasses that of their competitors, it is the feature most valued by students. Either way, they seem to be aware of a certain weakness in employment.

To summarize, the WBSCPS paints a rich and nuanced picture of SCPs and their providers in LAC. Most providers are relatively young. Consistent with the dynamism of this market, the programs are also young and have been recently updated. They typically feature a fixed curriculum, devote half of the time to practical training, and require mandatory internships. Before the COVID-19 pandemic, they offered a small proportion of classes online, suggesting that they might have struggled to adapt to online delivery. In general, they are well equipped in terms of practice facilities. They have low student-faculty ratios, and their faculties are academically qualified, relatively young, and quite engaged with industry. The programs evaluate faculty with care and student evaluations are an important evaluation criterion. They deliberately engage the private sector and do so in multiple ways, the main one being through internship agreements.

At the same time, there is substantial variation in SCPs' characteristics and practices—just as there is substantial variation in their outcomes (chapter 2). Indeed, chapter 4 exploits this variation to investigate whether program characteristics and practices are related to outcomes. And, although the programs provide various forms of job search support, the main type of support—provision of labor market information—is relatively passive and perhaps less useful than others, such as arranging job interviews or running an employment center. Importantly, most program directors believe that what students value the most is the quality of training—as opposed, for instance, to employment. This view of demand might guide supply. That is, if students value training quality the most, it is reasonable for the programs to concentrate on it, perhaps hoping that this alone will help students find employment. Relatedly, most programs consider themselves to be better than their competitors in training quality but not in employment. All in all, while the programs seem intent on providing good training and engaging with the private sector, they might need a more deliberate focus on labor market outcomes.

Conclusions

This chapter started by considering how the supply of SCPs could contribute to realizing their promise. In closing the chapter, this section concludes that SCPs in LAC have several positive features that could indeed contribute to that role, but they might also face some shortcomings.

On the positive side, the SCP market is dynamic—with more "churn" (entry and exit of programs) than the bachelor's program market. Institutions open new programs in response to the local economy and the labor market success of graduates in the corresponding field. Private institutions and non-university institutions are the most responsive to local conditions. Entry also responds to competitive patterns that are related to the existence, size, and geographic coverage of subsidized public HEIs. Further, programs are highly structured and focus on practical training. They interact quite closely with the private sector and support students in their job search. The combination of these features might be a reason why graduation rates are higher at SCPs than bachelor's programs, and why SCP graduates outperform bachelor's dropouts in the labor market (chapter 1).

Nonetheless, there is substantial variation in program characteristics and practices. Further, programs seem to focus more on training quality than employment—perhaps believing that training quality alone will help students find good jobs. Students, however, might need more. For example, they might need assistance applying for jobs, training for interviews, and connecting with potential employers. This lack of focus on employment might a "blind spot" —not just for SCPs but also for students, who seem to value training quality above employment.

Can this blind spot be eliminated? Perhaps, if students start gaining access to employment information and start expecting good employment outcomes or if regulation and funding provide the institutions greater incentives to focus on those outcomes. Rethinking their activities, particularly those related to graduates' labor market outcomes, seems to be a pressing need for these programs.

Notes

For their excellent research assistance, Andrea Franco, Manuela Granda, Angelica Sánchez, and Gabriel Suárez are gratefully acknowledged.

1. For the United States, Cellini (2009, 2010) finds that an increase in community college funding lowers enrollment at for-profit HEIs. Grosz (2019) finds that community college responses to local employment changes seem to operate through student demand rather than HEIs' supply. For Colombia, Carranza and Ferreyra (2019) find that HEIs are more likely to open bachelor's programs in markets that are larger, where they face less competition and there is a greater number of students similar to those served by the HEI, and in fields in which the HEI already has programs.

2. This section draws from the background paper by Carranza, Ferreyra, Gazmuri, and Franco (2021), written for this book.

3. In Chile, the first public HEIs for SCPs opened in 2018. As of 2018, they captured only 0.02 percent of SCP enrollment. Source: Ministry of Education of Chile.

4. For Colombia, the analysis does not study entry on the part of SENA. This is because SENA's decisions are made by the Ministry of Labor, on which SENA depends, based on policy-related considerations.

5. Although these locations might seem too large to represent local markets, they are actually reasonable. Most local markets correspond to metropolitan areas, and many students from the department (or region) who do not live in a metropolitan area actually travel there to take classes. Thus, in practice, the local market is indeed the whole department (or region).

6. The results reported here are based on partial coefficients from regressions that control for other regressors, including department, field, and year fixed effects. See Carranza et al. (2021) for further details.

7. These findings are similar to those for bachelor's programs exclusively in Carranza and Ferreyra (2019), described in Ferreyra et al. (2017).

8. Similarly, firm entry and exit in a given industry are positively correlated (Dunne, Roberts, and Samuelson 1988).

9. The share of small municipalities covered by SENA rose between 2003 and 2012 until reaching a peak of 56 percent and quickly declined in the following years as many programs were closed.

References

Bailey, T., S. Jaggars, and D. Jenkins. 2015. *Redesigning America's Community Colleges: A Clearer Path to Student Success.* Cambridge, MA: Harvard University Press.

Carranza, J. E., and M. M. Ferreyra. 2019. "Increasing Higher Education Coverage: Supply Expansion and Student Sorting in Colombia." *Journal of Human Capital* 13 (1).

Carranza, J. E., M. M. Ferreyra, A. Gazmuri, and A. Franco. 2021. "The Supply Side of Short-Cycle Higher Education Programs." Unpublished manuscript. World Bank, Washington, DC.

Cellini, S. R. 2009. "Crowded Colleges and College Crowd-Out: The Impact of Public Subsidies on the Two-Year College Market." *American Economic Journal: Economic Policy* 1 (2): 1–30.

Cellini, S. R. 2010. "Financial Aid and For-Profit Colleges: Does Aid Encourage Entry?" Journal of Policy Analysis and Management 29 (3): 526–52.

Dunne, T., M. J. Roberts, and L. Samuelson. 1988. "Patterns of Firm Entry and Exit in US Manufacturing Industries." *The RAND Journal of Economics* 19 (4): 495–515.

Ferreyra, M., C. Avitabile, J. Botero, F. Haimovich, and S. Urzúa. 2017. *At a Crossroads: Higher Education in Latin America and the Caribbean.* Washington, DC: World Bank Group.

Grosz, M. 2019. Do Postsecondary Training Programs Respond to Changes in the Labor Market?" FTC Bureau of Economics Working Paper 34, Federal Trade Commission, Washington, DC.

CHAPTER 4

Quality Determinants of Short-Cycle Programs in Latin America and the Caribbean

Lelys Dinarte Díaz and
Marina Bassi

Introduction

The evidence presented in the previous chapters indicates that expanding short-cycle programs (SCPs) in Latin America and the Caribbean (LAC) might be a promising avenue to improve the skills of the workforce. However, countries in the region face the challenge of expanding SCP systems while ensuring their quality. As described in chapter 2, SCP outcomes and value added in LAC show great dispersion, indicating wide variation in program quality. Yet, little is known about SCP quality determinants—what makes a program "good" after accounting for student characteristics. Quality seems to be a "black box" in which program features interact with each other and with student characteristics and result in good graduates' and student performance.

The lack of evidence establishing a clear link between specific program aspects and student-level outcomes stems, to some extent, from the limited availability of data on program practices, inputs, and characteristics. The data that are usually collected in administrative data sets include, at best, basic indicators of inputs and program characteristics, such as the number of students enrolled, program duration, and student-faculty ratio. In general, no information is collected on how institutions and programs recruit, train, and assess their faculty; how they support student learning; or how they establish links with local firms, which are the potential employers of their graduates. To fill this void, the World Bank Short-Cycle Program Survey (WBSCPS) collected unique data on such activities for five countries—Brazil (the states of São Paulo and Ceará), Colombia, the Dominican Republic, Ecuador, and Peru (licensed programs)—as reported by program directors.

This chapter aims to unveil the determinants of SCP quality. It draws on Dinarte et al. (2021), a background paper written for this book. The analysis identifies the SCP practices, inputs, and characteristics that are associated with good academic and labor market outcomes for the graduates, after accounting for student and institutional characteristics. The chapter starts by describing four outcomes that are used as measures of SCP quality: the dropout rate, extra time to graduate (ETG) beyond the official duration of the program, graduates' formal employment, and graduates' wages. Then, the SCP determinants are grouped into six areas that, as suggested by the literature, might contribute to quality. These areas are infrastructure, curriculum and training, costs and financing, engagement with industry, faculty, and other practices related to admission, graduation, and governance. Finally, the chapter presents the estimated contributions of the determinants in these six areas to SCP outcomes, after accounting for student and institutional characteristics.

The main findings show the following:

- On average, the programs report using good practices and having good inputs in terms of infrastructure, training and curriculum, costs and financing, engagement with industry, faculty, and other practices. However, there is much variation in these aspects among programs. While this variation enables estimating the association between the quality determinants and outcomes, it also raises concerns as it indicates that many programs do not use good practices or inputs. This, in turn, contributes to the large variation in returns documented in chapter 2.

- Among practices related to engagement with industry, specifically how programs support their students' job search, SCPs that have an employment center are more likely to report that almost all their graduates are employed in the formal sector and they earn higher wages. In contrast, some determinants related to engagement with industry seem to be negatively associated with graduates' outcomes. Specifically, programs for which firms provide equipment for students' training tend to report worse outcomes in terms of formal employment, while those that have agreements to hire graduates report lower wages, perhaps because the terms of these agreements are not necessarily beneficial to students or because the agreements could be substituting other arrangements, such as internship opportunities.

- Multiple determinants related to curriculum structure and content also seem to contribute to good outcomes. Programs that have a fixed curriculum have lower dropout rates than programs with mixed or flexible curricula. Moreover, offering academic remediation during the program to address previous cognitive deficits is associated with higher formal employment and wages for graduates. In addition, providing credits to continue onto longer higher education programs and teaching numerical competencies are associated with higher wages for graduates.

- Certain admission practices, graduation requirements, and governance features appear to be relevant to the outcomes. For example, programs that have more rigorous admission mechanisms (such as interviews and additional entry tests to ensure minimum content knowledge among incoming students) report shorter ETG and higher wages for graduates. In contrast, requiring a thesis for graduation seems to increase average ETG substantially, indicating that requirements that are less consistent with SCPs' practical focus might be ineffective. In addition, students in higher education institutions (HEIs) that have a governing board in addition to a provost or rector are more likely to complete the program or find formal employment, which could be indicating that a more diverse governance structure may attend better to the needs of the various stakeholders.

- In terms of program costs and financing, higher tuition is associated with lower dropout rates and higher wages for the graduates. The association between dropout and tuition possibly works as a signal of the program's high reputation among employers. On the flip side, the availability of HEI scholarships is associated with higher formal employment, perhaps because these scholarships ease financial restrictions and allow students to focus squarely on their training.

- Overall, infrastructure is positively associated with labor market outcomes. Programs that report having enough materials and equipment for training regardless of enrollment and that provide internet access show better labor market outcomes. Although the education literature overall agrees that increasing inputs is not by itself effective at improving students' outcomes (as the inputs might not be well utilized), the findings in this chapter suggest that the availability of adequate equipment and materials, which are key to practical training, gives students more skills that pay off in the job market. Providing internet access, in turn, may expand job search opportunities for students and thereby raise their formal employment.

- Among faculty-related practices, the use of peer evaluation to assess faculty performance is related to lower student dropout rates. Similarly, including class planning as an important element in faculty evaluation is associated with higher formal employment. Moreover, some faculty characteristics are correlated to the outcomes as well. Programs with a higher share of faculty with more work experience report faster student graduation and higher rates of formal employment. In addition, more female faculty is associated with faster graduation. On the contrary, a higher share of young faculty is associated with lower formal employment, as they might have less practical experience. Finally, a larger share of faculty working in industry is associated with higher dropout rates. These faculty might attract students to industry jobs while they are still in school, perhaps leading them to drop out.

- Most of the chapter reports findings using program-level data from the WBSCPS. In addition, the chapter uses individual-level administrative data to estimate the contributions of program characteristics to student outcomes for the case of Brazil (at the time of writing, Brazil was the only country that provided access to administrative data). The estimates show that specific quality determinants—such as providing labor market information and being deemed of high quality by the regulating authorities—as well as some characteristics, such as program size and HEI type, contribute to students' academic and labor market outcomes.

Defining and Measuring SCP Quality

Challenges of Measuring SCP Quality

Measuring the quality of higher education is challenging for a couple of reasons. First, there is little agreement over what is expected of higher education or how to measure quality in a standardized way. Moreover, the measures in a country are usually determined by data availability in its higher education information system.

A second challenge is related to whether quality should be measured through student outcomes or program value added. The distinction between outcomes and value added, outlined in this book's introduction and chapter 2, helps clarify this challenge. Consider the wage earned by a program's graduate immediately upon graduation. The wage constitutes the outcome, determined by student-level inputs (ability, effort, and other background characteristics), peers' characteristics, and program-level inputs. The program's contribution to the student's wage, net of the contributions made by the student herself and her peers, is the program's value added.

Estimating the value added of an SCP requires detailed individual-level data on all elements of the production function that could affect the graduate's wage. Unfortunately, this level of detail in higher education administrative data is difficult to obtain from the countries in the region. Some countries do not collect these data. Others do, but gaining access to these data is an enormous challenge as it usually contains confidential individual level information.[1] Collecting the data and facilitating their access remains a key task in LAC.

Due to the lack of data or the complexity of getting access to the data, this chapter follows an alternative approach, which is described in detail in Dinarte et al. (2021). The chapter uses the data reported by program directors to the WBSCPS on program infrastructure, curriculum and training, engagement with industry, costs and financing, faculty, and additional practices, as well as data on other characteristics of the programs, institutions, and students. Further, the chapter uses data collected by the WBSCPS on average academic and labor market outcomes for graduates at the program level, including dropout rates, extra time to graduate, formal employment, and wages.

Throughout, the term "determinant" refers to practices (for example, providing labor market information to students), inputs (for example, workshops for practical training), or input characteristics (for example, the percentage of faculty with more than five years of experience working in industry) that programs can choose and that could potentially affect graduates' outcomes.

Using WBSCPS data for the five countries covered in the survey—Brazil (the states of Ceará and São Paulo), Colombia, the Dominican Republic, Ecuador, and

Peru (licensed programs)—the chapter estimates the marginal contributions of SCP determinants to academic and labor market outcomes of graduates, net of student characteristics. For example, it estimates how programs' provision of labor market information to students is associated with improvements in students' formal employment, after accounting for student characteristics. The analysis focuses on two categories of outcomes: academic performance—measured by dropout rates and time to degree—and labor market outcomes—which include employment in the formal sector and graduates' salaries.

A couple of remarks are in order. First, the chapter estimates associations without claiming causality. To establish the *causal effect* of a determinant—for example, availability of an employment center—on an outcome of interest—for example, formal employment—ideally, individuals would be randomized between a group for which an employment center is available and a comparison group for which it is not available. Since individuals would be very similar between the two groups, any difference in formal employment would be attributable to the employment center. However, this approach is not feasible for thousands of programs and a large number of quality determinants.

Second, the program directors reported *average* outcomes for their programs and *average* student characteristics, not outcomes for individual students. To facilitate the explanation, imagine that program directors reported one average outcome (graduates' wage), one average student characteristic (percentage of part-time students), and one program characteristic (whether the program offers remedial education). The estimation answers the following question: If programs A and B have similar student bodies (the same percentage of part-time students), but program A offers remedial education while program B does not, what is the difference in average wages between graduates from A and B? In this sense, the estimation is an attempt to quantify program value added using aggregate data from the WBSCPS.

The rest of this section describes the outcomes of interest. It also documents the average outcomes of the programs using WBSCPS data. The next section describes the quality determinants, and the following one summarizes the main associations between quality determinants and the outcomes of interest. Annex 4A provides summary statistics for the outcomes, quality determinants, and other program characteristics.

Outcomes
Dropout Rate and Extra Time to Graduate
Data were collected on two academic outcomes: the dropout rate and extra time to graduate. To measure the dropout rate, the directors were asked to focus on the cohort that was supposed to graduate the previous academic year. For this cohort, the directors reported the percentage of students who attained each of the following outcomes: graduated on time, dropped out, and were still enrolled in the program. The percentage of students from this cohort that dropped out of the program is the dropout rate measure.

On average, the dropout rate is approximately 14 percent. As figure 4.1 shows, average dropout rates across countries are similar, ranging from 13 percent in Ecuador and Peru, to 14 percent in Colombia, and 15 percent in Brazil and the Dominican Republic.

The extra-time-to-graduate measure is the additional amount of time that, on average, a cohort takes to graduate relative to the official duration of the program (in percentage terms). The directors were asked to focus on students who graduated in the previous academic year, and to report the average time taken by those students to graduate. For example, if a program lasts two years and students on average took three years to graduate, then extra time to graduate is 50 percent. As shown in figure 4.2, panel a, across countries, there is more variation in this outcome than in dropout rates. The average extra time to graduate ranges from less than 10 percent in Peru to about 31 percent in the Dominican Republic.

Average extra time to graduate is not related to the average program duration by country. As figure 4.2, panel b, shows, the SCP average durations across the five countries are very similar, with an average of 5.2 semesters, although extra time to graduate varies substantially across countries.

Formal Employment

Graduates' employment is an important dimension of SCP quality. In this sense, high-quality SCPs should have a high share of graduates who are employed—or self-employed—in the formal sector, a low share of graduates who are working in the informal sector, and a low share of graduates who are neither working nor studying (the "*ninis*" for "no estudia, ni trabaja"). To understand how graduates are distributed across these three employment statuses (formal employment, informal employment, and neither working nor studying), the directors were

Figure 4.1 Student Academic Outcomes, by Country

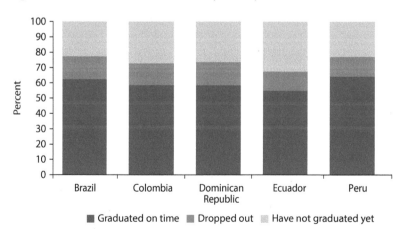

Sources: Dinarte et al. (2021); calculations based on the World Bank Short-Cycle Program Survey.
Note: The figure shows the average, over programs, of the percentage of students reaching each academic outcome as reported by program directors. The question refers to students who should have graduated the previous year. Only São Paulo and Ceará are included for Brazil, and licensed programs for Peru.

Figure 4.2 Average Extra Time to Graduate and Official Program Duration, by Country

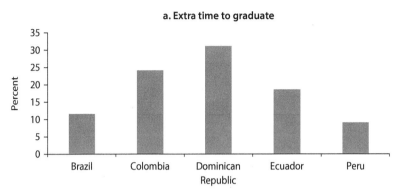

a. Extra time to graduate

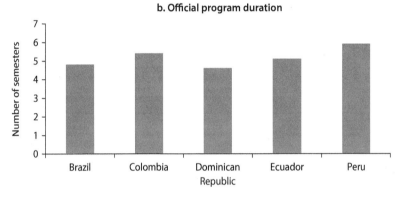

b. Official program duration

Sources: Dinarte et al. (2021); calculations based on the World Bank Short-Cycle Program Survey.
Note: Panel a reports the average extra time taken by students to graduate from their program, as a percentage of the official program (official) duration, and panel b reports the official program duration (semesters). The question on time to degree pertains to students who graduated the previous year. Only São Paulo and Ceará are included for Brazil, and licensed programs for Peru.

asked to indicate how many (with a scale including almost all, some, and almost none) of the graduates from the most recent cohort had each status.

Figure 4.3 presents the percentage of directors reporting "good" employment status outcomes of the graduates, namely the share reporting "almost all are employed in the formal sector," "almost none is employed in the informal sector," and "almost none is neither studying nor working." As panel a shows, 59 percent of the directors reported that almost all the graduates were employed in the formal sector, with the highest percentage reported in Brazil (74 percent) and the lowest in Ecuador (39 percent).

Informality has been one of the most significant and persistent challenges in LAC economies for decades. On average, close to 48 percent of workers are considered informal in Latin America. In the sample, about a third of the directors reported that almost no student is employed in the informal sector. In other words, in about two-thirds of the programs, there are at least some students in the informal sector. The country with the worst performance in terms of employment in the informal sector is the Dominican Republic (figure 4.3, panel b).

Figure 4.3 Programs Reporting Graduates'"Good" Employment Outcomes

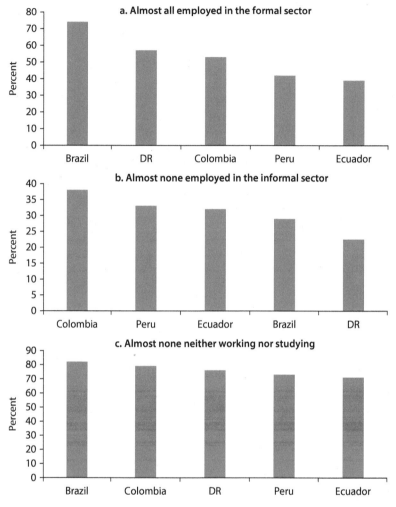

Sources: Dinarte et al. (2021); calculations based on the World Bank Short-Cycle Program Survey.
Note: The figure shows, for each country, the percentage of programs reporting each of three employment outcomes: almost all students are employed in the formal sector; almost no student is employed in the informal sector; almost no student is neither working nor studying. The outcomes were reported by the program directors. Only São Paulo and Ceará are included for Brazil, and licensed programs for Peru. DR = the Dominican Republic.

A report on youth employment documents that one in five youths in LAC—totaling more than 20 million people ages 15 to 24—was a *nini* in 2015, with greater incidence among poorer households.[2] The high incidence of *ninis* can bring some negative effects on their well-being due to its correlation with violence, crime, and the intergenerational persistence of inequality. The vast majority of the directors reported that almost no graduate from their programs was a *nini* (figure 4.3, panel c).

Taken together, these outcomes indicate that directors in Brazil and Colombia report the best employment outcomes. For Brazil, in particular, the probability that almost all SCP graduates are employed in the formal sector is close to 73 percent, as reported by the directors. Moreover, less than 18 percent of the program directors in those countries report that some of their graduates are neither working nor studying, which is lower than the rest of the countries in the sample.

Wages

Most of the recent evidence on value added in higher education analyzes the effects of program quality using wages as the outcome.[3] Thus, the directors were asked to report the average wage obtained by students in their first job after graduation from the last cohort of graduates. They reported a single average, without distinguishing between graduates employed in the formal and informal sectors.

Two wage measures are computed. First, to compare wages across countries, average wages are expressed in 2019 dollars (adjusted for purchasing power parity, PPP). Second, to compare SCP graduates' wages with other wages in the corresponding country, average wages are expressed as a multiple of the country's minimum wage. Table 4.1 presents a summary of the wage measures.

The average annual wage (PPP adjusted) in LAC for recent SCP graduates is close to US$10,700, ranging from US$7,481 in Peru to US$11,900 in the Ecuador. These salaries correspond to an average of 1.5 times the minimum wage in the region. In Brazil, an average SCP graduate earns about two times the salary of a minimum wage earner; the multiple is less (between 1.3 and 1.4) in the other countries.

SCP Quality Determinants

This section describes the different quality determinants that can potentially contribute to SCP quality as defined by the outcomes described in the previous section. It also summarizes previous knowledge, based on the relevant literature, on the association between quality determinants and measures of higher education quality.

Table 4.1 Average Annual Wages of SCP Graduates, by Country

Average wage measure	Brazil	Colombia	Dominican Republic	Ecuador	Peru
Purchasing power parity wage	$10,730	$10,313	$11,275	$11,910	$7,481
Multiple of the minimum wage	2.2	1.3	1.3	1.4	1.3

Sources: Dinarte et al. (2021); calculations based on the World Bank Short-Cycle Program Survey.
Note: The table reports the average annual wage per country, expressed in 2019 PPP dollars and as a multiple of the country's annual minimum wage. PPP adjustment of wages was done using the 2019 purchasing power parity (PPP) conversion factor. Average wage in terms of minimum wages (MW) was estimated using the last year's available minimum wage in the local currency. Average annual wage in minimum wages = average annual wage / MW, where MW = annual minimum wage = monthly minimum wage * 12. All descriptive statistics and estimations in this chapter are done excluding outliers, that is, excluding percentiles 1 and 99 of the wage distribution within each country. Only São Paulo and Ceará are included for Brazil, and licensed programs for Peru.

From the WBSCPS, data were collected on several practices, inputs, and characteristics chosen by the programs, which might work as quality determinants. These were grouped into six categories. Further, information was gathered on program, institution, and student characteristics to "control" for elements that can affect the outcomes but are not factors that the programs can select.

The following subsection describes the six categories, the specific determinants included in each one as well as their average level in WBSCPS countries, and, where available, the existing evidence on their impact based on other studies. Then the section describes additional program, HEI, and student characteristics that are included in the analysis as control variables. To facilitate interpretation of the estimation results, annex 4A summarizes the average levels of these determinants in the WBSCPS countries using only programs that are included in the estimations. Student characteristics are described in chapter 1, and the variation in some determinants across countries is discussed in chapter 3.

Categories of Quality Determinants

Based on previous research on what might constitute a good program,[4] the quality determinants are organized into six categories: infrastructure, curriculum and training, costs and financing, engagement with industry, faculty, and other practices related to admission, governance, and accreditation.

Infrastructure

Since SCPs provide practical training oriented toward specific occupations, they often need infrastructure and facilities such as labs, workshops, equipment, and internet access. They sometimes must provide classes online to adapt to students' needs.

Previous evidence from K–12 education suggests that interventions that only provide key educational inputs (such as textbooks, desks, or infrastructure) are overall ineffective to improve student learning. For higher education, and SCPs in particular, the evidence is very limited.[5] In general, SCPs in LAC have good infrastructure and materials for practical training. The average program has about 6.3 workshops for practice, and 73 percent of the programs report having enough materials in their labs. Almost 6 in 10 programs service their labs at least once per year.

Moreover, internet access provided by SCPs is almost universal in the survey. The data show that 92 percent of the programs provide internet access to faculty, students, or both. High internet access can benefit students' labor market outcomes. Previous evidence indicates that the current adoption of digital technologies across the LAC region is highly heterogeneous,[6] showing that there is still much potential for additional adoption in LAC and for the accompanying benefits of productivity and inclusive growth.

In addition, online delivery of classes and programs is of great importance for the flexibility it provides. Yet, studies in Colombia and the United States present mixed results on the effectiveness of higher education online programs compared with face-to-face instruction (see box 4.1).[7] A background paper written for this book (Cellini and Grueso 2020) indicates that, for SCPs in Colombia,

Box 4.1 Assessing the Effectiveness of Online and On-Campus SCPs in Colombia

Enrollment in higher education has expanded dramatically in Colombia in recent decades. It doubled between 2000 and 2013, partly due to the opening of new short-cycle programs (SCPs) and the expansion of existing ones (Ferreyra et al. 2017; Carranza and Ferreyra 2019). An important percentage of SCP students take classes online. According to the Colombian Ministry of Education, about 359,020 students were enrolled in some form of hybrid or fully online higher education in 2017 (bachelor's programs and SCPs), accounting for roughly 15 percent of the country's total enrollment in higher education (SNIES 2019).

The increased popularity of online education raises the question of its effectiveness. Despite the existence of several studies aiming to measure the effects of online education on student outcomes in Colombia, none of them has addressed the important issue of self-selection and thus, they do not provide causal estimates.

In a background paper for this book, Cellini and Grueso (2020) implement propensity score weighting methods to address self-election into on-campus and online SCPs, to estimate the effectiveness of online relative to face-to-face on-campus programs. The authors exploit the unique system of college exit exams in Colombia to compare student performance on the exit exam for online and on-campus students. Their data include many students, programs, and institutions.

Cellini and Grueso (2020) compare exam performance in quantitative analysis, reading, writing, and technical skills for students in online and on-campus SCPs. They find mixed results. First, in most institutions, online students appear to have significantly lower exit exam test scores (by about 0.04 standard deviation) than on-campus students, a result that holds for math, reading, and writing. These results are similar to the findings from Bettinger et al. (2017) using data from the United States.

However, after including institution fixed effects, the estimations indicate positive and significant test score gains from online enrollment by about 0.09 to 0.11 standard deviation. To explore how institutional characteristics might be affecting the results, the authors analyze the relative effect of online programs in two samples. The first includes all programs offered by the largest public vocational institution, the National Learning Service (SENA, *Servicio Nacional de Aprendizaje*), and the second contains all non-SENA programs. The estimations using the second sample indicate that online students perform worse than those enrolled in on-campus programs on exit exams by about 0.06 standard deviation. Yet, in the first sample, SENA students who take online classes have exit test scores that are about 0.169 standard deviation higher than SENA students taking only on-campus courses. This result holds and is remarkably consistent in magnitude even when differences are considered only within the same degree and major. In other words, online programs are more effective than on-campus programs at SENA, but they are less effective at non-SENA institutions.

Although Cellini and Grueso (2020) cannot rule out that SENA online students may be positively selected, interviews with SENA's staff at its Department of Training, Virtual and Distance Training Group suggest that their online programs might have features that make them more successful than other online programs. For example, most online SENA classes are synchronous, meaning that students are (virtually) face to face with an instructor rather than watching prerecorded videos. SENA classes make project-based learning central to the student experience.

certain design features make a difference. This is the case, for example, of synchronous teaching and opportunities for teacher-student interactions.[8]

In the WBSCPS, only 35 percent of the programs offer at least one online class as part of their curriculum. No conclusions can be drawn from the survey on how SCP providers in LAC adapted their teaching during the COVID-19 pandemic. However, it is highly likely that such low online provision would have complicated the transition to remote learning, and preliminary evidence suggests as much (see chapter 5).

Curriculum and Training

This category covers determinants related to the program's content—namely, the degree of flexibility in the curriculum (for instance, to take elective classes), the competencies that the program aims to develop, whether the program requires a mandatory internship, and the extent to which classes can count as credits for bachelor's programs.

Most of the SCPs in the sample have a fixed curriculum (70 percent). On average, the programs report devoting about half of the time to practical training. A flexible curriculum, if well implemented, could encourage students to establish their own goals within a certain structure. Yet, evidence from the United States shows that higher flexibility has unintended effects on students' outcomes.[9] Under what some authors call "the cafeteria model," in which students are expected to explore options with minimal or no guidance, students end up taking courses that are not coherently sequenced to master skills and knowledge relevant to their goals.

Results from the WBSCPS show that most programs claim to teach a variety of competencies, including numerical competencies and foreign languages. The programs update their curricula regularly, mostly trying to attend to the demands of employers.

In the survey, most of the directors reported that their students have important academic deficits (see chapter 1). However, these deficits could be addressed by the programs. As evidence from the United States shows, remedial education has positive effects on academic outcomes, such as early persistence in college.[10] About 91 percent of the directors surveyed in the WBSCPS reported that their programs offer some type of remediation, with 51 and 56 percent of the programs offering remediation before and during the SCP, respectively.

To promote practical training, some programs require a mandatory internship (61 percent), a professional or industry exit test (43 percent), or an independent research project (40 percent).

Costs and Financing

This category includes elements of the program's financial cost to the student, such as tuition, and the availability of funding options for students. As discussed in chapter 1, the SCPs are relatively affordable in some countries (Colombia, the Dominican Republic, and Ecuador) but less so in others (Brazil and Peru).

On average, the annual tuition is US$2,207 (PPP) and ranges between zero and US$25,516 (PPP).

Tuition can have important effects on enrollment, especially among nontraditional students. For example, evidence from the United States indicates that a reduction in community college tuition increased enrollment in those institutions in the first year after high school and increased transfers from community colleges to four-year institutions.[11]

The availability and type of financing instruments for students can have an impact on enrollment and students' outcomes. Evidence from the United States shows that linking financial aid with academic performance can improve grades and persistence.[12] Specifically, grants and loans can increase credits completed and grades in higher education.[13] In California, for instance, state-based financial aid has increased graduation and, for some student groups, has even raised annual earnings after graduation.[14]

As described in chapter 1, loans and scholarships from HEIs or governments are available in LAC, with scholarships being the most common source of financing aid for students. However, as documented in chapter 1, financing options reach very few students. This means that, for the most part, students cover tuition and other related expenses with their own resources. Perhaps this is why most of the directors reported that financial struggle is the main reason why students drop out. Moreover, less than 34 percent of the directors reported that their programs or institutions received additional funds from the government or industry.

Engagement with Industry

This category includes SCPs' practices that aim to connect the program with industry and students with the labor market. These determinants include the engagement of firms with curriculum design and updating, participation in the institution's governing body, and students' assessment. It also includes whether the program collects information on students' postgraduation employment or on employers' satisfaction, whether the program assigns staff to engage with industry, and how the program supports students in their job search.

Information from the survey shows that the programs relate to industry in multiple ways. Many programs have a person in charge of fostering private sector relations, such as a member of the board (84 percent). Other frequent practices are having firms represented on the HEI's governing board and collecting information about firms' needs or their satisfaction with program graduates.

The programs also engage with firms through agreements to provide internships to students, hire program graduates, train faculty, or provide program equipment for training. The share of directors reporting these types of agreements varies from 90 percent (agreements for internships) to 36 percent (agreements to train faculty).

The SCPs in the sample implement additional activities oriented to support their graduates' employability. The most frequent one is providing job market information to students, which is done by 81 percent of the programs. Eighty-three percent of the programs train students or coordinate with firms for job interviews, 76 percent collect data on the employment status of their graduates, and 63 percent run an onsite employment center.

Faculty

Although a large literature for K–12 education concludes that teaching practices are more effective predictors of student performance than teachers' characteristics (such as education and experience),[15] some of these characteristics seem to be associated with good outcomes for students in higher education. For example, evidence from Colombia documents that the share of full-time faculty is positively and significantly related to the graduation rate in universities.[16] Moreover, studies from the role models literature show that teachers' characteristics are associated with students' outcomes. For example, faculty or instructor gender impacts outcomes for female students.[17] Evidence from studies on higher education faculty suggests that personnel policies—which are largely underdeveloped in higher education—might be crucial for improving student learning.[18]

Considering this evidence, this section explores how faculty characteristics and practices are associated with SCP students' outcomes. The "faculty" category includes determinants such as faculty characteristics (for instance, gender and age) and practices related to faculty hiring, training, and evaluation.

In the survey, the average program has a faculty of about 20 professors or instructors, most of whom are highly educated and experienced. About 83 percent of the directors reported that most of their instructors have a bachelor's degree, and 48 percent reported that most have attended graduate programs. Most of the faculty members in the average program are part time and male, and more than half of the faculty has more than five years of industry experience. Not many are unionized, except in Brazil.

Almost all the directors reported assessing faculty performance. For faculty assessment, almost 65 percent of the programs reported that classroom observation or class planning are very important practices. However, only 34 percent of the programs reported that peer evaluations are a very relevant practice for faculty assessment. The programs also reported training their faculty: 55 percent of the surveyed directors reported that all or almost all their faculty received training in the previous year.

Other Practices

In addition to the quality determinants mapped to the five categories described, the programs implement other practices related to admission, governance, and high-quality certification processes. For admission requirements, 58 percent of the programs require a general or specific knowledge test, and 64 percent require a minimum high school grade point average or test score. Moreover, 52 percent of the programs require an interview.

Most programs (89 percent) reported having a governing board beyond the provost. While this practice has not been analyzed in the literature yet, a diverse governing body might voice the needs of different stakeholders (for example, students, faculty, and the private sector) in the design and implementation of program activities.

Finally, administrative data were collected to measure the share of programs that have gone through a high-quality accreditation process. Although having high-quality accreditation[19] can yield potential benefits to graduates' outcomes, the data from the survey show that only 20 percent of the programs have been accredited by local authorities.[20] Yet, almost 94 percent of the accredited SCP directors believe that accreditation has boosted their programs' reputation with industry.

Other Program, Institution, and Student Characteristics

The aim of this chapter is to estimate associations between programs' quality determinants and academic and labor market outcomes for graduates, after accounting for student characteristics, and to come as close as possible (given data limitations) to value-added contributions. To this end, information was collected on additional program, institution, and student characteristics, which is used to control the estimations for these elements.

The results from the survey show that the average program has a student body that consists mostly of male students, students who are younger than age 25, and part-time students. Most of the directors reported that students enter the programs with math, reading, and writing deficits. For example, 81 percent of the programs reported that math skills are lacking in incoming students. Finally, the directors indicated that the average HEI is 38 years old and offers programs in four cities.

Overall, the programs use good practices and have good inputs in terms of infrastructure, training and curriculum, costs and financing, engagement with industry, faculty, and other practices related to admission, graduation, and governance. However, there is much variation in these aspects among the programs (see annex 4A). This variation makes it possible to estimate the association between quality determinants and outcomes. At the same time, the variation is concerning because it indicates that many programs do not use good practices or inputs—which, as the next section shows, is associated with the variation in outcomes among programs.

Associations between SCP Quality Determinants and Student Outcomes

This section analyzes the extent to which the quality determinants described in the section titled "SCP Quality Determinants" are associated with the academic and labor market outcomes discussed in the section titled "Defining and Measuring SCP Quality." In other words, the section answers questions such as the following: Is the provision of job market information to students correlated with their dropout rate, extra time to graduate, formal employment, or wages? If so, how strong is the association?

The empirical strategy used to estimate these contributions or associations is described in box 4.2[21] and the results are summarized in figures 4.4 to 4.7. The values in the figures correspond only to the variables that showed a relevant correlation with the corresponding outcome (that is, the figures include only the associations that are statistically significant at the 10 percent level or less). The magnitudes of the coefficients are comparable within the figures, but they have different interpretations across the graphs, depending on the outcome under analysis. To approximate the estimations to a value-added approach, the main specifications include controls for student, program, and HEI characteristics, as described in box 4.2.

Academic Performance and Determinants of SCP Quality
Dropout Rate
Figure 4.4 summarizes the quality determinants associated with the dropout rate. The estimations show four determinants associated with lower dropout rates. The first one is related to the curriculum: programs with a fixed curriculum are more likely to have lower dropout rates. This result is in line with the literature from the United States, which finds evidence that programs with a completely

---

Box 4.2 Estimating the Contributions of the Quality Determinants to Academic and Labor Market Outcomes: A LASSO-Regression Approach

For estimating the contributions of the programs' practices and inputs to academic and labor market outcomes, the World Bank Short-Cycle Program Survey (WBSCPS) has the advantage of providing a large set of explanatory variables that can be assessed as potential quality determinants. However, the large number of explanatory variables posits two challenges. The first is selecting the "right" set of explanatory variables. On the one hand, using too few controls or the wrong ones may create omitted variable bias. On the other hand, using too many may lead to model overfitting. The second challenge is that the sample sizes in some countries are small. For instance, there are only 80 SCPs in the Dominican Republic. Since there might be more variables than observations, the model might not be identified.

The first challenge could be addressed by creating indexes within each of the five categories of determinants by using statistical techniques for data reduction, such as factor or principal components analyses. However, this technique requires interval-level data, a requirement not met by some of the survey variables. Moreover, the types of variables (interval level or dummy variables) would vary within each determinant, which would preclude the use of these techniques.

Hence, to address the challenges of selecting explanatory variables and potential underidentification or nonidentification of the model, the parameters of interest are estimated using the Least Absolute Shrinkage and Selection Operator (LASSO) technique. This is being used in

box continues next page

the literature for estimating parameters in linear models with several controls with the aim of improving model fit. Intuitively, LASSO throws out the variables that contribute little (or nothing) to the fit.

A two-stage process is followed. The first stage uses an adaptive LASSO methodology and estimates the following model for each outcome of interest:

$$y_{jc} = \alpha_0 + \sum_{d=1}^{6} \mathbf{Q}_{jc}^{d}{'}\alpha_1 + \mathbf{C}_{jc}{'}\alpha_2 + \phi_c + \epsilon_{jc}, \qquad \text{(B4.2.1)}$$

where y_{jc} represents the average academic (dropout rates and extra time to graduate) or labor market (formal employment and wages) outcome of interest for graduates from SCP j in country c. $\mathbf{Q}_{jc}^{d}$ is a vector that includes all the variables within each of the six quality determinant categories.

$\mathbf{C}_{jc}$ is a vector of control variables at the program and higher education institution (HEI) level. These controls are program or HEI characteristics that do not constitute a quality determinant, such as the number of years the HEI has been operating and program age, among others. Some of these characteristics (such as whether the HEI is for profit, public or private, or a university) are "fixed" in the first stage. That is, LASSO is "asked" to keep them as controls for the first and second stages. Other characteristics, including HEI age, number of branches, and student characteristics, are not fixed. In other words, they can be kept or dropped by the LASSO procedure.

The vector of coefficients α_1 corresponds to the associations between the outcome and each quality determinant. Similarly, the coefficients α_2 indicate the correlations between the control variables and the outcome. For the cross-country estimations, country fixed effects ϕ_c are included. Finally, ϵ_{jc} is the error term. In all the pooled (with all countries) and country-specific models, clustered standard errors are estimated at the HEI level.

Among all the quality determinants included in $\mathbf{Q}_{jc}^{d}$, LASSO calculates a "penalty" parameter that determines the set of variables that minimizes the out-of-sample minimum square error of the estimations. In this sense, LASSO conducts a data-driven selection of the set of determinants, $\mathbf{Q}^*$, that provides the best fit to the data.

In the second stage, each outcome of interest y_{jc} is regressed on the set of selected determinants and the following equation is estimated:

$$y_{jc} = \beta_0 + \sum_{d=1}^{6} \mathbf{Q}_{jc}^{*d}{'}\beta_1 + \mathbf{N}_{jc}{'}\beta_2 + \gamma_c + \omega_{jc}, \qquad \text{(B4.2.2)}$$

where $\mathbf{N}_{jc}$ is a vector of control variables at the program and HEI level that are fixed by LASSO during the first stage and kept for the second stage; for this second one, γ_c corresponds to country fixed effects, and ω_{jc} is the error term. The rest of the variables are defined as previously.

Equation B4.2.2 is estimated using ordinary least squares for the dropout rate, extra time to graduate, and wages, and probit is used for formal employment. The estimated parameters of interest are in vector $\widehat{\beta}_1$, which reflects the association between the quality determinants and outcomes in the sample. As in the first stage, in all the cross-country and country-specific models, clustered standard errors are estimated at the HEI level.

Figure 4.4 Associations between SCP Quality Determinants and Dropout Rates

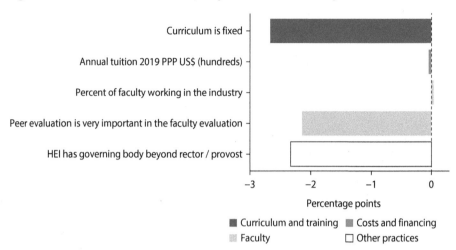

Source: Dinarte et al. (2021).
Note: The figure shows the change in the dropout rate associated with quality determinants (in percentage points). The estimation was done using only programs for which the dropout rate can be calculated and that have data on all the quality determinants. The average dropout rate for this set of programs is 14.1 percent. All variables are dummies except when noted. HEI = higher education institution; PPP = purchasing power parity; SCP = short-cycle program. A positive change denotes worsening; a negative change indicates improvement in dropout rates.

flexible curriculum can negatively affect student outcomes such as further education and employment.[22]

The second determinant associated with (slightly) lower dropout rates is related to costs. SCPs with higher tuition present lower dropout rates. One possible explanation is that higher tuition makes a student more likely to graduate to recuperate her investment. Another possible explanation is that higher tuition captures unmeasured aspects of program quality (for instance, lab quality or library size) that help the student graduate.

The third determinant pertains to faculty assessment. Programs in which teachers are evaluated by their peers exhibit lower dropout rates than programs that do not use this practice. Evidence on faculty evaluations in higher education shows that peer review is positively accepted and perceived as promoting good teaching practices.[23] As teachers receive feedback from peers on their teaching performance, they can improve the learning environment, which might help students complete the program.[24] Interestingly, the association between the dropout rate and peer evaluations in faculty assessments is driven by private HEIs (see figure 4B.1, in annex 4B).

The fourth determinant associated with lower dropout rates is the presence of a governing body beyond the provost or rector. A potential explanation is that the participation of stakeholders from different sectors—including faculty, students, and industry—allows programs to consider demands and needs from all of them, thereby adapting their training and curricula to help students graduate.

The analysis also finds that one faculty characteristic is slightly associated with higher dropout rates: the share of faculty working in industry. Anecdotal evidence suggests that faculty working in industry sometimes invite their students to work with them on specific industry projects while still enrolled in the program. Although this can increase their employability in the long term, it also restricts the time they can devote to the program, increasing their dropout probability.[25]

In sum, the analysis suggests that a fixed curriculum and having a governing body beyond the provost are associated with the largest dropout rate reductions. Having a fixed curriculum is the practice associated with the greatest reduction in the dropout rate (2.7 percentage points). Considering that the average program's dropout rate is 14.1 percent, having a fixed curriculum is associated with a 19.1 percent reduction in the average dropout rate. Although the analysis cannot establish that a fixed curriculum will lead to a reduction in the dropout rate, the association is nonetheless informative.

Dropout rates do not differ by administration type (public or private) according to WBSCPS data. After accounting for all the quality determinants and other HEI and program characteristics, there are no statistically significant differences in average dropout rates between public and private HEIs.

Extra Time to Graduate

Figure 4.5 shows that three determinants are associated with *lower* extra time to graduate (ETG). First, SCPs that have a higher share of faculty with industry experience have a (slightly) lower ETG. As these faculty may translate their know-how and expertise into more practical training, students may be more

Figure 4.5 Associations between SCP Quality Determinants and Extra Time to Graduate

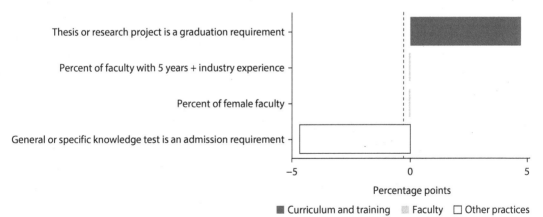

Source: Dinarte et al. (2021).
Note: The figure shows the change in the extra time to graduate relative to the official duration of the program that is associated with the quality determinants (in percentage points). The estimation was done using only programs for which data were available on program duration, average time to degree for the last cohort of graduates, and all the quality determinants. Average extra time to graduate for this set of programs is 18.6 percent. All variables are dummies except when noted. A positive change denotes worsening; a negative change indicates improvement in the outcome. SCP = short-cycle program.

motivated to learn and complete the program on time. Indeed, programs with a higher share of faculty with industry experience tend to be those whose students view training quality as the most important program feature, suggesting that those faculty enhance training quality.[26]

A second faculty characteristic associated with lower ETG is the share of female faculty. SCPs with a higher share of female faculty are (slightly) more likely to have cohorts that graduate on time. Existing evidence in the literature shows that the presence of female faculty can positively affect academic outcomes for female students.[27] Indeed, in the WBSCPS, programs with a higher share of female faculty also have a higher share of female students.

Requiring an admission test of general or specific knowledge is the third determinant associated with lower ETG. This association is driven by public HEIs (see figure 4B.2, in annex 4B), which are more likely than private HEIs to apply admission requirements. Among all the determinants, this practice has the largest association with ETG (4.8 percentage points). Choosing whom to admit presumably allows the program to choose the students best suited to the program and who will thus finish sooner. This finding is in line with evidence that students in SCPs taught by more "selective" institutions have better outcomes than those in less selective institutions (although, as discussed in chapter 1, SCPs are usually not selective in a conventional sense).[28]

On the flip side, SCPs that require a thesis as a graduation requirement have a *higher* ETG. On average, requiring a thesis for graduation is associated with an increase of 4.8 percentage points in ETG. Considering an average ETG of 18.6 percent, this determinant can increase the ETG by 26 percent. In the survey, this practice is more common in public HEIs and for the education, humanities, and social science fields. This finding calls into question the suitability of a thesis as a graduation requirement for higher education programs with a stronger practical focus, like SCPs.

Overall, the results of the associations between the quality determinants and ETG indicate that an entry exam is associated with a substantially lower ETG, while requiring a thesis for graduation is associated with substantially higher ETG.

Labor Market Outcomes and Determinants of SCP Quality
Employment in the Formal Sector
Figure 4.6 summarizes the estimated associations between the quality determinants and the probability of having almost all graduates employed in the formal sector. For simplicity, this outcome is called "formal employment."

Formal employment is associated with determinants in all the categories. First, two determinants of infrastructure for practical training are associated with formal employment. The results suggest that graduates from programs with internet available for faculty and students and those that provide enough equipment and materials for practice have higher formal employment. As these inputs complement practical training, students may be better prepared for the labor market.

Figure 4.6 Associations between SCP Quality Determinants and Formal Employment

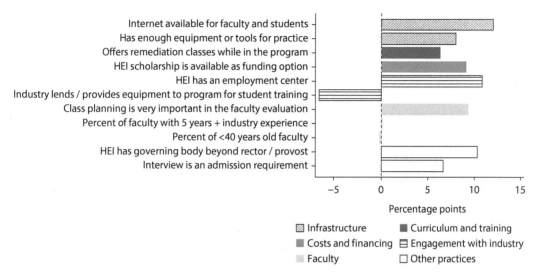

Source: Dinarte et al. (2021).
Note: The figure shows the change in the average probability that almost all graduates obtain formal employment (in percentage points) that is associated with the quality determinants. The estimation was done using only programs for which data were available on the probability that almost all graduates obtain formal employment and all the quality determinants. On average, 58 percent of the SCPs report that almost all their graduates are working in the formal sector. All variables are dummies except when noted. A positive coefficient denotes improvement; a negative association indicates worsening of the outcome. GPA = grade point average; HEI = higher education institution; SCP = short-cycle program.

Providing onsite internet access is associated with higher formal employment as well—presumably by facilitating students' job search.

A second category of determinants associated with formal employment pertains to the curriculum category. Graduates from SCPs providing remediation support during the program (as opposed to not having it or having it before the program only) have higher formal employment rates. Conditional on completing the program, these classes seem to strengthen students' training.

There is also a determinant associated with higher formal employment from a third category: costs and financing. Graduates from SCPs where students use HEI scholarships are more likely to be formally employed. As financial restrictions are eased by the availability of HEI scholarships, students are more likely to focus on completing their coursework and practical training, thereby consolidating their skill sets and improving their formal employment prospects.

The fourth category of determinants associated with higher formal employment is engagement with industry. There are mixed results here. On the one hand, programs in HEIs with an employment center report higher formal employment for their graduates. This is aligned to evidence that technical training, complemented with customized job search assistance, improves employment outcomes.[29] On the other hand, programs that have agreements allowing students' use of firms' equipment for practical training report lower formal employment for their graduates. The literature finds that successful vocational training includes well-designed contracts between training providers and local employers.[30] Agreements that just allow students to use equipment might entail too little industry commitment and detract from other types of agreements.

Fifth, there are positive associations between faculty characteristics and formal employment. Programs with a higher share of faculty with industry experience report (slightly) higher graduates' formal employment. In contrast, a higher share of young faculty is associated with (slightly) lower formal employment. Faculty with industry experience presumably know which skills are most relevant in the labor market and teach them, while young faculty may not be experienced enough for students' needs.[31] Moreover, programs where faculty evaluation depends highly on class planning report higher formal employment.

Finally, there are positive associations between the "other practices" category and formal employment. Requiring an interview for admission is associated with higher graduates' formal employment. As the literature shows, selectivity can be associated with better employment outcomes.[32]

Two key lessons can be drawn from these findings. First, at least one practice from each quality determinant category seems to be positively associated with formal employment. Among these determinants, providing internet access to faculty and students is associated with the largest increase in formal employment (about 12 percentage points).

Second, some practices can have unintended effects on formal employment when they are substituting for others that may be more effective at improving graduates' employability. For example, agreements with industry in which firms play a passive role, such as allowing students to use firms' equipment, may be possibly substituting other forms of agreements where industry is more engaged, such as providing internship opportunities.

After accounting for quality determinants and other program and HEI characteristics, there is no association between administration type (public or private) and formal employment rates. Moreover, some associations between the quality determinants and employment in the formal sector are similar for public and private institutions (see figure 4B.3, in annex 4B). Such is the case of the association between faculty evaluation based on class planning and formal employment.

Wages

Figure 4.7 summarizes the main results on the associations between wages and the SCP quality determinants. Eight program determinants are associated with higher wages.

As with formal employment, the salaries reported for graduates from programs with sufficient materials for practical training—regardless of enrollment—are high compared with those reported for graduates from other programs. More opportunities for practical training may be providing students additional skills that are rewarded in the labor market through higher salaries.

Figure 4.7 Associations between SCP Quality Determinants and Graduates' Wages

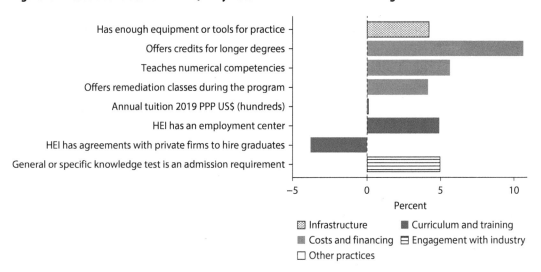

Source: Dinarte et al. (2021).
Note: The figure shows the percentage change in reported average wages that is associated with the quality determinants. The change associated with variable X is calculated as (*exp(coefficient on X)*-1)* 100. The estimation was done using only programs for which data were available on wages and all the quality determinants. The average wage of graduates for this set of programs (PPP adjusted) is US$10,435. All variables are dummies except when noted. A positive change indicates an increase in wages, whereas a negative change indicates a reduction in graduates' wages. HEI = higher education institution; PPP = purchasing power parity; SCP = short-cycle program

Three determinants from program curriculum and training are positively associated with higher salaries. They consist of providing credits for students' further education, teaching numerical competencies, and assisting poorly prepared students.

Graduates from SCPs that offer credits for bachelor's degrees earn higher salaries according to directors' reports. Employers might value the fact that if their employees wanted to pursue a bachelor's degree, they would not need to start from scratch—something that might lead them to quit the job. Alternatively, credits for bachelor's degrees might only be given by high-reputation programs, in which case this positive association might reflect the payoff to program reputation.

Offering remediation to poorly prepared students during the program is associated with higher graduates' wages. As recent evidence shows, students who receive remedial education are more likely to persist in college.[33] By remediating students' deficits, these programs may be enabling them to learn more over the course of their studies and obtain higher salaries after graduation. And in line with findings from *World Development Report 2019: Changing the Nature of Work* in terms of skills, results indicate that graduates from programs that teach numerical competencies seem to be more likely to earn higher wages than graduates from programs that do not teach them.

In addition, a determinant related to costs and financing is associated with higher salaries. Higher annual tuition is associated with higher salaries after graduation, perhaps because programs with a higher reputation might charge higher tuition. Alternatively, higher tuition might provide resources to improve program quality—for instance, by hiring better trained faculty, upgrading infrastructure, or providing more student services, all of which might enhance skill formation and contribute to higher graduates' wages.

As with formal employment, there are mixed associations between wages and determinants related to engagement with industry. On the one hand, graduates from programs or institutions with an employment center have reported higher salaries than those from programs without this service, a result that is aligned with evidence that job search assistance improves employment outcomes.[34] On the other hand, programs that have agreements with firms to hire their graduates report lower wages among their graduates. Those agreements might create a trade-off: although the firms agree to hire the graduates, they do so at a lower wage.[35]

The association between the type of administration (public or private) and wages is not statistically significant when accounting for all the other determinants. However, the estimations show that most of the associations between the determinants and wages are driven by private HEIs (see figure 4B.4, in annex 4B). That is, although governance type (public or private) per se is not associated with wages, the relationship between the quality determinants and wages is different for public and private programs.

So far, the chapter has reported findings using program-level data from the WBSCPS. In an ideal setting, the outcomes would be gauged from individual-level administrative data. At the time of writing this report, Brazil was the only country for which data were accessible. Box 4.3 describes the use of these data to estimate the contributions of program characteristics and practices to student outcomes for Brazil. The estimates show that specific quality determinants—such as providing labor market information and receiving a high grade from the regulating authorities—as well as some characteristics, such as program size and HEI type, are associated with students' academic and labor market outcomes.

Box 4.3 Quality Determinants and Value Added: The Case of Brazil

As discussed in "Defining and Measuring SCP Quality," a possible measure of program quality is value added to student outcomes. The estimation of value added requires detailed data at the individual level on all the elements that could affect student outcomes, to disentangle the contributions of all the inputs involved, including student background characteristics and ability, peer background and ability, and others.

Such data were obtained for Brazil, specifically the states included in the World Bank Short-Cycle Program Survey, São Paulo and Ceará. Data from several sources were merged: the Annual Reports of Social Information (*Relação Anual de Informações Sociais*, RAIS), a matched employer-employee data set of all workers and firms in the formal sector; the Higher

---

box continues next page

Box 4.3 Quality Determinants and Value Added: The Case of Brazil *(continued)*

Education Census; and the National Educational Entrance Examination (ENEM, *Exame Nacional de Ensino Médio*), the national assessment taken by students at the end of secondary education. In addition to test scores, ENEM includes student and family characteristics. Thus, the data set contains detailed information on academic readiness for higher education and socioeconomic background for the student and her peers, as well as labor market outcomes (wages and employment) for short-cycle program (SCP) graduates who are employed in the formal sector after graduation.

With these data, a two-stage approach is used to estimate program-level contributions net of the contributions made by the student herself and her peers. Three outcomes are considered for SCP graduates: graduation, employment in the formal sector, and wages. In the first stage, following the background paper by Ferreyra et al. (2020), the following model is estimated:

$$Y_{ijt}^k = \boldsymbol{R}_i^{k\,\prime}\alpha_1 + \boldsymbol{Z}_{ijt}^{k\,\prime}\alpha_2 + \hat{u}_j^k + \in_{ijt}^k, \tag{B4.3.1}$$

where Y_{ijt}^k is the outcome of interest, $k = \{1,2,3\}$, for student i, in program j, and cohort t. $\boldsymbol{R}_i^k$ includes individual characteristics, such as ENEM score, gender, age, socioeconomic status, and parental education. $\boldsymbol{Z}_{ijt}^k$ is a vector of peers' characteristics, including average ENEM score, age, socioeconomic status, and parental education of student i's peers. Finally, u_j^k is program fixed effects. The vector of fixed effects estimates ($\hat{u}$) constitutes the main vector of interest from the first stage—the estimated program-level contributions (the application of this methodology to Colombia is described in chapter 2).

In the second stage, the vector $\hat{u}$ is merged with the program characteristics collected through the World Bank Short-Cycle Program Survey (WBSCPS). Then the Least Absolute Shrinkage and Selection Operator (LASSO) approach is implemented to identify the determinants that jointly explain the most variation in $\hat{u}$ (see box 4.2).

The results show that SCP graduation rates in Brazil are associated with one important determinant and two program or higher education institution (HEI) characteristics (see figure B4.3.1). Programs that received a high grade from the regulator the previous year and those provided by universities have higher graduation rates. Moreover, graduation rates are higher for programs with higher enrollment.

Formal employment is higher for programs that provide labor market information for students, aligned with findings from the WBSCPS. Interestingly, offering online classes has a negative association with graduates' formal employment, aligned with Ferreyra et al.'s (2020) findings for SCPs in large cities in Colombia.

The results for wages show that the single determinant that makes a sizable contribution is having a high grade from the regulator. How can this result be explained? As discussed in chapter 1, the National Institute of Educational Research and Studies (INEP, *Instituto Nacional de Estudos e Pesquisas Educacionais Anísio Teixeira*) evaluates programs annually in Brazil. For this evaluation, INEP uses data from the National Higher Education Assessment System, which assigns a Preliminary Course Score (CPC, *Conceito Preliminar de Curso*) to each program based on multiple indicators. These are related to program inputs and value added to student learning but not labor market outcomes.

box continues next page

Box 4.3 Quality Determinants and Value Added: The Case of Brazil (continued)

The General Course Index (IGC, *Índice Geral de Cursos*) score is a summary at the HEI level of other indicators, including the corresponding CPCs. Hence, the IGC score is a general indicator of HEI quality. Due to data availability, the IGC is used and a program is defined as has having a high grade if it is in the top quartile of the IGC score distribution for all programs in the WBSCPS universes of São Paulo and Ceará. Considering that the IGC reflects some program determinants, including inputs and potentially practices, it is not surprising that it is the only determinant associated with program value added to wages.

Do these findings mean that all regulatory evaluations (such as the CPC, IGC, and accreditation processes) have the ability to identify programs that make positive contributions to labor market outcomes? Not necessarily—it depends on the evaluation structure and content. When well designed, these evaluations should indeed identify high value-added programs. In the case of Brazil, the evaluations seem to be fulfilling that role.

Figure B4.3.1. SCP Quality Determinants and SCP Value Added in Brazil

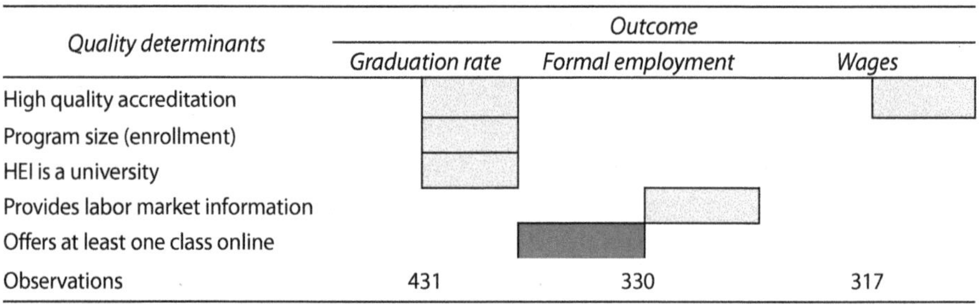

Quality determinants	Outcome		
	Graduation rate	Formal employment	Wages
High quality accreditation	▭		▭
Program size (enrollment)	▭		
HEI is a university	▭		
Provides labor market information		▭	
Offers at least one class online		▮	
Observations	431	330	317

Source: World Bank calculations based on Dinarte et al. (2021).
Note: The figure presents a summary of the quality determinants that are correlated with value-added estimates of graduation rate, formal employment, and wages. Green indicates that the feature "improves" the outcome, while red indicates that the feature "worsens" the outcome. HEI = higher education institution; SCP = short-cycle program.

Conclusions

In the literature, little is known about what determines SCP quality—namely, the program practices, inputs, and characteristics that contribute to good outcomes for the graduates. The rich data collected by the WBSCPS provide a unique opportunity to make inroads into this issue. As described in this chapter, specific determinants that might be adopted by a program and specific program, student, and HEI characteristics are associated with better academic and labor market outcomes for graduates.

The variation in determinants among programs is useful to researchers because it enables estimating the correlations of the determinants with student outcomes. At the same time, it is concerning from the point of view of policy. That specific practices, inputs, and characteristics are associated with good outcomes indicates that programs that do not have such elements may also not have the associated good outcomes. In other words, at least some of the large variation in returns among SCPs documented in chapter 2 could be related to the variation in program determinants. Improving outcomes to eliminate the lower tail requires, at least to some extent, the adoption of good practices such as those documented in this chapter.

Two final caveats are in order. First, a negative association between a determinant and an outcome does not indicate that the determinant is undesirable. Nonetheless, it indicates the need to focus on certain specific determinants and assess how it fits with the program's goals. For example. the results do not mean that having agreements with industry to hire graduates are unwanted, but they do indicate that understanding how these agreements are related to the program's outcomes is of greatest importance.

Second, while this chapter cannot claim to have identified the program determinants that make one program better than another, these findings—the first of their kind—are still of great interest. They could inform regulation and oversight mechanisms to ensure that good practices are more frequently adopted and reported by programs and institutions. They could also inform the design and replication of high-quality SCPs—which are ultimately the only ones capable of realizing the SCP promise. Finally, the findings could inspire more detailed and nuanced collection of data on programs and institutions, which would provide more information on these practices and characteristics than is typically found in administrative data. Ideally, the findings would encourage education authorities to build more effective data collection systems and facilitate merging various administrative data sets, an endeavor that would yield much deeper insights on the quality of higher education.

Annexes

Annex 4A. Quality Determinants and Outcomes

Table 4A.1 Descriptive Statistics

Panel A. Quality Determinant Categories	Mean	Median	SD	Min	Max
Curriculum and training					
Curriculum is fixed	0.70	1.00	0.46	0.00	1.00
Teaches numerical competencies	0.80	1.00	0.40	0.00	1.00
Teaches reading and writing competencies	0.97	1.00	0.18	0.00	1.00
Teaches foreign language	0.62	1.00	0.48	0.00	1.00
Teaches communication competencies	0.99	1.00	0.08	0.00	1.00
Offers remediation classes before starting the program	0.51	1.00	0.50	0.00	1.00
Offers remediation classes during the program	0.56	1.00	0.50	0.00	1.00
Test required for graduation	0.43	0.00	0.49	0.00	1.00
Thesis or research project is a graduation requirement	0.40	0.00	0.49	0.00	1.00
Second language is a graduation requirement	0.12	0.00	0.32	0.00	1.00
Offers credits for longer degrees	0.90	1.00	0.30	0.00	1.00
Curriculum updated more often than the median time	0.70	1.00	0.46	0.00	1.00

table continues next page

Table 4A.1 Descriptive Statistics *(continued)*

Panel A. Quality Determinant Categories	Mean	Median	SD	Min	Max
More than once per year: analyze student performance to solve problems	0.88	1.00	0.33	0.00	1.00
More than once per year: collect student satisfaction data	0.71	1.00	0.45	0.00	1.00
Time assigned to practical training (%)	46.80	50.00	16.67	0.00	90.00
Internships outside institution are mandatory	0.61	1.00	0.49	0.00	1.00
Infrastructure					
Program offers at least one online class	0.35	0.00	0.48	0.00	1.00
> 30% of classes can be taken online	0.16	0.00	0.37	0.00	1.00
Internet available for faculty and students	0.92	1.00	0.27	0.00	1.00
Number of workshops / labs available for practice	6.33	4.00	7.30	0.00	76.00
Has more labs than the median in the country	0.60	1.00	0.49	0.00	1.00
Has enough materials for practice	0.73	1.00	0.45	0.00	1.00
Costs and financing					
Annual tuition 2019 PPP US$ (hundreds)	22.07	22.44	18.19	0.00	255.16
HEI scholarship is available as funding option	0.79	1.00	0.41	0.00	1.00
Government scholarship is available as funding option	0.64	1.00	0.48	0.00	1.00
Loan by HEI is available as a funding option	0.29	0.00	0.45	0.00	1.00
HEI has received funding from government	0.34	0.00	0.47	0.00	1.00
HEI has received funding from private sector	0.20	0.00	0.40	0.00	1.00
Faculty					
Number of faculty	19.80	14.00	18.96	1.00	200.00
Percent of full-time faculty	38.65	31.25	30.16	0.00	100.00
Percent of faculty < age 40 years	40.51	35.71	29.25	0.00	100.00
Percent of female faculty	34.63	30.77	23.21	0.00	100.00
Percent of faculty with T&T degree	19.93	5.71	29.90	0.00	100.00
Percent of faculty with BA degree	83.03	100.00	28.83	0.00	100.00
Percent of faculty with graduate degree	47.70	41.67	32.21	0.00	100.00
Percent of faculty with 5+ years of experience	56.27	57.14	33.68	0.00	100.00
Percent of faculty working in the industry	42.58	37.50	31.32	0.00	100.00
Important for hiring faculty: practical experience	0.88	1.00	0.33	0.00	1.00
Important for hiring faculty: classroom experience	0.91	1.00	0.28	0.00	1.00
Classroom observation is very important in faculty evaluation	0.65	1.00	0.48	0.00	1.00
Class planning is very important in faculty evaluation	0.65	1.00	0.48	0.00	1.00
Student evaluation is very important in faculty evaluation	0.75	1.00	0.44	0.00	1.00
Students' and peers' informal comments are very important in faculty evaluation	0.34	0.00	0.47	0.00	1.00
Peer evaluation is very important in faculty evaluation	0.34	0.00	0.48	0.00	1.00
Almost all or all faculty participated in professional training last year	0.55	1.00	0.50	0.00	1.00
Engagement with industry					
More than once per year: collect data on employment or employers' satisfaction	0.59	1.00	0.49	0.00	1.00
More than once per year: communicate with local firms about their needs	0.54	1.00	0.50	0.00	1.00

table continues next page

Table 4A.1 Descriptive Statistics *(continued)*

Panel A. Quality Determinant Categories	*Mean*	*Median*	*SD*	*Min*	*Max*
Industry participates in evaluating students' skills design	0.71	1.00	0.45	0.00	1.00
Industry has internship agreements with HEI	0.90	1.00	0.29	0.00	1.00
Industry has agreements with HEI to hire program grads	0.39	0.00	0.49	0.00	1.00
Industry has agreements to train faculty	0.36	0.00	0.48	0.00	1.00
Industry lends or provides equipment to the program for student training	0.51	1.00	0.50	0.00	1.00
In charge of relations with industry: member of the board	0.84	1.00	0.36	0.00	1.00
In charge of relations with private sector: whoever is available	0.07	0.00	0.26	0.00	1.00
HEI trains students or coordinates with firms for job interviews	0.83	1.00	0.37	0.00	1.00
HEI has agreements with private firms to hire graduates	0.50	0.00	0.50	0.00	1.00
HEI has an employment center	0.63	1.00	0.48	0.00	1.00
HEI provides job market information	0.81	1.00	0.39	0.00	1.00
Program has staff assigned to collect grads' employment data	0.76	1.00	0.43	0.00	1.00
Other practices					
High-quality accreditation	0.19	0	0.39	0	1
General or specific knowledge test is an admission requirement	0.58	1.00	0.49	0.00	1.00
Interview is an admission requirement	0.52	1.00	0.50	0.00	1.00
Minimum scores in high school GPA or national entry test is an admission requirement	0.64	1.00	0.48	0.00	1.00
HEI has a governing body beyond rector provost	0.89	1.00	0.32	0.00	1.00
Panel B. Other program, institution, and student characteristics					
HEI age	38.01	32.00	31.33	1.00	300.00
Number of cities where the HEI offers the program	4.04	1.00	14.79	1.00	401.00
Percentage of full-time students is greater than median	0.47	0.00	0.50	0.00	1.00
Percentage of students > age 25 years greater than median	0.47	0.00	0.50	0.00	1.00
Percentage of female students greater than median	0.47	0.00	0.50	0.00	1.00
Mathematics is lacking in incoming students	0.81	1.00	0.39	0.00	1.00
Reading is lacking in incoming students	0.69	1.00	0.46	0.00	1.00
Oral expression is lacking in incoming students	0.56	1.00	0.50	0.00	1.00
Writing is lacking in incoming students	0.67	1.00	0.47	0.00	1.00
Panel C. Outcomes					
Dropout rate (%)	14.06	10.00	13.08	0.00	75.00
Extra time to degree (%)	18.56	16.67	27.14	-60.00	200.00
Almost all graduates employed in formal sector	0.58	1.00	0.49	0.00	1.00
Average annual wage (first job) – (US$ PPP)	10,434.86	9,763.74	3,242.97	5,000.88	22,782.06

Source: Dinarte et al. (2021).
Note: The table presents descriptive statistics of the main variables used in the analysis. Panel A presents the variables in each of the quality determinant categories. Panels B and C summarize the statistics for other characteristics and main outcomes used in the analysis, respectively. The sample used in this table has been restricted to *programs* that are included in the estimations. Variables are binary unless indicated otherwise. BA = bachelor's; GPA = grade point average; HEI = higher education institution; Max = maximum; Min = minimum; PPP = purchasing power parity; SD = standard deviation; T&T = teaching and technology.

Table 4A.2 Summary of Results

Categories	Quality determinants	Dropout rate	Time to graduate	Formal employment	Wages
Infrastructure	Internet available for faculty and students			improves	
	Has enough materials for practice			improves	improves
Training and curriculum	Curriculum is fixed	improves			
	Teaches numerical competencies				improves
	Offers credits for longer degrees				improves
	Offers remediation classes during the program			improves	
	Thesis or research project is a graduation requirement		worsens		
Costs	Annual tuition 2019 PPP US$ (hundreds)	improves			improves
	HEI scholarship is available as funding option			improves	
Link with industry	HEI has an employment center			improves	improves
	Industry lends/provides equipment for student training			worsens	
	HEI has agreements with firms to hire graduates				worsens
Faculty	Peer evaluation is very important in faculty evaluation	improves			
	Class planning is very important in the faculty evaluation			improves	
	Percentage of faculty working in industry	worsens			
	Percentage of female faculty		improves		
	Percentage of faculty with 5+years of experience		improves	improves	
	Percentage of faculty < age 40 years			worsens	
Other practices	General or specific knowledge test is an admission requirement		improves		improves
	Interview is an admission requirement			improves	
	HEI has a governing body beyond rector/provost	improves		improves	

Source: World Bank calculations based on Dinarte et al. (2021).
Note: The table presents a summary of the results on the correlates of the quality determinants and program academic and labor market outcomes. Green indicates that the feature "improves" the outcome, while red indicates that the feature "worsens" the outcome. HEI = higher education institution; HS GPA = high school grade point average; PPP = purchasing power parity.

Annex 4B. Quality Determinants of Short-Cycle Programs, by Type of Higher Education Institution

Figure 4B.1 Dropout Rate and Quality Determinants

Quality determinants	Type of administration	
	Private	Public
Peer evaluation is important in the faculty evaluation		
HEI has a governing body beyond rector/provost		
Curriculum is fixed		
Percentage of faculty working in the industry		
Programs	750	430
Average dropout rate	13.8	15.5

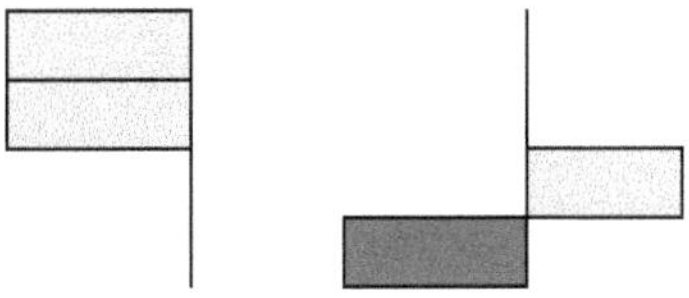

Source: World Bank calculations based on Dinarte et al. (2021).
Note: The figure presents a summary of the quality determinants that are correlated with dropout rates, separated by type of administration. Green indicates that the feature "improves" the outcome, while red indicates that the feature "worsens" the outcome. HEI = higher education institution.

Figure 4B.2 Extra Time to Degree and Quality Determinants

Quality determinants	Type of administration	
	Private	Public
Percentage of faculty with 5+ years of experience		
General or specific knowledge test is an admission requirement		
Thesis or research project is a graduation requirement		
Observations	770	382
Average ETG	16.6	21.5

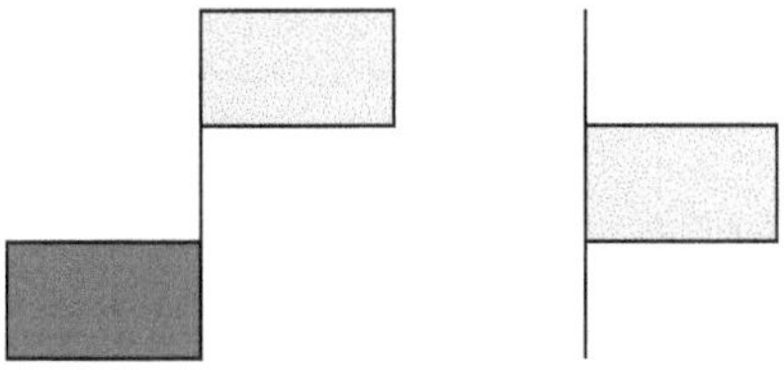

Source: World Bank calculations based on Dinarte et al. (2021).
Note: The figure presents a summary of the quality determinants that are correlated with the percentage of extra time to graduate relative to the theoretical duration of the program, separated by type of administration. Green indicates that the feature "improves" the outcome, while red indicates that the feature "worsens" the outcome. ETG = extra time to graduate.

Figure 4B.3 Formal Employment and Quality Determinants

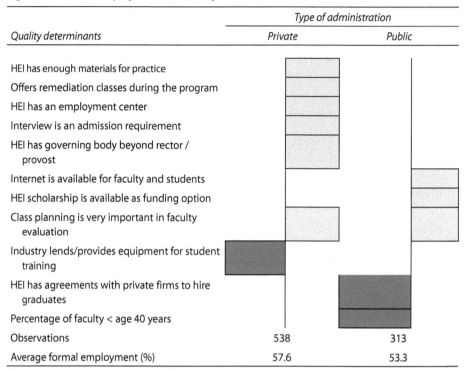

Quality determinants	Type of administration	
	Private	Public
HEI has enough materials for practice		
Offers remediation classes during the program		
HEI has an employment center		
Interview is an admission requirement		
HEI has governing body beyond rector / provost		
Internet is available for faculty and students		
HEI scholarship is available as funding option		
Class planning is very important in faculty evaluation		
Industry lends/provides equipment for student training		
HEI has agreements with private firms to hire graduates		
Percentage of faculty < age 40 years		
Observations	538	313
Average formal employment (%)	57.6	53.3

Note: The figure presents a summary of the quality determinants that are correlated with the probability of graduates being employed in the formal sector, separated by type of administration. Green indicates that the feature "improves" the outcome, while red indicates that the feature "worsens" the outcome. HEI = higher education institution.

Figure 4B.4 Wages and Quality Determinants

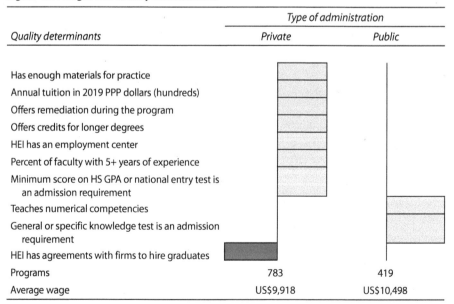

Quality determinants	Type of administration	
	Private	Public
Has enough materials for practice		
Annual tuition in 2019 PPP dollars (hundreds)		
Offers remediation during the program		
Offers credits for longer degrees		
HEI has an employment center		
Percent of faculty with 5+ years of experience		
Minimum score on HS GPA or national entry test is an admission requirement		
Teaches numerical competencies		
General or specific knowledge test is an admission requirement		
HEI has agreements with firms to hire graduates		
Programs	783	419
Average wage	US$9,918	US$10,498

Source: World Bank calculations based on Dinarte et al. (2021).
Note: The figure presents a summary of the quality determinants that are correlated with wages, separated by type of administration. Green indicates that the feature "improves" the outcome, while red indicates that the feature "worsens" the outcome. HS GPA = high school grade point average; HEI = higher education institution; PPP = purchasing power parity.

Notes

The authors gratefully acknowledge the superb research assistance of Gabriel Suarez and Angelica Sánchez.

1. In December 2020, the team was granted access to individual data on salaries and employment from the Dominican Republic and Ecuador. Only Brazil granted access in time for writing this book. The results for all three countries will be available in the background paper by Dinarte et al. (2021).

2. In the report "Out of School and Out of Work," De Hoyos, Popova, and Rogers (2016) compare Latin America with other regions and estimate that LAC is the region with the largest concentration of *ninis* among households in the bottom 40 percent of the income distribution.

3. See Melguizo et al. (2017) and Ferreyra et al. (2020), a background paper for this book.

4. See, among others, Bailey (2015), Cellini and Grueso (2020), Deming et al. (2015), Denning (2017), Dynarski and Scott-Clayton (2013), and Bettinger et al. (2017).

5. Dobbie and Fryer (2013) collected data on the inner workings of 39 charter schools; they correlate these data with school effectiveness. They find that traditionally collected input measures are not correlated with school effectiveness. See also Hanushek (1997) and Krueger (2003).

6. See Dutz, Almeida, and Packard (2018). They demonstrate with economic theory and data from Argentina, Brazil, Chile, Colombia, and Mexico that lower skilled workers can benefit from adoption of productivity-enhancing technologies biased toward skilled workers, and often do.

7. See specifically the studies by Bettinger et al. (2017) and Cellini and Grueso (2020).

8. Jaggars and Xu (2016) examine the relationship between four online course design features and student course grades and find that the quality of online interpersonal interaction is positively related to students' grades.

9. Bailey (2015) defines the *cafeteria* or *self-service* community college model as one in which students are left to navigate often complex and ill-defined pathways mostly on their own.

10. Calcagno and Long (2009) use data from community colleges in Florida and find that remediation might promote early persistence in college. Yet, the paper concludes that additional effort is needed to estimate the impact of remedial courses on weaker students who score far below the placement cutoff necessary to take college-level courses. The authors also explain that future research should focus on institutional policies and practices and classroom strategies, to explore differences in the effects of remediation by remediation program design.

11. See Denning (2017). The author also documents that marginal community college enrollees induced to attend by reduced tuition have similar graduation rates as average community college enrollees.

12. For example, findings from Dynarski and Scott-Clayton (2013).

13. See Marx and Turner (2019). A novelty of their results is that they separately identify the effects of grant aid and loans on short-run attainment.

14. For example, the results in Bettinger et al. (2017).

15. See Kane and Staiger (2012), Murnane and Ganimian (2014), and Araujo et al. (2016).

16. See Saavedra (2009).

17. For example, Bettinger and Long (2005), Allgood, Walstad, and Siegfried (2015), and Porter and Serra (2020) show how role models can positively impact the outcomes of (undergraduate) students.

18. See De Vlieger, Jacob, and Stange (2020).

19. As discussed in chapters 1 and 3, this process varies across WBSCPS countries.

20. Chapter 1 briefly discusses the accreditation processes in the different countries.

21. See Belloni, Chernozhukov, and Hansen (2014a, 2014b) and Ahrens, Hansen, and Schaffer (2020).

22. See Bailey (2015).

23. See Daniel, Mittag, and Bornmann (2007).

24. Other studies of the United States find that students' evaluations of teachers are not effective in predicting teachers' effectiveness, as shown by De Vlieger, Jacob, and Stange 2020. In line with this evidence, the findings here suggest that students' evaluations of teachers are not relevant for the dropout rate.

25. Among the additional characteristics, programs that report receiving students with large deficits in math content also report higher dropout rates than those that do not report this knowledge gap. Longer programs and those taught by public institutions also show higher dropout rates. Finally, having mostly female students is associated with higher dropout rates.

26. The programs' most important features are discussed in chapter 3.

27. Bettinger and Long (2005) find that having a female faculty member in an initial course affects the likelihood that a female student will take additional credit hours or major in a particular subject.

28. In their background paper for this book, Ferreyra et al. (2020) find that the contributions of SCPs in Colombia are greater for programs taught by selective and specialized institutions. A similar finding in terms of selectivity is identified by Hoxby (2009) using data from college programs in the United States.

29. See Almeida et al. (2012) and Betcherman, Olivas, and Dar (2004).

30. See Almeida et al. (2012).

31. Surprisingly, programs that reported that they receive students with math content deficits report better employment outcomes for their graduates. It is possible that the programs that are more aware of students' academic deficits (and report them) do more to address them and, as a result, help their students obtain more formal employment.

32. Barrera-Osorio and Bayona-Rodriguez (2019) estimate that salaries are higher for graduates from the most prestigious universities in Colombia.

33. See Bettinger and Long (2005).

34. See Almeida et al. (2012) and Betcherman, Olivas, and Dar (2004).

35. As in the case of formal employment, programs provided by universities tend to report lower wages among their graduates on average. Again, this could be because universities are being conservative when reporting graduates' outcomes or universities are investing less effort in their SCP graduates' outcomes than non-universities.

References

Ahrens, A., C. B. Hansen, and M. E. Schaffer. 2020. "lassopack: Model Selection and Prediction with Regularized Regression in Stata." *The Stata Journal* 20 (1): 176–235.

Allgood, S., W. B. Walstad, and J. J. Siegfried. 2015. "Research on Teaching Economics to Undergraduates." *Journal of Economic Literature* 53 (2): 285–325.

Almeida, R., J. Arbelaez, M. Honorati, A. Kuddo, T. Lohmann, M. Ovadiya, L. Pop, M. L. Sanchez Puerta, and M. Weber. 2012. "Improving Access to Jobs and Earnings Opportunities: The Role of Activation and Graduation Policies in Developing Countries." Social Protection Discussion Papers and Notes 67610, World Bank, Washington, DC.

Araujo, M. C., P. Carneiro, Y. Cruz-Aguayo, and N. Schady. 2016. "Teacher Quality and Learning Outcomes in Kindergarten." *Quarterly Journal of Economics* 131 (3): 1415–53.

Bailey, T. R. 2015. *Redesigning America's Community Colleges: A Clearer Path to Student Success*. Cambridge, MA; Harvard University Press.

Barrera-Osorio, F., and H. Bayona-Rodríguez. 2019. "Signaling or Better Human Capital: Evidence from Colombia." *Economics of Education Review* 70: 20–34.

Belloni, A., V. Chernozhukov, and C. Hansen. 2014a. "High-Dimensional Methods and Inference on Structural and Treatment Effects." *Journal of Economic Perspectives* 28 (2): 29–50.

Belloni, A., V. Chernozhukov, and C. Hansen. 2014b. "Inference on Treatment Effects after Selection among High-Dimensional Controls." *Review of Economic Studies* 81 (2): 608–50.

Betcherman, G., K. Olivas, and A. Dar. 2004. "Impacts of Active Labor Market Programs: New Evidence from Evaluations with Particular Attention to Developing and Transition Countries." Social Protection Discussion Papers and Notes 29142, World Bank, Washington, DC.

Bettinger, E. P., L. Fox, S. Loeb, and E. S. Taylor. 2017. "Virtual Classrooms: How Online College Courses Affect Student Success." *American Economic Review* 107 (9): 2855–75.

Bettinger, E. P., and B. T. Long. 2005. "Do Faculty Serve as Role Models? The Impact of Instructor Gender on Female Students." *American Economic Review* 95 (2): 152–57.

Calcagno, J. C., and B. T. Long. 2009. "Evaluating the Impact of Remedial Education in Florida Community Colleges: A Quasi-Experimental Regression Discontinuity Design." NCPR Brief. National Center for Postsecondary Research, Columbia University, New York.

Carranza, J. E., and M. M. Ferreyra. 2019. "Increasing Higher Education Access: Supply, Sorting, and Outcomes in Colombia." *Journal of Human Capital* 13 (1): 95–136.

Cellini, S., and H. Grueso. 2020. "Assessing Student Learning in Online Short-Cycle Programs in Colombia." World Bank, Washington, DC.

Daniel, H. D., S. Mittag, and L. Bornmann. 2007. "The Potential and Problems of Peer Evaluation in Higher Education and Research." In *Quality Assessment for Higher Education in Europe*, edited by A. Cavalli, 71–82. London: Portland Press.

De Hoyos, R., A. Popova, and H. Rogers. 2016. "Out of School and Out of Work: A Diagnostic of Ninis in Latin America." Policy Research Working Paper 7548, World Bank, Washington, DC, https://openknowledge.worldbank.org/handle/10986/23723.

De Vlieger P., B. Jacob, and K. Stange. 2020. "Measuring Instructor Effectiveness in Higher Education." In *Productivity in Higher Education*, edited by C. Hoxby and K. Stange. Chicago: University of Chicago Press.

Deming, D. J., C. Goldin, L. F. Katz, and N. Yuchtman. 2015. "Can Online Learning Bend the Higher Education Cost Curve?" *American Economic Review* 105 (5): 496–501.

Denning, J. T. 2017. "College on the Cheap: Consequences of Community College Tuition Reductions." *American Economic Journal: Economic Policy* 9 (2): 155–88.

Dinarte, L, M. M. Ferreyra, S. Urzua, and M. Bassi. 2021. "What Makes a Program Good? Evidence from Short Cycle Higher Education Programs in Latin America and the Caribbean." Research paper, World Bank, Washington, DC.

Dobbie, W., and R. G. Fryer, Jr. 2013. "Getting Beneath the Veil of Effective Schools: Evidence from New York City." *American Economic Journal: Applied Economics* 5 (4): 28–60.

Dutz, M. A., R. K. Almeida, and T. G. Packard. 2018. *The Jobs of Tomorrow: Technology, Productivity, and Prosperity in Latin America and the Caribbean*. Directions in Development, Information and Communication Technology. Washington, DC: World Bank, https://openknowledge.worldbank.org/handle/10986/29617.

Dynarski, S., and J. Scott-Clayton. 2013. "Financial Aid Policy: Lessons from Research." No. W18710, National Bureau of Economic Research, Cambridge, MA.

Ferreyra, M., C. Avitabile, J. Botero, F. Haimovich, and S. Urzúa. 2017. *At a Crossroads: Higher Education in Latin America and the Caribbean*. Washington, DC: World Bank.

Ferreyra, M. M., T. Melguizo, A. Franco, and A. Sanchez. 2020. "Estimating the Contribution of Short-Cycle Programs to Student Outcomes in Colombia." Policy Research Working Paper 9424, World Bank, Washington, DC.

Hanushek, E. A. 1997. "Assessing the Effects of School Resources on Student Performance: An Update." *Educational Evaluation and Policy Analysis* 19 (2): 141–64.

Hoxby, C. M. 2009. "The Changing Selectivity of American Colleges." *Journal of Economic Perspectives* 23 (4): 95–118.

Jaggars, S., and D. Xu. 2016. "How Do Online Course Design Features Influence Student Performance?" *Computers & Education* 95: 270–84.

Kane, T. J., and D. O. Staiger. 2012. "Gathering Feedback for Teaching: Combining High-Quality Observations with Student Surveys and Achievement Gains." Research Paper, MET Project, Bill & Melinda Gates Foundation, Seattle, WA.

Krueger, A. B. 2003. "Economic Considerations and Class Size." *Economic Journal* 113 (485): F34–F63.

Marx, B. M., and L. J. Turner. 2019. "Student Loan Nudges: Experimental Evidence on Borrowing and Educational Attainment." *American Economic Journal: Economic Policy* 11 (2): 108–41.

Melguizo, T., G. Zamarro, T. Velasco, and F. J. Sanchez. 2017. "The Methodological Challenges of Measuring Student Learning, Degree Attainment, and Early Labor Market Outcomes in Higher Education." *Journal of Research on Educational Effectiveness* 10 (2): 424–48.

Murnane, R. J., and A. Ganimian. 2014. "Improving Educational Outcomes in Developing Countries: Lessons from Rigorous Impact Evaluations." Working Paper WP20284, National Bureau of Economic Research, Cambridge, MA.

Porter, C., and D. Serra. 2020. "Gender Differences in the Choice of Major: The Importance of Female Role Models." *American Economic Journal: Applied Economics* 12 (3): 226–54.

Saavedra, J. E. 2009. "The Returns to College Quality: A Regression Discontinuity Analysis." Harvard University, Cambridge, MA.

SNIES 2019. *Sistema Nacional de Informacion de la Educacion Superior.* https://snies .mineducacion.gov.co/portal/ESTADISTICAS/Bases-consolidadas/. Accessed on November 2020.

CHAPTER 5

Policy to Realize the Promise of Short-Cycle Programs

Taking Stock

In closing, this chapter returns to the book's initial motivation—Latin America and the Caribbean's (LAC's) urgent need for skilled human capital.[1] This need, which had been pressing following the end of the region's "Golden Decade," is decidedly urgent now. The COVID-19 pandemic has accelerated structural changes in the economy that were already underway, showing the type of skills—analytical, technical, socioemotional, and interpersonal—that are needed in today's world. In the current crisis and its aftermath, the livelihoods of many individuals depend precisely on acquiring those skills—and doing it fast.

Can short-cycle programs (SCPs) provide those skills? The evidence presented in this book gives several reasons for hope:

- On average, SCPs have good outcomes. They graduate students at higher rates than bachelor's programs. SCP graduates obtain better labor market outcomes (employment, formal employment, and salary) than high school graduates and, remarkably, also better than bachelor's dropouts. These results are noteworthy given that, on average, SCPs take more disadvantaged, less traditional students than bachelor's programs.
- Although the Mincerian returns to bachelor's degrees (their salary premium relative to a high school diploma, after accounting for student characteristics) are higher than those of SCPs, the former have fallen since the early 2000s in most LAC countries. In contrast, the Mincerian returns to SCPs have risen in several countries over the same period. Further, Mincerian returns to complete SCPs are higher than those of incomplete bachelor's programs, a finding of great significance given that less than half of bachelor's students complete their degree.
- Even taking their cost into account, some SCPs yield high returns—higher than those of some bachelor's programs. There is a strong demand for SCP

graduates—greater than that for bachelor's graduates—particularly in the fields of computer science, technology, and business.

- Local availability of SCPs makes some students more likely to enroll in them and provides them a better match than that of bachelor's programs. The greatest SCP returns accrue to disadvantaged students, who are mostly male, poorly prepared, and do not live in large urban settings. If SCPs were not available, those students would attend bachelor's programs, most likely low-quality ones. Further, an improvement in the local labor market for SCP graduates leads disadvantaged females who would otherwise not attend higher education to enroll in SCPs.

- Based on directors' reports to the World Bank Short-Cycle Program Survey (WBSCPS), on average, SCPs in the region offer a good balance of theoretical and practical training. They hire faculty with industry experience and have low faculty-student ratios. They evaluate faculty performance periodically and train their faculty. They have adequate infrastructure. They engage with the private sector in multiple ways, including gauging its needs, soliciting feedback on graduates, and having internship agreements. SCPs also assist students' job search in several ways such as providing information, arranging job interviews, and running employment centers.

- Based on statistical analysis using WBSCPS data, some programs deploy practices that are associated with better academic and labor market outcomes, after accounting for student characteristics. Programs whose graduates have higher wages and formal employment rates, for instance, tend to have sufficient equipment for practical training, teach numerical competencies, and offer academic remediation during the program. They assess faculty's class plans as part of their faculty evaluation and run an employment center. They admit students based on exams and interviews and are provided by institutions that have a governing board beyond the rector or provost.

- The supply of SCPs is dynamic—more so than that of bachelor's programs. The opening and closing of programs are associated with patterns of local economic activity, suggesting that SCPs might respond to them. On average, SCPs update their curricula frequently in response to the local economy. Because they are flexible, nimble, and attuned to the needs of the local economy, they have the potential to respond quickly and creatively to the current emergency.

At the same time, the evidence from this book gives several reasons for caution:

- Despite their good average outcomes, and despite the evidence that some SCPs have very high returns, others have very low ones. For an uninformed student, this great variation poses a substantive risk. There is similar variation in the practices implemented by the programs. While some programs engage in good, desirable practices, others do not. The variation in returns and practices is aggravated by the fact that the current oversight and regulation of the sector often focuses on inputs (such as faculty and infrastructure) rather than outcomes.

- Most SCPs offered no classes online before the pandemic and must have had a difficult adjustment to online provision in the midst of the pandemic. Further, the evidence indicates that online provision of SCPs before the pandemic was only effective when certain features (such as synchronous teaching and project-based learning) were present. In addition, online teaching of the hands-on skills that are typically taught in labs or workshops could be quite challenging.
- Although SCPs open in response to local economic activity, the openings also respond to cost considerations, raising the concern that institutions might open some low-quality programs just because they are profitable. The concern is more acute when the regulatory authority does not carefully screen program entry and examine program outcomes periodically to identify the low-quality ones.
- The average program might focus too much on student training rather than employment, perhaps believing that students value training more than employment. While some programs might currently have a greater employment focus for reputational reasons, the average program will not have it unless it receives the incentives to do so, coming, for instance, from a regulatory authority that periodically examines students' labor market outcomes.
- The main reason for student dropout is financial struggle—which might have become even more severe during the pandemic. Although governments face an extremely tight budget constraint at the moment, addressing SCP funding is critical given the urgent need for skilled workers.
- Although the programs claim to provide a pathway to a bachelor's program, in practice, these pathways are extremely limited. As a result, students might perceive SCPs as an academic "dead end" and enroll in bachelor's programs instead. However, a bachelor's program might not be the best fit for all students, as evidenced by the fact that more than half of bachelor's program students drop out.

In sum, although SCPs appear to be promising, they also have shortcomings. These may well have contributed to the long-standing, persistent stigma whereby students view SCPs as the lesser higher education choice. However, rather than dismissing SCPs or relegating them to a minor role—as may have been done in the past—the use of policy is suggested in order to address their shortcomings and realize their promise. This amounts to examining the very reasons why SCPs fall short of their promise and tackling them directly.[2] Since the shortcomings have been likely aggravated by policy failures, the rest of this chapter discusses four broad policy categories that have potential for mitigating them: information, funding, oversight and regulation, and skill development pathways. Box 5.1 presents the theoretical framework behind government intervention in higher education markets, providing a rationale for these four policy categories.

In the face of multiple shortcomings, multiple policy tools are needed. In other words, not all shortcomings will be solved just by providing information to students, or by providing them more generous funding. Moreover, relying on a

Box 5.1 Why Should the Policy Maker Intervene in Higher Education Markets?

At its best, higher education realizes individuals' potential and meets the economy's skill needs. But if higher education institutions and students are left to markets alone, this potential cannot be realized—for several *market failures* as discussed below.

Externalities arise because a student's decision to pursue higher education benefits society as a whole, yet it does not take such consequences into account. For example, a higher education degree not only provides higher earnings and opportunities to the student but also benefits society—for example, by making the student a better citizen and a more involved parent. By not taking this social benefit into account, the student may acquire less education than what is best for society.

Some students may not have the financial resources to acquire higher education. These *liquidity constraints* detract not only from equity among individuals but also from economic efficiency, as the economy fails to realize its full productive potential. While the credit market could, in principle, mitigate short-term liquidity constraints, this market is imperfect. Student loans typically lack the collateral or guarantee required by lenders because students borrow to finance an investment embodied in themselves. Thus, if the student does not repay the loan, the bank cannot take possession of the student as it can seize a house, for example, when a mortgage is not paid back.

Since higher education offers complex "products" whose nature and quality are difficult to assess, the market is plagued with *information asymmetries*. Consider, for instance, a student interested in biology who is trying to choose an industry-oriented program. The student may not know which specific program, among the many available, provides that training. Even after locating a few such programs, the student may not be able to differentiate them—because, for example, the institutions do not provide information on graduates' salaries and employment prospects. Even if the student knows which programs deliver high-paying jobs, it may not be clear whether this is because those programs attract very well-prepared students, or because they provide excellent training. And even if all this information exists and is easily accessible, the student may not be able to understand and use it. Further, the student may overestimate her prospects in a program by not realizing, for instance, that she is poorly prepared or ill-suited for it.

In a well-functioning market, programs command high returns when the skills they develop are relatively scarce in the labor market. As a result, at least some students gravitate toward those programs, thereby satisfying the economy's needs. Information asymmetries on program returns and characteristics break this virtuous cycle. Further, a different kind of information asymmetries may prevent students from accessing high-paying jobs even if they choose high-return programs: vacancies might only be advertised to a narrow network of students and higher education institutions (HEIs); some HEIs might not promote their graduates in the labor market; or students might not be able to prove their command of the required skills. The latter happens, for instance, when a student who has the corresponding skills lacks a credential certifying them, therefore complicating both her job search and the potential pursuit of a longer degree.

Higher education markets display *imperfect competition*. Since setting up and running an HEI is costly, this alone can concentrate supply around a few providers with high market

box continues next page

Box 5.1 Why Should the Policy Maker Intervene in Higher Education Markets? *(continued)*

power, particularly in small localities that can only support a few providers. Legal and regulatory barriers to institutions' entry determine actual concentration. If barriers are low and entry of institutions and programs is easy, the market will be more competitive. Nonetheless, the fact that HEIs offer *differentiated products* (in aspects such as geographic location, program type and field, curriculum focus, academic rigor, and labor market connections) gives HEIs a certain degree of market power even under plentiful entry. For instance, in Latin American and the Caribbean, most students attend higher education close to home, thus giving local HEIs considerable market power. Also, governments generously subsidize tuition in public HEIs but rarely offer financial aid for students in private HEIs, thereby endowing public HEIs with considerable market power. Further, since the early 2000s, higher education enrollment has grown dramatically in the region and has attracted a "new" student, of low income and poor academic readiness (Ferreyra et al 2017), who was previously underrepresented in the system. This type of student, who has little information or familiarity with higher education, invites the entry of low-quality, high-price institutions and programs, thereby deserving close regulatory attention.

Such market failures justify policy intervention, particularly in the areas of terms of information, funding, oversight and regulation, and skill development pathways.

---

tool to address one problem may exacerbate others. For instance, more generous funding may not only increase SCP demand, as desired, but also encourage the entry of low-quality providers. Addressing this unintended effect would require the use of funding and regulation policies in a complementary fashion.

This chapter argues that program-level information is necessary for policy makers—who must regulate and oversee the programs—and for students—who need to make informed choices. Mere information provision is not enough; students must be engaged directly to ensure that they receive and process the information. Currently, higher per-student subsidies at public higher education institutions (HEIs) are provided to students in bachelor's programs rather than SCPs. Further, no financial aid is provided to SCP students in private HEIs. These practices must be corrected to restore equity and promote skill acquisition. Oversight and regulation must eliminate the lowest quality programs and promote an environment where only "good" programs are supplied. Flexible pathways must be implemented to facilitate skill acquisition in blocks or modules, at the end of which students can obtain credentials leading to a degree, and to promote lifelong learning. Overall, the goal of policy should be to create a system in which program-level information is disseminated and used by students and policy makers alike, and in which policy makers monitor all programs closely and actively intervene to eliminate the lowest-quality programs. Knowing the scrutiny they face from students and policy makers, programs in this environment would strive to offer a good product.

While the implementation of these policies would be challenging in any setting, it is even more so in the current one, as the COVID-19 pandemic has had a profound effect on higher education in LAC (box 5.2). Nonetheless, their

Box 5.2 The Impact of the COVID-19 Pandemic on Higher Education in LAC

COVID-19 has caused major disruptions in higher education in Latin America and the Caribbean.[a] Most governments closed higher education institutions (HEIs) beginning in March 2020. The immediate effect was that most classes were canceled, with only a few institutions implementing online learning. Although most HEIs implemented remote learning over the following months, about 27 million students have not attended in-person classes in about a year at the time of this writing (March 2021).

Despite limited resources, most governments in the region made efforts to support higher education throughout the pandemic. For example, they have provided connectivity kits to students, developed TV and radio remote learning, provided additional resources to HEIs to conduct online teaching, and increased student financial aid. Nonetheless, the transition to online teaching has been far from easy. Before the pandemic, higher education in LAC had made very limited use of technology in teaching and learning. Technology is expensive in LAC and not accessible to many students and teachers, which has always been an important obstacle for HEIs to invest in e-learning. During the pandemic, inequalities in student access to technology have been profound and have exacerbated preexisting inequalities in education access and quality. Education quality has been further affected as institutions, faculty, and students have had to adapt abruptly, with few resources and little training, to the on-line modality. While 90 percent of faculty believes in the importance of integrating technology into teaching, only 25 percent feels fully prepared to use digital tools in their classes. Programs that require practice in labs or workshops have been even more affected given the limited alternatives available for students to develop practical skills.

Access to and graduation from higher education are also expected to suffer. High school students have been out of school for many months, with big disruptions in learning, exit examinations, graduation, and overall transition to higher education. Similarly, many students and families have suffered severe financial hardship, leading many students to drop out of school. For private HEIs, which attract about half of higher education students in LAC and represent the bulk of higher education supply in several countries, losses in tuition revenue might lead to the short-term reduction of faculty, staff, and academic offerings, and to the closing of many HEIs in the medium to long run. Fiscal constraints, which were already tight before the pandemic, have become even more severe. In the absence of additional resources, public higher education systems will need to gain efficiency, possibly reducing faculty and staff, adjusting the variety and length of programs, and shifting resources away from research and students' supports to on-line learning and technology. While some of these actions might create long-term benefits, short-term adjustments will doubtless be challenging.

a. This box draws from Becerra, Alonso, and Frias (2021).

implementation is crucial because skills are crucial. The policy discussion that follows offers general principles; specific policy design and implementation are beyond the scope of this book. Ultimately, the discussion seeks to attract greater attention, from the point of view of policy, to a type of program that may not have figured prominently on the recent policy agenda but may prove distinctly helpful in the current context and beyond.

Information

Information about programs is crucial for students, the policy maker, and the economy as a whole. Students cannot choose "good" programs unless they know program characteristics and outcomes. The policy maker cannot oversee and regulate the sector without knowing how it performs. The economy cannot obtain the advanced skills it needs unless those who supply them (that is, higher education students) know which skills are demanded in the labor market. Suppose, for example, that the labor market needs data scientists more than tourism managers. In a well-functioning market, data scientists would command higher salaries than tourism managers. Armed with this information, at least some students would become data scientists. Without salary information, too many students might become tourism managers. In this scenario, neither would students obtain the highest possible salary nor would firms obtain the required skills—a "lose-lose" situation. Information is thus critical to a good functioning of the education and labor markets.

In LAC, the vast dispersion in returns to SCPs and bachelor's programs, as well as the persistent SCP stigma, indicates that students are likely ignorant of the good average outcomes of SCPs, particularly relative to an incomplete bachelor's program. Even if they know such outcomes, they may believe they would actually graduate from a bachelor's program should they enroll in one. Students, however, should be familiar with some key facts when making their decisions: in LAC, the chances of completing a bachelor's program are less than 50 percent (chapter 1); they are lower for low-income, poorly prepared students than for others;[3] and not all bachelor's graduates fare better than SCP graduates (chapter 2). Further, students may ignore not just programs' returns but also their content. It is easy to imagine what an accountant does, but not necessarily what a cybersecurity specialist or a logistics technician does.

These issues are all the more serious in LAC, where students choose a higher education major right at the beginning of their studies (chapter 1). While switching majors is possible, it involves starting the new one almost from scratch, as credits do not transfer easily among majors owing to a lack of general education classes. Also, students in LAC typically attend higher education only once in their lifetime. As a result, most students make the high-stakes choice of a major only once, when they are very young. Lack of information about the programs' content and returns as well as unrealistic perceptions of their readiness for the various programs can certainly lead students to make poor choices.

Mitigating these problems requires that students gain access to program-level information, including program content, costs and funding options, average labor market outcomes, background characteristics of the average graduate (for example, average academic readiness), and requirements for student success (for example, a strong math background). Based on this information, students should be able to assess their readiness and fit for the program. Program-level information should be made available in high school—at least two or three years before graduation—for the students to have enough time to make these important choices. The information should reach not only students but also the families, who might make considerable financial sacrifices on their children's behalf, and the high school teachers, who know the students and can help them process the information. Information processing is particularly important because students might experience an information overload owing to excessive information or might not know how to interpret information, particularly in the case of students with less educated parents.

Choosing the program-level outcomes and metrics to report is not straightforward. Several are possible, including graduation rate, time-to-degree, learning achievement (for example, scores in an exit or licensing exam), short-term labor market outcomes, long-term labor market outcomes, and value-added contributions to one or several of these outcomes. Some of these metrics can be manipulated quite easily. A program can, for instance, lower graduation standards in order to raise graduation rates. From this perspective, labor market outcomes are preferable, as are learning outcomes certified by a third party (for example, test scores in a national exit exam). Among labor market outcomes, however, short- and long-term outcomes may paint different pictures. For instance, a program may provide better employment prospects right after graduation than 10 or 15 years later. More generally, different metrics may be at odds with each other, as documented by Ferreyra et al. (2020) for Colombia in their background paper for this book, and by others for the United States and LAC.[4] To a certain extent, what information is reported depends on what is available. Yet, even if all possible outcomes and metrics were available and reported, students might still need assistance interpreting them.

Because of their simplicity and ease of interpretation, rankings are an appealing way to present program-level information. But, for the same reasons described in the previous paragraph, rankings can be easily altered by choosing different metrics. Even if one built an index of multiple indicators (such as various academic and labor market outcomes) and constructed a ranking based on it, the ranking would be sensitive to the weight given to each indicator in the index. Precisely because rankings do affect the behavior of HEIs and students alike,[5] policy makers should refrain from building them. Whereas third parties might build rankings, students should at least be aware of their content and pitfalls.[6]

An important question, of course, is who would provide the program-level information underpinning all information-related policies. Building this information requires student-level data on wages, employment, and higher education program completed. In countries such as Chile and Peru, the governments collect the relevant information and make it publicly available, at the program level, on a website. However, this is rare in the rest of LAC. The relevant data typically come from multiple government agencies (for example, the ministries of education and labor) and is therefore subject to substantial coordination problems. Indeed, the team preparing this book encountered multiple instances of these problems. Many countries do not collect the information at all, and some that do choose not to report it, either at the program or HEI level.

Governments have a natural advantage in collecting the relevant information because they can enforce HEIs' obligation to report it and can solve the interagency coordination problem. However, they might choose not to do it, perhaps for political economy reasons. Private entrepreneurs could collect at least part of it—for example, through internet scraping. Further, good programs have every incentive to track down and advertise their graduates' outcomes— particularly if their revenues depend on enrollment, as is the case for private institutions. Although low-quality programs have incentives to (falsely) depict themselves as good, this might be averted by requiring a third-party audit of self-reported information (coding boot camps in the United States are already following this practice). Although private solutions to information provision are therefore possible, governments have an unsurpassed advantage at collecting the information and ultimately need it for regulation purposes.

It should be mentioned, however, that collecting all the relevant information and making it easily available might not necessarily affect students' decisions. The evidence indicates that what information is provided, to whom, and how, matters greatly (box 5.3). Light-touch interventions, such as posting information on a website, sending an email, or nudging students with text messages, generally fail to alter students' behavior. These interventions are impersonal and do not engage the student directly; she might not see the information or consider it useful or reliable. In contrast, high-touch interventions, which are more direct and intensive, affect students' choices. Frequent sessions with a counselor are an

---

Box 5.3 What Do We Know about Information Interventions?

Most information interventions that are reported in the literature have aimed at providing prospective students information related to college access. Scholars seem to disagree about the effectiveness of informational interventions in affecting student behavior, yet part of the disagreement may stem from a lack of agreement on what constitutes an informational intervention. Interventions vary in what information they provide (such as availability and characteristics of programs), when they provide it (how far in advance before high school graduation), and how (whether in a light- or high-touch fashion). Light-touch interventions mail information to students (Hoxby and Turner 2013; Gurantz et al. 2021; Bergman, Denning, and Manoli 2019; Hyman 2020), nudge them (Castleman, Deutschlander, and Lohner 2020; Oreopoulos and Petronijevic 2019), or post information on a website (as is the case of government information provision, studied by Hurwitz and Smith 2018 and Baker 2020). In contrast, high-touch interventions engage the student directly and intensively, for instance through repeated counseling sessions (Bettinger and Baker 2014; Oreopolous and Ford 2019; Bettinger and Evans 2019; Mulhern 2020).

In general, the evidence shows that light-touch interventions do not affect behavior (Page and Scott-Clayton 2016), but high-touch interventions do. However, there are some nuances to consider.

Although merely posting of information on a website is not effective, interactive websites that tailor information to the student and mimic the role of a counselor are effective

box continues next page

Box 5.3 What Do We Know about Information Interventions? *(continued)*

(for example, Naviance in the United States, studied in Mulhern 2021). Further, mailing information to students is effective when the message is personalized and targeted to specific students who find it credible and relevant, and when it is also sent to "influencers" close to the student (as in the HAIL experiment at the University of Michigan, studied by Dynarski et al. 2020).

A few studies have examined the impact of providing major or program-specific information to students. Researchers using an experimental design have found that information led students to switch to higher return options in Chile (Hastings, Neilson, and Zimmerman 2015) and the United States (see Conlon 2019 for four-year colleges and Baker et al. 2018 for community colleges). In Chile, the provision of information also leads to higher persistence in college (Hastings, Neilson, and Zimmerman 2015).

Some recent interventions in the Dominican Republic and Peru have provided middle and high school students videos that teach them about education's value and returns (see J-PAL 2017 for Peru). The interventions have lowered dropout rates among low-performing students and affected the field of study among high-performing students. Such interventions have been scaled up in Peru and the Dominican Republic and have recently been implemented in Chile.

Of critical importance is the quality of the information provided. As discussed in the main text, an ideal information system would keep track of all the higher education programs that are available in a country and their basic characteristics, such as duration and cost. It would also keep track of all the students in higher education—particularly those who graduate—and follow them into the labor market to allow for the calculation of program-level average returns and employment rates. Ideally, countries would also have disclosure platforms (for instance, websites such as www.mifuturo.cl and www.ponteencarrera.pe in Chile and Peru, respectively) where program-level information can be easily found. Although data collection and disclosure do not affect behavior by themselves, they provide the inputs necessary for the interventions that do affect it.

---

example, as are interactive websites (such as Naviance in the United States) tailoring information to the specific student, parents, and counselors. Students often overestimate the returns to their chosen programs, do not know about similar programs offering higher returns, and are generally misinformed about returns to various fields and programs. Nonetheless, they do alter their choices in response to well-designed interventions, as indicated by evidence from the United States and Chile.

There are cases in which even a well-designed intervention might fail to affect student choices. Students might still choose a program with relatively low returns just because it is local or offers something they value (for example, convenient schedule, online teaching, on-site child care, quiet place to study.)[7] Alternatively, students may simply not have other choices, as is the case of those who live in small or medium-size municipalities (chapter 3), or cannot afford anything more expensive than their current program. As discussed later in this chapter, ultimately it is the regulator's duty to ensure that the options available are good and that students have the financial means to choose among them.

These caveats notwithstanding, program-level information is still necessary. As stressed at the beginning of this chapter, it will not solve all problems—but will solve several of them, particularly when combined with others such as regulation and funding. Collecting the relevant data is the first step. The policy makers' own need for program-level information might spearhead data collection efforts, as it is impossible to monitor individual programs without knowing their outcomes. More generally, the goal is to create an information-based higher education culture in which information is provided and used to make consequential decisions, and providers, knowing they are being monitored by students and policy makers, strive to offer a good product.

Funding

Policy makers around the world subsidize higher education for efficiency and equity reasons. Since higher education benefits society as a whole, they subsidize it to induce individuals to pursue it in order to build the economy's optimal level of human capital. They also subsidize it because many students, left to their own resources, cannot afford higher education. To subsidize higher education, they can make transfers to HEIs and students, or can intervene in the student loan market by providing, guaranteeing, or subsidizing student loans. In LAC, policy makers' subsidize public HEIs, provide little or no subsidies to private HEIs or their students, and sometimes intervene in the student loan market—which is very small, at least in the WBSCPS countries.[8]

At the moment, the higher education funding in LAC is not equitable and is often regressive. It is not equitable at public HEIs, where the annual per-student subsidy for SCPs is lower, on average, than for bachelor's programs (chapter 1). The subsidy gap becomes even larger when the total subsidy is considered—over the whole program duration—because SCPs are shorter than bachelor's programs.

This situation is inequitable for several reasons. Students in SCPs are more disadvantaged than those in bachelor's programs and hence have greater financial needs. SCPs have lower dropout rates than bachelor's programs, which means that a greater subsidy is devoted to students who are more likely to drop out. And, among bachelor's students, those who graduate come from higher income families than those who drop out and hence need the subsidy even less.[9]

Neither is SCP funding equitable for students at private HEIs. In LAC, on average, these students account for 48 percent of total SCP enrollment and mostly pay tuition out of their own pocket (chapter 1). Although public HEIs are highly attractive because of their generous tuition subsidies, many students might have legitimate reasons to choose private HEIs. For example, local public HEIs might be oversubscribed, not offer the student's program of interest, or offer low-quality programs. As a result, subsidizing SCP students at public but not private HEIs creates inequities among students. Crucially, because public HEIs might not have enough capacity for a potential SCP expansion, private HEIs might be indispensable to absorb the increased demand.[10] In other words, the large-scale upskilling and reskilling of the workforce required in the current emergency might only be possible by subsidizing students in public as well as private HEIs.

The concern remains, for many, that public financial aid for students in private HEIs might flow to low-quality programs. Of course, public funds might flow to low-quality programs taught not only at private but also public HEIs. Averting this concern requires that funding and regulation complement each other— vigorously overseeing *all* programs—to identify the low-quality ones and prevent public funds from flowing into them.

Given the current fiscal constraints, it is not realistic to consider additional funding for higher education. Instead, raising subsidies for SCP students requires more efficient public spending in higher education, including a funding reallocation among higher education students based on their income and program type. Restoring equity in higher education funding would matter in any circumstance but is crucial now, since the COVID-19 pandemic has affected individuals unequally and deepened the already high, persistent inequality in the region.

Fiscal constraints, along with the need to expand SCPs, indicate that public resources alone might not suffice. Expanding student loans—whose current coverage is low—would provide additional resources. Income-contingent loans, provided by public or private entities, is an option worth exploring. With these loans, the student pays once she starts working, but only to the extent allowed by her income. This type of loan is almost nonexistent in LAC at the moment.[11] Nonetheless, boot-camp providers in the region already provide income-contingent loans to students, as they finance students' training and begin to collect payments only when the student gets a job.[12]

Another funding option might operate through the social protection system. Given policy makers' current concern with protecting employment, subsidizing employment conditional on the employees attending an SCP would fulfill both employment and human capital goals. This is similar to the well-known conditional cash transfers (CCTs), in which households receive a cash transfer as long as they fulfill certain conditions such as sending their children to school. Well-designed and implemented CCTs have been successful at increasing school attendance and enrollment.[13]

More generally, the pandemic has shown the need to redesign social protection systems to include funding for skill development, since skills are the ultimate insurance mechanism.[14] For example, SCP funding could be used as a counter-cyclical tool—or an automatic stabilizer—that rises during recessions as more individuals, particularly those who are out of employment, need to upskill or reskill. Given that some fields of knowledge (such as science and technology) command a higher program cost than others, an efficient use of public funds would provide a different per-student funding by field. Since private HEIs tend not to open programs in high-cost fields (chapter 3), this funding scheme would expand the supply of these high-cost yet high-value programs.

Regardless of how they fund SCPs, policy makers might only want to commit resources to SCPs if they are cost-effective. Box 5.4 illustrates how they might evaluate cost-effectiveness using program-level data.

Box 5.4 Are SCPs Cost-Effective?

When allocating funds among projects, policy makers face the question of whether a particular project is cost-effective, that is, whether its benefits are greater than or equal to its costs. Consider, for instance, a policy maker who is pondering whether to provide a full subsidy for short-cycle programs (SCPs) for at least some students. Are SCPs cost-effective? As discussed in chapter 2, answering this question is not simple for two reasons. First, it requires information on program costs. Second, it requires measuring program benefits from the government's point of view.

To showcase how governments might analyze SCP cost-effectiveness, the analysis in this box relies on World Bank Short-Cycle Program Survey (WBSCPS) data, including program-level data as reported by the program directors (chapter 4). Two definitions of SCP benefits are considered. The first is the increase in workers' productivity as measured by salaries. The second is the increase in tax revenues because of the higher salaries earned by workers as a result of completing an SCP.

For the first definition, the program is cost-effective if the average lifetime increase in earnings owing to the program (relative to a high school diploma) is greater than the program's cost; that is, the program is cost-effective if it provides a positive net present value or premium relative to a high school diploma. Calculations assume that program costs at private HEIs are equal to tuition, and that program costs at public HEIs can be proxied by the country's average tuition charged by *private* programs. According to these calculations, SCPs are cost-effective, on average, in all the WBSCPS countries (see table B5.4.1).

Table B5.4.1 Net Present Value of SCPs, from the Policy Maker's Perspective

	Brazil	Colombia	Dominican Republic	Ecuador	Peru
1. Average net present value for SCPs	$ 125,551.40	$ 115,623.20	$ 144,872.50	$ 132,518.70	$ 78,272.44
2. Average net present value for HS diploma	$ 76,241.70	$ 81,468.18	$ 78,261.04	$ 93,024.07	$ 72,881.87
3. Average SCP premium	$ 49,309.70	$ 34,155.02	$ 66,611.46	$ 39,494.63	$ 5,390.57
4. Average SCP premium relative to HS	64.7%	41.9%	85.1%	42.5%	7.4%

Source: Staff calculations based on data from the World Bank Short-Cycle Program Survey and SEDLAC (2018).
Note: The net present value of a program is the present discounted value of the wages of program graduate minus tuition costs. In the table, (3) = (1) − (2); (4) = (3) / (2) * 100. Since tuition is subsidized at public higher education institutions, their cost to the policy maker is proxied with the country's average tuition in private higher education institutions. The calculations assume the following: (a) the student completes the program on time; (b) the discount rate is 10 percent; and (c) values are discounted at age 18. All values are in 2019 PPP dollars. HS = high school; PPP = purchasing power parity; SCP = short-cycle program.

box continues next page

Box 5.4 Are SCPs Cost-Effective? *(continued)*

For the second definition, tax rates are a critical piece. For simplicity, the same tax rate is assumed for workers at all income levels. Under this definition, by construction, fewer programs are cost-effective compared with using the first definition. For example, if a program yields a 30 percent increase in lifetime salaries and the tax rate is 10 percent, tax revenues will rise by only 3 percent. Clearly, a 3 percent tax revenue increase is less likely to surpass the program's cost than a 30 percent salary increase. Hence, it is possible that many programs that are, on average, cost-effective under the first definition are not cost-effective under the second definition. However, any program that is not cost-effective under the first definition would not be cost-effective under the second definition. Hence, the first definition allows the policy maker to rule out programs that would not be cost-effective from a productivity or fiscal standpoint.

Perhaps the main drawback of these calculations is that they do not include other program benefits, such as improved health for the individual and her family, or the individual's positive spillovers on her community. These types of benefits are notoriously difficult to measure. Thus, the calculations can be viewed as a lower bound of total SCP net returns.

Oversight and Regulation

Some might believe that, once students receive and process the appropriate program-level information, they will act as informed consumers, making "good" choices that will discipline the market and eliminate the need for oversight and regulation. Appealing as this sounds, it is not correct. The SCP market—and, in general, the higher education market—is not perfectly competitive, as providers often enjoy market power and many students have few or no options (see box 5.1). These "market failures" are particularly salient among SCPs given the students they serve. And, of course, the assumption that these disadvantaged students would have the time and ability to monitor programs and institutions is rather implausible. Oversight and regulation are therefore critical—not only for the sake of a well-functioning market but also for the sake of equity.[15]

One of the main SCP shortcomings is their large quality variation, which poses a risk to students and may account for much of the SCP stigma. Regulating SCPs and holding them accountable are critical for the existence of a competitive SCP market where only high-quality programs are offered—or, at least, one in which all programs are above a minimum quality threshold. In principle, good regulatory and quality assurance systems should perform the following tasks:

- Authorize only the entry of programs with expected high quality. The screening of new programs should be based not only on the proposed curriculum and training, but also on proposed activities to interface with the private sector, promote graduates' employment, compete against similar programs, and perhaps provide financial aid to students. It should also be based on the institution's record with previous programs and the expected labor market outcomes of the graduates. The goal of screening would be to prevent programs with clearly poor prospects from entering the market.

- Establish minimum standards that programs should meet. For instance, a program should provide a student with an expected salary increase relative to what she would have earned without the degree, net of tuition costs. Collecting data on recent salaries for graduates from the program, and on loan repayment where applicable, is critical for monitoring whether these standards are met. This focus on minimum standards (the "do no harm" criterion) has been proposed recently for higher education accountability in the United States.[16]

- Oversee the programs periodically—not just every 5 or 10 years as is typically done for accreditation or license renewal, but annually to detect problems early and let the programs .adjust as needed. The annual monitoring would focus on outcomes and "flag" programs that do not meet the minimum standards in order to follow them closely. An important outcome to monitor is program net return, which relates to whether a program's tuition is too high relative to its outcomes.

- Publish the results of periodic evaluations. This would help the students of "flagged" programs make decisions accordingly (to intensify their own job search efforts, for instance, or switch to another program). It would also help nonflagged programs advertise their status. More broadly, it would incentivize programs to perform well every year for the sake of their own reputation, which would in turn attract or retain students.

- Close poorly performing programs. This would prevent students from enrolling in those programs and public funds from flowing into them.

Importantly, the minimum standards described above are outcome based. This does not mean that relevant inputs (such as faculty size or infrastructure) or practices (such as job search assistance) should be excluded from periodic evaluations or quality assurance. Rather, it reflects a focus on the ultimate object of interest from the student's point of view—expected outcomes—and provides incentives for programs to adjust inputs and practices to reach the desired outcomes.

When choosing outcomes for regulatory purposes, it might be argued that labor market outcomes are too narrow because students might have other, nonpecuniary reasons to pursue specific programs (see the Introduction and chapter 2 of this book). While these additional reasons are legitimate, a regulatory focus on labor market outcomes is justified by the very goal of SCPs, which is to provide skills for the labor market in a short amount of time. The focus is all the stronger when the HEIs receive public funding and/or attract disadvantaged students, as argued below.

As a regulation criteria, merely setting minimum standards might seem too lax. At the same time, it might be difficult to evaluate programs on a more granular basis—distinguishing, for instance, very good from excellent programs. Identifying the worst programs should be simpler and would facilitate the closing of programs in the lower tail of the quality distribution—those that harm students and perhaps contribute the most to the SCP stigma. To illustrate how impactful minimum standards might be, consider the program average net lifetime returns reported in chapter 2 for Chile and Colombia. If, for example, only programs with positive returns were allowed to function, then a substantive fraction of SCPs (12 and 53 percent in Chile and Colombia, respectively) would have to be closed.

Outcome-based evaluations might seem unfair for programs whose students are particularly disadvantaged from an economic or academic standpoint. At the same time, lowering the outcome standard to adjust for student disadvantage would do a disservice to the students for whom the standards matter the most. Minimum standards are preferable to more nuanced ones, such as those based on value added, precisely because minimum standards do not require adjustments based on student characteristics. In effect, requiring a program to do no financial harm to the student is reasonable regardless of the student's initial disadvantage. If any adjustment by student characteristics is to be made, it might be best to benchmark each program against "similar" ones—for instance, programs in the same field, in a comparable geographic location, and serving students with similar characteristics—which is akin to comparing programs based on their value added. Simulated evaluations conducted in the United States show that "demography is not destiny" because there is great outcome variation even among programs that have disadvantaged students. Although these programs have lower-than-average outcomes, some of them are well above average.[17]

Oversight and regulation are critical when programs receive public funding—direct funding to the HEI or indirect funding through student financial aid—to prevent money from flowing to low-quality programs. They are also critical when SCP providers enjoy some kind of market power, which is quite often. Programs in small or even medium-size municipalities, where few options are available, have market power because they are subject to little competition. Programs with publicly subsidized tuition enjoy market power as well by undercutting their competitors and absorbing the captive demand from students who cannot afford other options. Programs without tuition subsidies that serve disadvantaged students, unfamiliar with higher education, also enjoy market power, as they might be able to charge disproportionately high tuitions. Box 5.5 exemplifies how regulation (or the lack thereof) on HEIs receiving public funding has indeed affected the lowest-quality SCPs in the United States.[18]

The dynamism and "churn" of the SCP market (chapter 3) might pose accountability challenges, as it might be hard to ensure quality or provide information when programs open, close, and change frequently. Careful entry screening and detailed annual evaluations would alleviate these challenges. In a different but also dynamic context, this is how the most effective charter school authorizers in the United States handle these issues.[19] Moreover, good regulation benefits new, high-quality HEIs. Since new HEIs do not have a past reputation, publicly recognizing those that are of high quality helps them attract students and further encourages the entry of high-quality HEIs and programs.

Box 5.5 Oversight and Regulation: The Case of For-Profit Institutions in the United States

As in Latin America and the Caribbean (LAC), many higher education programs in the United States exhibit unsatisfactory outcomes. For-profit higher education institutions (HEIs) teach many of these programs. Seeking to protect the substantial federal resources devoted to higher education financial aid as well as students' and families' own resources, the US government has attempted to regulate HEIs.[a] For-profit institutions have been a particular concern because they cost more yet generate lower earnings, higher debt, and lower loan repayment rates than comparable programs at other institutions, even after controlling for confounding factors (Cellini and Koedel 2017; Armona, Chakrabarti, and Lovenheim 2020; Cellini and Turner 2019; Gaulke, Cassidy, and Namingit 2019; Cellini and Chaudhary 2014; Cellini, Darolia, and Turner 2020).

Past regulations succeeded at limiting the activities of low-performing programs and HEIs. In the early 1990s, many programs and HEIs with low student repayment rates lost federal student aid eligibility or were closed (Darolia 2013; Looney and Yannelis 2019; Cellini, Darolia, and Turner 2020). The displaced students, in turn, mostly shifted to local community colleges (Cellini, Darolia, and Turner 2020).

For-profit HEIs grew rapidly during the early 2000s owing to the rising popularity of online learning and lax federal oversight. They gained even more enrollment during the Great Recession as workers found their advertising attractive and sought them to retrain online. Seeking to mitigate their negative impact, in the mid-2010s, the federal government imposed sanctions on several institutions and closed others. In addition, it restricted for-profit HEIs' aggressive recruiting, created the College Scorecard website to disseminate information on institutions' outcomes, and established the Gainful Employment Rule to hold colleges accountable.[b] Policy makers and academics emphasized the importance of providing information to help students make better choices, perhaps with an emphasis on establishing minimum quality standards and eliminating the "lower tail" of the quality distribution (Deming and Figlio 2016). As a result, between 2010 and 2016, for-profit enrollment declined and some large for-profit chains were closed. Although the Gainful Employment Rule was never fully implemented, it might have provided a threat that led many low-performing programs to close (Kelchen and Liu 2019).

As most of these regulations were eliminated or not enforced in later years, for-profit enrollment bounced back. During the COVID-19 pandemic, for-profit enrollment has grown by 3 percent relative to a 9 percent decline in community college enrollment. Since for-profits were already teaching mostly online before the pandemic, they have adjusted easily to full online teaching and have not suffered the enrollment losses experienced by in-person programs. Further, they have continued to outspend community colleges in advertising (Vazquez-Martinez and Hansen 2020). Overall, the US experience with for-profit HEIs shows that oversight and regulation can indeed improve the supply of higher education, but only to the extent that norms are well designed and appropriately enforced.

a. Much of this box draws from Matsudaira and Turner (2020) and Cellini (2020).

b. The College Scorecard is an online tool with institution-level information on cost and outcomes (https://collegescorecard.ed.gov/). The Gainful Employment Rule identifies programs leading to earnings that do not allow individuals to pay back student loans.

To a large extent, the main regulatory tools currently used for higher education institutions and programs in LAC are quality assurance and accreditation. These clearly have a role, particularly when well designed and properly executed. However, they should not become a substitute for periodic (for example, annual) oversight, coupled with information disclosure and a readiness to deploy the "first line of attack"—closing the worst-performing programs—as needed. If there is one task that the regulator must accomplish, it is the closing of the worst programs. LAC countries have grappled with regulatory issues in recent years, as illustrated in box 5.6.

Box 5.6 Oversight and Regulation Reform: Recent Attempts in LAC

Higher education systems in Latin America and the Caribbean (LAC) have experienced drastic, complex growth over the last decades (see chapter 1). Enrollment rates have approximately tripled over the past 30 years, and many new higher education institutions (HEIs)—including those offering short-cycle program (SCP) degrees—have entered the market.

An important factor behind this enrollment growth were the public initiatives aimed at lowering students' financial burden from higher education. Chile offers an example of such initiatives. During the early 2000s, new student loan programs prompted fast enrollment growth in Chile. Over time, however, widespread concern arose because of high interest rates, deficient quality assurance mechanisms, and a mismatch between the skills produced by the higher education system and those demanded by the market. To address the generalized discontent created by these issues, in 2016, the Chilean government implemented a major funding reform, *gratuidad*, at the heart of which is the notion of tuition-free higher education (see chapter 3). A few years into this new system, substantial fiscal costs and technical design issues, along with the preexisting problems not addressed by *gratuidad*—such as those related to quality assurance and the disconnect between the supply and demand of skills—emerge as barriers for a high-quality, inclusive higher education system.

Another factor behind the rapid higher education growth in some countries was the lack of a modern, up-to-date regulatory framework for HEIs. Such was the case of Peru. For a number of years, the absence of a modern, cohesive, and effective regulatory framework enabled the fast, somewhat disorganized entry of many new HEIs and programs, a number of which were of questionable quality. Beginning in 2014, the government has implemented a series of reforms with the goal of enhancing the quality of higher education supply. These include the licensing of HEIs contingent on minimum standards and a new, more effective institutional accreditation system. Reform implementation has been rather slow, in part because of the large number of HEIs that have requested a license. The licensing of universities concluded in January 2021, while that of other HEIs (including SCP providers) is still ongoing. By mid-2020, more than 13 universities had been closed, 37 HEIs had received hefty fines, and many HEIs had been penalized for offering unauthorized programs.[a] It is still too early to assess the long-term impact of these reforms.

a. See https://www.sunedu.gob.pe/sunedu-seis-anos-reforma-universitaria-servido-para-construir-sistema-universitario -diferente-ordenado-sin-ilegalidad/

Skill Development Pathways

One reason why students might not choose SCPs is that they might view them as an academic "dead end" given the difficulty of transferring to a bachelor's program. For example, although most program directors interviewed for the WBSCPS report that their programs offer credits for longer degrees, administrative data show that most SCP students do not pursue or finish such degrees (chapter 1).

Creating smoother, more flexible pathways between SCPs and bachelor's degrees would mitigate the perception of SCPs as a "dead end" and lower their stigma. More importantly, flexible pathways would facilitate lifelong learning by shifting the focus away from degrees and onto skills. Under flexible pathways, a student receives a credential when she completes a skill acquisition block or module (such as the first year in college or a series of computer-related classes). She completes blocks flexibly as allowed by work or family obligations. Once she completes the required portfolio of blocks, she becomes eligible for a final degree (for example, an SCP or bachelor's degree). In this way, the SCP itself becomes a block in the portfolio toward a bachelor's degree.

Creating flexible pathways is easier said than done. Two main obstacles emerge. The first is that, when an SCP graduate seeks admission to a bachelor's program, the latter must trust that the student learned what she was supposed to learn in the former. The second is that the programs in question—SCPs and bachelor's—may in and of themselves not be flexible enough. The first problem can be solved through exams in which the student demonstrates her readiness for the bachelor's program. It can also be solved by institutional arrangements between the two programs or HEIs. A mere agreement, however, is not enough. In the United States, many states have an equivalence of credits between community colleges and four-year institutions, yet the actual student transfers only work well in some of them—namely, in the states where the faculties of the sending and receiving institutions coordinate as needed.[20] Yet another solution to the first problem is the use of standardized "descriptors," similar to those used among countries in the European Union, that establish general parameters and intended learning outcomes by program type (for instance, SCP and bachelor's) in order to ensure the acceptance of degrees across institutions.[21]

Proving that the student has not only completed a block but also acquired the corresponding skills is relatively simple when the student accumulates blocks at the same or related institutions. In other cases, the reputation of the certifier (be it an HEI or a private company), along with detailed information on the skills acquired, are perhaps the best available solutions. Multiple arrangements of this kind exist in the United States (box 5.7). These include stackable credentials, which allow students to "stack" certificates or degrees toward a more advanced credential, and digital badges, which provide a

Box 5.7 Flexible Academic Pathways in the United States

Flexible pathways have been—at least nominally—a feature of the US higher education system for several decades. Before describing them, some definitions are in order. A *credential* is a document awarded by an authorized body attesting that an individual has achieved specific learning outcomes and skills relative to a given standard. This broad concept includes degrees, diplomas, licenses, certificates, badges, and professional or industry certifications. A *certificate* is a credential that "certifies" or documents expertise for a particular occupation. The corresponding program usually lasts between a few months and a year and may not provide credits for further education. While an *associate degree* is also focused on specific occupations, it requires additional classes on the subject matter and general education (for example, math, English, and science). It usually gives credits for further education. Certificates can be pursued to enter a field or acquire additional, specialized knowledge for those with previous expertise in the field. In the field of radiology, for example, the entry certificate trains individuals as limited scope X-ray technicians, whereas the certificate for magnetic resonance imaging (MRI) trains individuals with previous expertise who seek to specialize in MRIs. In contrast, the associate degree in radiologic technology provides qualifications for several radiologic specializations, such as MRIs and radiation therapy, and includes clinical practice.

Perhaps the best-known pathway is that of *transfers* from community colleges to four-year institutions. Bailey, Jaggars, and Jenkins (2015) document that over two-thirds of the US states have adopted policies to facilitate these transfers so that community college graduates can enter college as juniors (third-year students). Although transfers are quite seamless in some states, they are not so in others, where transfer students are often asked to take first- or second-year classes in college because their specific major does not accept the community college classes. The evidence suggests that policies are not enough for transfers to work. The key issue is coordination between the faculties of community colleges and four-year institutions.

The recent *certificate-first* approach decomposes a bachelor's degree into certificates and "flips" the curriculum by reversing the order of classes. Whereas the typical curriculum starts with general classes and moves toward more specific and practical ones, the flipped or "upside-down" curriculum starts with more practical classes. It gives students a certificate for completing them and continues with the more general classes. In this way, students who pause or end without a degree attain at least one credential. Consider, for instance, a bachelor's degree in applied technology. Under the certificate-first approach, the degree comprises the following certificate sequence: certificate in computer programming, certificate in web front end, and certificate in web development. The last two certificates teach the general education and elective courses that would typically be taught at the beginning. Completing the first certificate gives a credential; completing the first and second yields an associate degree; and completing all three provides a bachelor's degree. This approach has been implemented by Brigham Young University–Pathway Worldwide, Champlain College, and Western Governors University (Gilbert and Horn 2019).

Stackable credentials are traditional certificates or credentials that can be "stacked" to build qualifications and help an individual in her career path. Typically, the credentials are given by a

box continues next page

Box 5.7 Flexible Academic Pathways in the United States *(continued)*

higher education institution, but they can also be given by industry. The most common example is that of an individual who already has a certificate or associate degree and returns to community college to obtain further training or credentials. So-called "stacked" associate degrees are designed to be pursued regularly or by the stacking of specific credentials. For stacked degrees in the Wisconsin Technical College System, Kiddo (2017) finds that individuals who choose the stacking option and first earn a certificate are more likely to complete their final degree than those who choose the regular option. The Tennessee Transfer Pathways creates well-defined pathways in multiple areas, allowing students to earn community college or industry certificates on the way to a bachelor's or associate degree. Bailey and Belfield (2017) examine returns to stackable certificates and find no effects. However, Meyer, Bird, and Castleman (2020) provide more recent evidence—using data after the Great Recession—that a second credential for adults in Virginia has large and positive effects on employment and wages. So far, 17 states have allocated funding for colleges to develop stackable credential pathways, and many states have already implemented them.

Digital badges are akin to traditional paper diplomas but use digital technologies and usually represent competencies or expertise not shown on a transcript, such as data collection skills or volunteer work. As a result, they are sometimes known as "microcredentials." For example, a digital badge for leadership skills is associated with metadata describing the skill content and naming the certifying authority. The badge can be posted online, on job platforms, or on social networks. Badges can be given by institutions, organizations, or individuals, who partner with another organization in charge of displaying and verifying the badges. Digital badge examples are Open Badges by IMS Global and Acclaim Platform by Credly.[a]

Digital badges have been driven largely by the need to match individuals with firms based on skills rather than degrees. They sometimes work as stackable credentials and can count toward a degree. Motivated by numerous conversations with local employers on skill deficits, the Colorado Community College system offers digital badges for skills such as drill press, manual machining, and computer numerical control turning, which can be stacked toward an associate degree. IBM issues digital badges (for skills such as design thinking, data analytics, and program management) that can be used toward certificates and degrees, including bachelor's and master's, at Northeastern University. In addition, IBM has partnered with the University of Louisville to establish the IBM Skills Academy, which focuses on digital learning and technology skills.[b]

a. For more on digital badges, see, for instance, https://internal.cccs.edu/academic-affairs/academic-initiatives/digital-badges/.
b. See, for instance, https://internal.cccs.edu/academic-affairs/academic-initiatives/digital-badges/ and https://www.forbes.com/sites/michaeltnietzel/2019/05/06/four-reasons-why-the-university-of-louisvilles-ibm-skills-academy-is-a-very-smart-move/?sh=7e02715c14f5.

digital certification that an individual possesses a particular skill (for instance, leadership skills), even if she did not acquire it through formal training. A recent arrangement is the "certificate-first" approach, which teaches a program's most practical classes in the first year and provides a certificate for them, while teaching the more general, theoretical content later. The "certificate-first" approach provides an example of how bachelor's programs can become more flexible in order to accommodate SCP students without losing rigor or depth.

As for the second obstacle to flexible pathways, namely the rigidity of the programs in question, SCPs may have been usually regarded as the main culprit by not facilitating two different paths, namely entry into the labor market and continuation toward a bachelor's degree. But, in fact, the problem might lie not with the SCPs but rather with the bachelor's programs because these might not be flexible enough to accommodate SCP students—which could be accomplished, for instance, through a block structure or a "certificate-first approach". The experience of giving utmost flexibility to SCPs has been tried and found wanting in US community colleges. Indeed, community college students typically choose classes that would allow them to transfer to a four-year institution, as 80 percent of incoming community college students express an intention to transfer. However, only 31 percent of incoming students do transfer, and less than half of them complete a bachelor's degree.[22] Among the remaining 69 percent, many leave community college without a degree, after accumulating classes that would have been useful had they transferred yet have little market value otherwise.

The great flexibility of the "cafeteria-style" curriculum of community colleges, which allows students to choose and accumulate classes at will, does not seem to serve them well. Indeed, some of the most successful community colleges in the United States deliberately avoid this approach and instead provide "guided pathways" similar to those commonly used by SCPs in LAC (chapter 3).[23] Moreover, the evidence from the WBSCPS suggests that SCPs' structured curricula and training contributes positively to students' graduation (chapter 4), perhaps accounting for the greater graduation of SCP than bachelor's students in the region. In light of these considerations, and given the aggregate success of SCPs, flexible pathways might be better attained by emphasizing flexibility on the side of bachelor's programs rather than SCPs. Indeed, not all programs might need the same flexibility, and a "one-size-fits-all" approach in this regard might not be convenient.

When discussing pathways, the path commonly considered is that from SCPs onto bachelor's programs. However, the opposite path should be considered as well, particularly for students who do not complete their bachelor's program. SCPs in this case could function as an "exit ramp" that would give students an SCP degree upon leaving higher education rather than letting them leave without any type of credential. The "exit ramp" notion seems especially promising given the better labor markets of SCP graduates relative to bachelor's dropouts (chapter 1).

To promote lifelong learning, programs not only must be flexible; they must also be short. At the moment, some programs might simply be too long. Particularly given the current urgency to form skilled human capital, streamlining programs—redesigning and shortening them—is a simple, inexpensive way to make higher education more flexible and attractive. Box 5.8 illustrates some recent innovations in curriculum design.

Box 5.8 What Should Be Taught, and How?

As the higher education focus shifts from degrees to skills, an additional question emerges—how can programs identify the specific skills they are supposed to teach? How can they teach the skills efficiently and effectively, so that graduates perform at the highest level in their jobs? One answer to this question comes from the World Bank Short-Cycle Program Survey (WBSCPS). The program directors reported engaging with firms to assess their needs, sometimes cooperating with them on curriculum design and student evaluation. Another answer comes from the United States, where some community colleges apply a "guided pathways" framework to their curricula.[a] This involves "program mapping," that is, identifying the competencies needed by graduates to succeed in the labor market or future studies, mapping those competencies onto skills, and finally designing the courses, teaching methods, and activities to impart the skills. In this approach, individual classes are not stand-alone elements but rather steps along a coherent path. Faculty spend less time delivering content and more time leading activities (for example, project-based learning and case-based teaching) that build student motivation and focus on those competencies. Project-based learning is a specific example of the "experiential learning" that Northeastern University has pioneered through their "co-op" model. In this model, students split their time between the classroom and work, with great fluidity between both components, deliberately making each one impact the other.[b]

In a similar spirit, McKinsey Generation applies a targeted, task-based approach to its workforce development programs.[c] The approach identifies the most important activities required by the corresponding job and designs a curriculum that teaches the skills needed to perform them at the highest level. Importantly, those are the activities that separate high from low performers—individuals who succeed in the market from those who fail. For instance, a web developer's critical task is designing user-friendly interfaces. This requires technical skills, such as Java coding and database management, and behavioral skills, such as assessing the user's needs, welcoming her feedback, and delivering iterative versions on time. Thus, task-based training repeatedly practices those skills until the trainee acquires them at the highest possible level.

a. Bailey, Jaggars, and Jenkins (2015).
b. See https://www.northeastern.edu/experiential-learning/.
c. See https://www.mckinsey.com/about-us/new-at-mckinsey-blog/15000-lives-transformed-and-counting. These programs are short and do not qualify as SCPs.

SCP Stigma

SCPs bear the stigma of being the lesser choice relative to bachelor's programs. It is rarely a student's dream to be an SCP graduate, or a parent's dream to see her child graduate from an SCP program. SCPs are viewed as the option to take when the better one—a bachelor's program—is not available.

Is the stigma fair, given the evidence presented in this book? In other words, does it reflect reality? This chapter has highlighted some strong reasons for viewing SCPs favorably, all of which might deem the stigma unfair. At the same time, SCPs have shortcomings that might justify the stigma. In addition, students might perceive SCPs as narrow given their focus on specific occupations—in contrast with the supposedly broader, more theoretical training of a bachelor's program. This concern is heightened when the student believes she only has one chance at higher education and advanced learning.

To the extent that students evaluate higher education programs based on who enrolls in them, the SCP stigma might be related to the fact that relatively disadvantaged students choose SCPs. More advantaged students might interpret this as evidence that these programs are less challenging and rewarding than bachelor's programs—in other words, the lesser choice. Moreover, policy may have inadvertently contributed to the stigma. Particularly in countries with easy access to zero-tuition bachelor's programs in public HEIs, students may be naturally inclined to choose them. In other words, admission and funding policies for bachelor's vis-à-vis SCPs in public HEIs may give students incentives to choose bachelor's programs rather than SCPs. By focusing more resources and attention on bachelor's programs, policy makers may have contributed to the perception that SCPs are the lesser choice.

The policies described in this chapter should help mitigate the SCP stigma. Providing information on SCPs and bachelor's programs and helping students process it, restoring equity to higher education funding, facilitating academic pathways and lifelong learning, and regulating SCPs to ensure the supply of quality programs should help. But, perhaps, a new mindset for higher education is needed as well—one that prizes variety in offerings so that every student can find her best match, as stressed in Ferreyra et al. (2017). The policy maker's goal should not be to maximize the number of bachelor's graduates, but to maximize the number of highly skilled individuals—through bachelor's programs or SCPs. Similarly, a student's goal should not be to obtain a bachelor's degree at any cost, but rather to graduate from the program that best matches her needs, academic preparation, interests, and goals.

The private sector may play a critical role in the removal of the SCP stigma by vigorously affirming its need for the skills developed by SCPs. Box 5.9 illustrates how the private sector participation in public communications campaigns can raise the desirability of a particular type of degree. Further, an unexpected ally for SCPs might have emerged in recent years: students' waning interest in long programs. Many of the program directors who were interviewed for the WBSCPS emphasized that students were no longer interested in years' worth of training but rather in short-term credentials with immediate employment. Given these new preferences, SCPs might become attractive to a much wider and more varied segment of the population than that of its current students.

Ultimately, nothing will help eliminate the SCP stigma more than a resounding success. The current crisis might just be the opportunity for SCPs to accomplish this.

Box 5.9 Combating a Degree's Stigma: Germany's Experience

In 1999, 31 European countries signed a declaration in Bologna titled "The European Higher Education Area," which aimed to establish comparable higher education degrees in Europe by 2010 while also raising program quality to enhance graduates' employability. The "Bologna process" introduced a two-cycle degree structure (undergraduate and graduate); bachelor's and master's degrees are available for almost all fields and majors, and generally last six and four semesters, respectively.

In Germany, the reform was implemented so that both traditional universities and professional schools, known as "universities of applied sciences," could deliver both types of programs. Bachelor's programs were designed so as to provide skills relevant to the European labor market. The problem, however, was the emergence of a stigma for bachelor's degrees, which were perceived as inferior relative to master's degrees.

The industry played an important role in combating this stigma. To help remove it, in 2004, the German Trade and Industry Association, the Centre for Higher Education Development, and the Confederation of German Employer's Associations launched the "Bachelors Welcome" joint initiative. The goal was to portray bachelor programs as an attractive professional option, capable of delivering good entry jobs and subsequent career prospects. Through a joint declaration, these organizations supported the reforms introduced by the Bologna process and sought to elevate the status of bachelor's programs by highlighting their practical orientation, shorter length, and international relevance. The declaration was originally signed by the directors of human resources of 15 leading companies, and was reaffirmed and expanded over the following years. In 2012, 62 leading German companies signed a new declaration named "Bologna@Germany", reiterating their commitment to collaborate with higher education institutions (HEIs) in the expansion of bachelor's programs and advocating in favor of stronger practical content and greater access for a diverse group of students.

Conclusions

There are reasons to be optimistic about SCPs as well as reasons to be cautious. Thoughtful policy design could mitigate SCP shortcomings and help realize their potential. Providing and disseminating information, correcting funding inequities, holding programs accountable based on outcomes, closing the lowest-performing programs, and facilitating flexible academic pathways are examples of such policies.

SCPs entered the LAC higher education scene relatively late and have not had a prominent role in a region where bachelor's programs have been held as the superior—and perhaps only—key to social and economic mobility. Nonetheless, SCPs might prove extremely helpful, not just to overcome the employment and production crisis generated by the COVID-19 pandemic, but also to prepare individuals for today's world of work—a world whose arrival has been accelerated by the pandemic. Success at this juncture would generate a different public perception of SCPs—no longer as the lesser choice, but as the right choice for many at a time of great need. Now is the time for SCPs. If not now, when?

Notes

Angelica Sanchez and Gabriel Suarez are acknowledged for their excellent research assistance.

1. In a different context, the best charter school authorizers in the United States have adopted a similar philosophy by "removing the valid reasons why some people hate charter schools" (Pearson, S. 2020. "5 Things We Learned in D.C. about How to Advance Charter Schools." Blog, Education Next, September).

2. Ferreyra et al. (2017); Carranza and Ferreyra (2019); Ferreyra et al. (2020), background paper for this report.

3. Minaya and Scott-Clayton (2019) and Riehl, Saavedra, and Urquoila (2019).

4. Deming and Figlio (2016) provide evidence of how institutional rankings, particularly those produced by *U.S. News and World Report*, lead to strategic responses on the part of institutions and affects students' applications.

5. Before the College Scorecard was released, the initial purpose of the Obama administration was to use that information to rate colleges and allocate funding based on performance. Considerations such as those presented here led to the dismissal of those purposes, opting instead to just release the College Scorecard.

6. See Carrell and Kurlaender (2019) and Hastings, Neilson, and Zimmerman (2015) for evidence on the importance of nonpecuniary program attributes in the United States and Chile, respectively.

7. Chile is an exception in that it subsidizes students in private HEIs and has a large student loan market.

8. Ferreyra et al. (2017), Carranza and Ferreyra (2019), and Ferreyra et al. (2020), background paper for this report, document the variation in dropout rates by income and academic readiness.

9. In the United States, for example, states and local governments provide transfers to public HEIs. In addition, the federal government provides financial aid to students in all HEIs—public and private—through direct grants and loans.

10. Exceptions are Chile's Ingresa loans and Colombia's ICETEX loans. However, the latter cover a very small fraction of the SCP student population (see chapter 1).

11. See, for instance, https://www.soyhenry.com/ and https://www.laboratoria.la/en.

12. See the review by Baird et al (2014), and the references therein.

13. See Beylis et al. (2020) and Silva et al. (2021).

14. Ferreyra and Liang (2012), Deming and Figlio (2016).

15. See the higher education accountability proposal in Matsudaira and Turner (2020). A concern is that a policy of minimum standards could create an adverse selection problem, whereby some programs of high expected quality do not open to avoid being closed in the future, whereas others of low expected quality open to make a profit before the regulator closes them. A careful screening of programs before authorizing their entry should mitigate this issue. This is, for example, how effective charter school regulators operate. See Ferreyra and Kosenok (2018) for a discussion of the District of Columbia Public Charter School Board as well as https://dcpcsb.org/.

16. Matsudaira and Turner (2020).

17. It would be interesting to know whether SCP outcomes improve when regulatory provisions such as minimum standards are present. Novel, robust empirical

evidence on this issue would require longitudinal information and cross-country taxonomy for regulations. Such data are currently not available. Nonetheless, this study provides evidence on returns that could be used in the future to analyze that question.

18. For example, the Public Charter School Board in Washington, DC, is the sole charter school authorizer in the city (https://dcpcsb.org/). To apply for a charter, a prospective entrant must submit an exhaustive business and academic plan and participate in multiple interviews with the authorizer. Only a third of entry applications are approved. Every year, the authorizer conducts a thorough annual review of every school according to well-defined guidelines contained in the Performance Evaluation Framework. In addition, the authorizer visits the schools multiple times a year. Based on the annual evaluation, the authorizer classifies the charter schools into three tiers and publishes all evaluations.

19. Bailey, Jaggars, and Jenkins (2015).

20. See http://ecahe.eu/w/index.php/Dublin_Descriptors as well as chapter 1.

21. See https://ccrc.tc.columbia.edu/Community-College-FAQs.html

22. Bailey et al (2015).

References

Armona, L., R. Chakrabarti, and M. Lovenheim. 2020. "Student Debt and Default: The Role of For-Profit Colleges." Staff Report No. 811, Federal Reserve Bank of New York.

Bailey, T. R., and C. Belfield. 2017. "Stackable Credentials: Do They Have Labor Market Value?" CCRC Working Paper No. 97, Community College Research Center, Columbia University, New York.

Bailey, T., S. Jaggars, and D. Jenkins. 2015. *Redesigning America's Community Colleges: A Clearer Path to Student Success.* Cambridge, MA: Harvard University Press.

Baird, S., F. H. Ferreira, B. Özler, and M. Woolcock. 2014. "Conditional, Unconditional and Everything in Between: A Systematic Review of the Effects of Cash Transfer Programmes on Schooling Outcomes." *Journal of Development Effectiveness* 6(1): 1–43.

Baker, D. J. 2020. "'Name and Shame': An Effective Strategy for College Tuition Accountability?" *Educational Evaluation and Policy Analysis* 42 (3): 393–416.

Baker, R., E. Bettinger, B. Jacob, and I. Marinescu. 2018. "The Effect of Labor Market Information on Community College Students' Major Choice." *Economics of Education Review* 65: 18–30.

Becerra, M., J. Alonso, and M. Frias. 2021. "COVID-19 Response. Latin America and the Caribbean: Tertiary Education." World Bank, Washington, DC.

Bergman, P., J. T. Denning, and D. Manoli. 2019. "Is Information Enough? The Effect of Information about Education Tax Benefits on Student Outcomes." *Journal of Policy Analysis and Management* 38 (3): 706–31.

Bettinger, E. P., and R. B. Baker. 2014. "The Effects of Student Coaching: An Evaluation of a Randomized Experiment in Student Advising." *Educational Evaluation and Policy Analysis* 36 (1): 3–19.

Bettinger, E. P., and B. J. Evans. 2019. "College Guidance for All: A Randomized Experiment in Pre-College Advising." *Journal of Policy Analysis and Management* 38 (3): 579–99.

Beylis, G., R. Fattal-Jaef, R. Sinha, M. Morris, and A. Sebastian. 2020. *Going Viral: COVID-19 and the Accelerated Transformation of Jobs in Latin America and the Caribbean.* World Bank Latin American and Caribbean Studies. Washington, DC: World Bank.

Carranza, J. E., and M. M. Ferreyra. 2019. "Increasing Higher Education Access: Supply, Sorting, and Outcomes in Colombia." *Journal of Human Capital* 13 (1): 95–136.

Carrell, S., and M. Kurlaender. 2019. "Estimating the Productivity of Community Colleges in Paving the Road to Four-Year College Success." In *Productivity in Higher Education,* edited by C. Hoxby and K. Stange. Chicago: University of Chicago Press.

Castleman, B. L., D. Deutschlander, and G. Lohner. 2020. "Pushing College Advising Forward: Experimental Evidence on Intensive Advising and College Success." National Education Working Paper Series No. 20326, Annenberg Institute, Brown University, Providence, RI.

Cellini, S. R. 2020. "The Alarming Rise in For-Profit College Enrollment." Brookings, Brown Center Chalkboard Blog Post, http://www.brookings.edu/blog/brown-center-chalkboard/2020/11/02/the-alarming-rise-in-for-profit-college-enrollment/.

Cellini, S. R., and L. Chaudhary. 2014. "The Labor Market Returns to a For-Profit College Education." *Economics of Education Review* 43: 125–40.

Cellini, S. R., R. Darolia, and L. J. Turner. 2020. "Where Do Students Go When For-Profit Colleges Lose Federal Aid?" *American Economic Journal: Economic Policy* 12 (2): 46–83.

Cellini, S. R., and C. Koedel. 2017. "The Case for Limiting Federal Student Aid to For-Profit Colleges." *Journal of Policy Analysis and Management* 36 (4): 934–42.

Cellini, S. R., and N. Turner. 2019. "Gainfully Employed? Assessing the Employment and Earnings of For-Profit College Students Using Administrative Data." *Journal of Human Resources* 54 (2): 342–70.

Conlon, J. J. 2019. "Major Malfunction: A Field Experiment Correcting Undergraduates' Beliefs about Salaries." *Journal of Human Resources* 0317-8599R2.

Darolia, R. 2013. "Integrity versus Access? The Effect of Federal Financial Aid Availability on Postsecondary Enrollment." *Journal of Public Economics* 106: 101–14.

Deming, D. J., and D. Figlio. 2016. "Accountability in US Education: Applying Lessons from K-12 Experience to Higher Education." *Journal of Economic Perspectives* 30 (3): 33–56.

Dynarski, S., C. J. Libassi, K. Michelmore, and S. Owen. 2020. "Closing the Gap: The Effect of a Targeted, Tuition-Free Promise on College Choices of High-Achieving, Low-Income Students." Working Paper 25349, National Bureau of Economic Research, Cambridge, MA.

Ferreyra, M. M., C. Avitabile, J. Botero Álvarez, F. Haimovich Paz, and S. Urzúa. 2017. *At a Crossroads: Higher Education in Latin America and the Caribbean.* Washington, DC: World Bank.

Ferreyra, M., T. Melguizo, A. Franco, and Angelica Sanchez. 2020. "Estimating the Contribution of Short-Cycle Programs to Student Outcomes in Colombia." Policy Research Working Paper 9424, World Bank, Washington, DC.

Ferreyra, M. M., and G. Kosenok. 2018. "Charter School Entry and School Choice: The Case of Washington, D.C." *Journal of Public Economics* 159: 160–82.

Ferreyra, M. M., and P. J. Liang. 2012. "Information Asymmetry and Equilibrium Monitoring in Education." *Journal of Public Economics* 96 (1-2): 237–54.

Gaulke, A., H. Cassidy, and S. Namingit. 2019. "The Effect of Post-Baccalaureate Business Certificates on Job Search: Results from a Correspondence Study." *Labour Economics* 61, 101759.

Gilbert, C. G., and M. B. Horn. 2019. "A Certificate, Then a Degree." Blog Post, https://www.educationnext.org/certificate-then-degree-programs-help-tackle-college-completion-crisis/.

Gurantz, O., J. Howell, M. Hurwitz, M., C. Larson, M. Pender, and B. White. 2021. "A National-Level Informational Experiment to Promote Enrollment in Selective Colleges." *Journal of Policy Analysis and Management* 40 (2): 453–79.

Hastings, J., C. A. Neilson, and S. D. Zimmerman. 2015. "The Effects of Earnings Disclosure on College Enrollment Decisions." No. 21300, National Bureau of Economic Research, Cambridge, MA.

Hoxby, C., and S. Turner. 2013. "Expanding College Opportunities for High-Achieving, Low Income Students." Discussion Paper, 12, 014, Stanford Institute for Economic Policy Research, Stanford, CA.

Hurwitz, M., and J. Smith. 2018. "Student Responsiveness to Earnings Data in the College Scorecard." *Economic Inquiry* 56 (2): 1220–43.

Hyman, J. 2020. "Can Light-Touch College-Going Interventions Make a Difference? Evidence from a Statewide Experiment in Michigan." *Journal of Policy Analysis and Management* 39 (1): 159–90.

J-PAL. 2017. "Decidiendo para un futuro major," https://www.poverty-action.org/sites/default/files/DFM-Policy-Brief.pdf.

Kelchen, R., and Z. Liu. 2019. "Did Gainful Employment Regulations Result in College and Program Closures? An Empirical Analysis." Working Paper, https://kelchenoneducation.files.word-press.com/2019/11/kelchen_liu_nov19.pdf.

Kiddoo, S. 2017. Exploring Associate Degree Outcomes of Stacked Credential Models at Two-Year Colleges. PhD dissertation, The University of Wisconsin–Madison. ProQuest Dissertations Publishing.

Looney, A., and C. Yannelis. 2019. "The Consequences of Student Loan Credit Expansions: Evidence from Three Decades of Default Cycles." Working Paper No. 19-32, Federal Reserve Board of Philadelphia, Philadelphia, PA.

Matsudaira, J. D., and L. J. Turner. 2020. "Towards a Framework for Accountability for Federal Financial Assistance Programs in Postsecondary Education." Economic Studies at Brookings, Brookings Institution, Washington, DC.

Meyer, K., K. A. Bird, and B. L. Castleman. 2020. "Stacking the Deck for Employment Success: Labor Market Returns to Stackable Credentials." EdWorking Paper No 20-317, Annenberg Institute, Brown University, Providence, RI.

Minaya, V. and J. Scott-Clayton. 2019. "Labor Market Outcomes and Postsecondary Accountability: Are Imperfect Metrics Better than None?" In *Productivity in Higher Education*, edited by C. Hoxby and K. Stange. Chicago: University of Chicago Press.

Mulhern, C. 2020. "Beyond Teachers: Estimating Individual Guidance Counselors' Effects on Educational Attainment." Unpublished manuscript, RAND Corporation.

Mulhern, C. 2021. "Changing College Choices with Personalized Admissions Information at Scale: Evidence on Naviance." *Journal of Labor Economics* 39 (1): 219–62.

Oreopoulos, P., and R. Ford. 2019. "Keeping College Options Open: A Field Experiment to Help All High School Seniors through the College Application Process." *Journal of Policy Analysis and Management* 38 (2): 426–54.

Oreopoulos, P., and U. Petronijevic. 2019. "The Remarkable Unresponsiveness of College Students to Nudging and What We Can Learn from It." No. 26059, National Bureau of Economic Research, Cambridge, MA.

Page, L. C., and J. Scott-Clayton. 2016. "Improving College Access in the United States: Barriers and Policy Responses." *Economics of Education Review* 51: 4–22.

Riehl, E., J. E. Saavedra, and M. Urquiola. 2019. "Learning and Earning: An Approximation to College Value Added in Two Dimensions." In *Productivity in Higher Education*, edited by C. Hoxby and K. Stange. Chicago: University of Chicago Press.

Silva, J., L. Sousa, T. Packard, and R. Robertson. 2021. *Crises and Labor Markets in Latin America and the Caribbean: Lessons for an Inclusive Recovery from the COVID-19 Pandemic*. Washington, DC: World Bank.

Vasquez-Martinez, A., and M. Hansen. 2020. "For-Profit Colleges Drastically Outspend Competing Institutions on Advertising." Brookings, Brown Center Chalkboard Blog Post, https://www.brookings.edu/blog/brown-center-chalkboard/2020/05/19/for-profit-colleges-advertising/.